The
Nine Lives
of
Naomi Mitchison

THE
NINE LIVES
OF
NAOMI MITCHISON

Jenni Calder

A *Virago* book

Published by Virago Press 1997
Reprinted 1997

Copyright © Jenni Calder 1997

Photograph of Naomi Mitchison in the USSR with Pioneer Camp children, 1952, on p. 8
of the picture section, included courtesy of the late Margot Kettle.

The moral right of the author has been asserted.

A CIP catalogue record for this book is available from the British Library

ISBN 1 85381 724 4

Typeset by Solidus (Bristol) Limited
Printed and bound in Great Britain by Clays Ltd, St Ives plc

Virago
A Division of
Little, Brown and Company (UK)
Brettenham House
Lancaster Place
London WC2E 7EN

Acknowledgements

THE SEED of this book was planted by Joan Lingard: my grateful thanks to her for initiating such a rewarding experience. Many people have been involved in its making, not least the subject herself. For over four years she has given me time, hospitality, generous access to material and absorbing conversation. I owe her a huge debt for all this and for permission to quote from published and unpublished material, from her own pen and by G.R. Mitchison and J.B.S. Haldane. My thanks, too, to the members of her family who have helped and encouraged: Denis Mitchison, Murdoch and Rosalind Mitchison, Val Arnold-Forster, Graeme Mitchison, Tabitha Lucas, Sally Mitchison and in particular Lois Godfrey.

Thank you to everyone who talked, listened, remembered, drew attention to material, supplied information and tracked down out-of-print copies of NM's work, especially: Rosemary Addison, Frances and Chris Allen, Louise Annand, John Burnett, Rachel Calder, Gabriel Carritt, Jim Ford, John Gibson, Dr Lesley Hall of the Wellcome Institute for the History of Medicine, Sue Innes, the late Margot Kettle, Hilda McDonald, Jemima Maclean, Angus Martin, Isobel Murray, Fiona Rudd, Naomi Tarrant.

In Botswana I was immeasurably aided in my research by Sandy and Elinah Grant, who also contributed greatly to the enjoyment of my stay. Sandy Grant also commented invaluably on my chapter on N.M. in Botswana. I am grateful to all those in Botswana and South

Africa who gave me help, especially Kgosi Linchwe and his wife Kathy, Skara Aphiri, Charles Bewlay, Brian Egner, Didon and Michael Faber, Janet Hermans, David Maine, Kwapeng Modikwe, Fiona Moffat, David Molefi, Norman Molomo, Gertrude Mulindwa of Botswana's National Library, Patrick von Rensburg, Struan Robertson and Greek Ruele. The visit to Botswana was made possible by a travel grant from the Scottish Arts Council.

For permission to quote from papers in their holdings I am grateful to the Harry Ransom Humanities Research Centre, University of Texas, Austin; the Mass-Observation Archive at the University of Sussex; the Trustees of the National Library of Scotland. Thank you to all these institutions for their help. Dorothy Sheridan of the Mass-Observation Archive made personal contributions to this book, and Robin Smith of the National Library of Scotland helped to chart a course through uncatalogued material. Thank you to the following for allowing me to quote from correspondence: Diarmid Gunn, Kenneth Komo, Kgose Linchwe, Norman Molomo, Christopher Pilley, Greek Ruele, David Higham Associates for permission to quote ms comments by John Lehmann, and A.M. Heath & Co. Ltd for permission to quote a letter by George Orwell, © Mark Hamilton as literary executor of the estate of the late Sonia Brownell Orwell and Martin Secker and Warburg Ltd.

Finally, some personal thanks: to Marina Benjamin who was in at the beginning and at the end; to Lan Ying and Jim Douglas, who looked after me so wonderfully in Austin, Texas; to my son Gideon Calder for his comments and corrections; and to Arthur Blue, for his comments, companionship and unfailing support.

Contents

Introduction

Among the roots, the dirt, the despised,
The lathe and the loom and the trawling net,
The fishers, the shepherds, the carpenter's baby:
The people who have not spoken yet.

THESE LINES by Naomi Mitchison were printed on a Christmas card she sent to Lewis Gielgud. There is no date, but it was probably in the 1930s when Gielgud, an old friend, was living in Paris. Naomi's origins were patrician and her life has been privileged, though she has tried very hard to ensure that it has not been protected. But if there has been one single impulse behind all of her lives, it is the urge to speak for 'the people who have not spoken yet'. Whether it is those who struggled for a voice long in the past, to whom she gave words in her fiction, or working-class women who sought advice on birth control, or crofters and fishermen in isolated areas of Scotland, or Africans striving for education – these and many other people and causes have impelled her life and work.

She has been equally driven to speak for herself. Behind these urges lie complex needs and motives which have much to do with her family and the times in which she has lived – virtually the whole of the twentieth century. 'Lived' hardly seems an adequate word, because for Naomi Mitchison living has meant not existing, enduring, putting up with, compromising – the way most of us live. It has meant adventuring, protesting, galvanizing others, often shouting, crying and stamping her foot, never accepting if it did not seem right to accept, making her voice heard in love, anger and the taking of risks. And of course it has meant writing, an activity she sustained from childhood to her nineties. She has written novels and short stories, plays and poetry, history and biography, many books for children and a vast range of journalism. In her twenties she was acclaimed as a fresh, innovative, challenging novelist and story writer, but she never became 'established', as her friend Aldous Huxley did. It is only recently that her clear focus and forthright style have begun again to be seen as valuable and resonant story-telling, and an illumination of many aspects of this century's history.

She has lived through 'the age of extremes', and again 'lived' does not do justice to her participation. She has always been more than an observer. Two world wars, two ages of economic crisis and drastic unemployment, the rise and fall of Soviet communism, the emergence and in some cases the destruction of African nations, the rolling back of frontiers in science and the roller-coaster of changing opportunities for women: these have all shaped the substance of her life and work. Scotland, the country of her ancestry and birth, has provided much of the cultural and intellectual fuel, but she has drawn inspiration from all over the world.

She has travelled in five continents; not just travelled, but paused long enough to take in and take part in whatever caught her attention as worthwhile. Wherever she has been she has shown an uncanny talent for peeling away the surfaces and getting at the essentials. She has never tried to hide her feelings. Grief, anger and love are all worn on her sleeve. The Anglo-Saxon and the Scottish Calvinist world, in particular, have found this difficult to deal with. She has exasperated many people. She has also had many admirers. It is not only her husband Dick who had cause to think of her as 'true and brave and infinitely kind'.

By the time Naomi Haldane reached adolescence, it was clear

that one life would not be enough for her. Her teenage love for theatre pointed the way to adopting different roles. She wrote herself into her plays and fiction, but was inseparable from invention. She lived the lives she wrote about and wrote about the lives she lived. The division of this book into nine lives is in part a biographer's convenience, in part an emblem of her multiplicity of being. Its intention is to suggest the extraordinarily rich and creative activity of a remarkable woman. Her literary output in itself - over eighty books, editorial work on several others, plays and poems, dozens of short stories, hundreds of reviews and articles and much unpublished work - suggests much more than a single life. In addition, she has had a political life in England and Scotland, she has farmed and fished, she has served the interests of women in many ways, she has campaigned for the Scottish Highlands and Islands and in particular for her own community of Carradale in Kintyre, she has worked for a quarter of a century for the southern African country of Botswana, she has led an unorthodox personal life which has included a committed and sustaining marriage, several lovers, five surviving children and numerous grandchildren and great-grandchildren.

This book has had the benefit of many hours of conversation with its subject, members of her family and people who have known her. Like the century in which Naomi has lived, it is an unfinished story, not only because she is still with us, but because it takes time and distance to complete a narrative and understand its full significance. I hope that writing an unfinished story now will alert subsequent generations to the need to complete it in the future. As the millennium draws to a close we need, perhaps more than ever, to be reminded of what individuals can achieve. Naomi Mitchison does that.

CHAPTER ONE

Daughter

I avoided the lines as, presumably, most right-thinking people
do. Yet there must be some who actually step on the lines.

Small Talk

1

THE HOUSE at 10 Randolph Crescent in Edinburgh's New Town
was a place of steep stairs and dark corners. In its depths were
cellars where stalactites dripped from the roof: 'long thin dark
black things caused by water with lime in it dripping between the
stones in the roof,' as recorded by six-year-old Naomi Haldane in
her diary.[1] A trapdoor covered a well from which came water that
tasted of 'esparto grass and drains'.[2] In spite of this, Naomi's mother
thought it a romantic house, but for the young Naomi the stalactites
were ghosts and prisoners were incarcerated in the cellars. The
large, cavernous bathroom upstairs was also full of ghosts, and the
interests and pleasures of the city itself were not enough to allay
the fears let loose by her powerful imagination. Remembering her
childhood in 1956, Naomi felt that 'as a family we made the most of
what we saw and heard, putting a flourish on to any bare boughs'.[3]
She seems to have learnt early to add flourishes, or perhaps it was
instinctive. She remembered an uncle who was convinced that the

workmen cleaning the dome of St George's Church in Charlotte Square, where her parents had been married (it is now West Register House) were 'men climbing up to heaven'.[4]

Randolph Crescent is a terrace of Georgian houses rising above the Water of Leith, a modest river which winds down from the Pentland Hills to the port of Leith. It is built at the top of a steep slope, and the back of number ten descends four storeys from street level, while the front rises four storeys up. The house had originally belonged to Naomi's great-grandmother, Louisa Trotter, who died in 1895, then to her grandparents. Naomi Haldane was born in the house on 1 November, All Saints Day, 1897, five years after her brother Jack. Most of the houses of her childhood contained sources of terror, and nightmares haunted her. She has all her life been sensitive to the influence of magic and the supernatural. If the nightmares were an affliction, it is difficult to dissociate them from the imagination, which was a gift.

Naomi's parents, John Scott Haldane and Louisa Kathleen Trotter, had been living in Oxford for ten years before Naomi was born, but returned to Edinburgh for her birth. Her mother wanted a woman doctor to attend her, and had to come to Edinburgh to find one. Her father had graduated in medicine at Edinburgh University and started his medical career as a doctor at the city's Royal Infirmary. The stronger Edinburgh connection was in fact through her mother, descended from Henry Dundas, 1st Viscount Melville, a figure who looms large over Scotland's history in the early eighteenth century. The Trotters were linked with many notable Scottish families, including Coutts the bankers, and had for several generations owned estates in the Pentlands – Bush, Castlelaw and Dreghorn. They were establishment figures, benefiting from the Dundas legacy, if not directly, then by association. It was an inheritance that Louisa Kathleen Haldane, herself part Irish and, going back another generation, part Jewish, vigorously maintained.

The family returned to Oxford, but as a child, Naomi Mary Haldane often visited Edinburgh, spending Christmases there – 'how long the grey Edinburgh light took to seep through until one could see the shape of one's stocking at the foot of the bed'[5] – and exploring the streets and the shops. Randolph Crescent was just around the corner from Telford's soaring Dean Bridge. Childhood hopes to see 'a would-be suicide floating down from the Dean Bridge, parachuted by a petticoat as the story had it'[6] revealed a fascination for drama which was richly nourished by visits to Scotland. The Dean Village down below, occupied by mills and tanneries and their workers, was out of bounds. Edinburgh had always been a city of theatrical contrast, and there was no shortage of stimulus for a youthful imagination. There was, the young Naomi was convinced, an encampment of Indians in the central gardens of Randolph Crescent. More tangible were enticing shops, kilted pipers, fancy dress parties, and Edinburgh Castle presiding over Princes Street Gardens.

Another part of Naomi's Scottish inheritance came from Cloan, the country house near Auchterarder in Perthshire where Naomi's father had grown up and his mother and sister still lived. The Haldanes had been influential in that part of Perthshire for generations, owning the adjacent estate of Gleneagles and occupying nearby Foswell as well as Cloan. They had made their marks in the political, religious and intellectual life of Scotland over three centuries, and it was their history that Naomi Mitchison drew on when she came to write her first wholly Scottish novel more than forty years after her earliest visits.

The house at Cloan had its terrors too, with its own ghosts, and there were older cousins who happily preyed on Naomi's susceptibilities. Adults, perhaps inadvertently, contributed. There was a 'Gorgonzola' in the tower room, invented as a joke by Naomi's Aunt Bay, but the cause of dream-invading fear. Aunt Bay was her father's sister Elizabeth, scholar, author and a professional women in a number of fields, who became something of a role model for Naomi, in spite of the Gorgonzola.

Cloan, the house itself, its history and its people offered scope for adding less conventional dimensions to an upper-class Edwardian childhood. The resonance of a place that contained so much family history was bound to alert the child to her inheritance and make her aware of some of the layers of personality and achievement that were stacked behind her. Her grandmother, Granniema, was a presiding presence, keeper of the Haldane past, and clearly a wise and perceptive woman. She recognized and encouraged her granddaughter's artistic leanings, and the two became very close. Aunt Bay was also a powerful influence; an independent, well-travelled professional woman, she had lead a many-stranded life. In 1920, she would become Scotland's first woman Justice of the Peace. She had been active in initiating the public library movement, working with the Carnegie Trust, of which she became a trustee. She was involved in improving housing and in nursing, becoming manager of the Royal Infirmary. She was the author of several books, including a translation of Hegel and a biography of Descartes. Looking back on her life from the perspective of the 1930s, she wrote of the aspiration of the time 'to develop a sense of a concrete life in which we should all play our part. That is, we did not wish to exist as isolated units but as part of an organism which should develop in the right way.'[7] This may have flavoured conversations with her niece; certainly Naomi would articulate, in many different contexts, a similar goal. At some stage, though it is not clear when, Naomi overcame her aversion to her aunt. 'I did not care for Aunt Bay,' she wrote decades later, 'who later on became my dear friend.'[8]

The journey from Oxford to Perthshire was by train, arriving at Auchterarder in the cold early morning after travelling overnight. There was always a sense of anticipation. A carriage and horses took them out of the little town, which had once sustained dozens of hand-loom weavers, and south the couple of miles to Cloan. The house was often full of visitors – statesmen, intellectuals, dignitaries. Many of them would have been invited by Uncle Richard, a leading Liberal politician who became Secretary of State for War in 1905, and then Lord Chancellor. After the First World War, he shifted his support to the young Labour Party. Naomi and the other youngsters 'used to throw stones at the bee-hives in the hope of seeing distinguished generals and philosophers running away'.[9]

The mischief-making did not preclude closer association with the Cloan visitors, and a particular favourite of Naomi's was the writer Andrew Lang. 'Picture me,' she wrote in a memoir of Lang, 'with two fair plaits in a blue pinafore dress, rather long, with a white blouse and probably brown, leather, boy's shoes, the better to run about the hills and glens at the back of Cloan'.[10] Lang may have been best known to Naomi as the author of fairy-tales (though she told him later that she did not care for them) but two more significant interests perhaps rubbed off. In his sixties when Naomi met him, he was a classical scholar, author with S. H. Butcher, of the standard translations of the *Odyssey* and the *Iliad*. He was also a folklorist and anthropologist. He wrote several books on myth and ritual and a history of Scotland. The ancient Greeks, the Celtic heritage, mythology, custom and ritual: these were all to become vital ingredients of Naomi's own first books. Lang's work lent credence to Naomi's early tendency to merge with mythology, which she described in the first of her memoirs, *Small Talk* (1973). When the oats were harvested, she was expected to help glean 'for the old ladies in the Poor House'.[11] Out in the field she met a hare. She married the hare and they kept house inside a corn stook. The hare is a Celtic symbol of fertility, which at that time she did not know, but it is possible that something she heard or read sparked her imagination. On Lang's part, he took her proclivities seriously enough to ask her to participate when he conducted a viva with a student who had written a thesis on fairy-tales.

If Naomi was a perpetrator of mischief, she was also a victim. Cloan meant cousins, mainly male, larger and allies of her brother Jack. In spite of the age difference, Jack was a close companion, giving more time to a much younger sister than was probably usual. But he cheerfully joined in teasing and pranks aimed at Naomi. On one occasion, the boys purloined the dummy head used for making Granniema's caps and put it in Naomi's bed. They may have felt that Naomi's terrified screams were a satisfactory result, but they went on for so long that there was real concern. At the same time, in Naomi's recounting of these memories decades later, there is a hint almost of pleasure, as if the drama of the moment is still savoured, however real the fear. The compensatory imagination can be detected at work, transforming terror into theatre almost as it was happening. There were sometimes intense quarrels with Jack, in which he lost his temper in an alarming way, but when they were children peace and close companionship were always restored.

Sheer space was one of the liberating factors of Cloan. There were large lawns, shrubberies and a walled garden, plenty of territory for games and exploration. There were dogs to join in – Granniema's scotties and cairn terriers and Uncle Richard's St Bernard, Kaiser, whose name underwent a rapid change to Albert in August 1914. The green slopes of the Ochil Hills were on the doorstep, and to the north and west more formidable mountains. Walks were a part of life at Cloan. J. S. Haldane and his brothers thought little of walking fifty or sixty miles in a day, or crossing over to Loch Earn on foot to climb Ben Vorlich, a good twenty-five miles, or to Ben Ledi near Callander, even further. Such distances were beyond a small girl, but walks in the gentler, nearer hills were less demanding and in the early years she could be carried if the going got tough. Jack's diary records climbing neighbouring Craig Rossie with Naomi when she was five – 'we had to carry her and haul her a lot of the way'.[12] When brother and sister were teenagers the Ochils became their favourite walking territory. They would be out for hours and declaim poetry as they went, competing with each other in capping verses. Swimming and hunting for wild flowers were also part of the Cloan summers.

Cloan was a community in itself as well as part of a community. There was a network of routines, responsibilities and ceremonies in which Naomi was expected to play a part: her childhood was framed by clear-cut notions of people and their place. She visited the local poorhouse with her grandmother. She went to church. 'It was a lovely walk down, past the little railway station, over the glen and up again on to the ridge, with more and more black-gloved, Sunday-suited family groups to whom we talked a little, though with a certain awareness that they were not quite our social class.'[13] But in the kirk, 'we were certainly all equals'. The conformity of dress, uniformly dark, proclaimed that 'in the face of another hierarchy

... our own was as nothing'.[14] Church was followed by Sunday lunch, another ritual, always sheep's head and barley, with Uncle Richard teasingly offering the sheep's eye as the choicest delicacy.

There were family prayers on Sunday evening, again underpinned by a sense of appropriate social gradation. 'The ceremony happened after dinner; the great gong would thunder and warn us to compose ourselves. Then the plush benches were brought in; in these and a few plain chairs the servants seated themselves in a long row, beginning with the black silk housekeeper, the butler and my uncle's chauffeur, who had induced the horn of the new motor car to play the opening bars of Lead Kindly Light. Then came the head house maid, my aunt's maid and a descending hierarchy of under house maids, kitchen maids and scullery maids.'[15]

Her parents were free thinkers and she was brought up in a strongly agnostic household, but she enjoyed the Sunday ritual and remembered it with affection. She did not share the belief, but absorbed something of the nature of faith, and respected the austere traditions of Calvinism even though she would fight them. Her grandfather was a lay preacher. Her great-grandfather and his brother, Robert and James Haldane, sold their house and land to evangelize through Scotland, travelling on foot to the country's remote corners. There was a dedication in this, a selflessness and a kind of heroism which were amongst the currents that shaped Naomi herself. She was equally shaped by the social order, apparently accepted and unshakeable, of the Cloan community. There was no way that the family from Oxford, another world, challenged or rebelled against the established ways of Cloan. And of course, the essential ambience of Cloan was its blend of the traditional and the unconventional, the conservative and the liberal. This blend, replicated to some extent by her own immediate family, ran in Naomi's veins.

Cloan and Edinburgh were not the limits of visits to Scotland. The Trotter grandparents rented houses in the summer, usually not far from Edinburgh. There were some interesting expeditions, to the Bass Rock, and by boat to Stirling, under the Forth Bridge, still new enough – it was completed in 1890 – to excite a sense of wonder. There were fishing trips, and a visit to the pottery at Prestonpans where Naomi was allowed to make a pot. But there were also restrictions: no damming of streams, a favourite ploy of Jack and Naomi, or playing on the sands at North Berwick, because of pollution. There were visits to Trotter friends and acquaintances in grand and sometimes exotic houses which offered diversions in the shape of an eccentric individual or a strange plant in a greenhouse. But Naomi was not so comfortable with the Trotter relatives. She found her Trotter grandmother alarming, in her rustling grey and purple silk and satin.

2

Cloan, Edinburgh, the Lothians – these were interludes, however stimulating and however deep their roots. The mainstream of Naomi's childhood was Oxford, where life was more circumscribed as well as being at a distance from so much that hooked Naomi into her heritage. Oxford provided a particular kind of intellectual milieu which proved to be a source of both sustenance and frustration. Most families are a knot of contradictions. The Haldanes, unusually liberal and adventurous in many ways, were no different in this. To a cocooned Edwardian child, the adult world seemed unattainable. The Haldane parents were unexceptionally aloof from the day-to-day lives of their children, whose needs were seen to by nurses and servants. At the same time, all the family had pet names, which suggests a cosy intimacy. John Scott Haldane was 'Uffer' to his children, and his wife 'Maya'. Jack was 'Boy' or 'Boydie' (boy dear), and Naomi was, and has remained to many, 'Nou'.

To the small Nou, Uffer was a source of security and comfort, though preoccupied with work and often away. He seemed ill at ease in the environment of conventionally coded behaviour and appearances upheld by his wife. 'He was unable to look at home in tails or even a dinner jacket',[16] a problem in a household where such formalities were standard. Maya was more formidable, uncompromising in what she expected from her children, perhaps particularly her daughter, whom she assumed would be more malleable. It is clear that Naomi's relationship with her mother was never comfortable, although she did not question Maya's views until she was an adolescent. Years later, Naomi reflected on 'the impossible mother-daughter relationship' and her own 'insufficient love'.[17]

John Scott Haldane had left Edinburgh to work with his uncle, Sir John Burdon-Sanderson, Professor of Physiology. He became involuntarily embroiled in academic politics and rivalries, but eventually was offered a fellowship at New College. His distaste for the academic establishment remained. His experimental work in the physiology of respiration was groundbreaking, particularly in its concern for some of the consequences of industrial development. He worked on the effects of gases on the lungs and heart, investigating conditions in coal mines and sewers, and was often on call to examine problems and accidents. A mining accident could mean a summons to the scene to help men who had been trapped underground. The family were used to his absences and to the risks that he took in the interests of improving his own understanding. 'Exploring the lungs ... led him from the Dundee sewers into coal mines, tin mines, and submarines, up Pike's Peak and down to the bottom of the sea.'[18]

The children were tolerated in their father's lab, yet in Naomi's memoirs Uffer remains a remote figure, only occasionally emerging as an intimate presence, for example when Naomi describes nestling on his knee. He actively involved Jack in his scientific interests; Naomi was not discouraged, but there was an assumption that she could not share in her father's activities as her brother could. She hung around in his lab at home, played with the experimental animals, 'helped' here and there. But if she absorbed the ethos of experimental science, which remained with her all her life, she also seems to have assimilated an understanding that this was a world in which women were, if not excluded, not expected to participate seriously.

Yet much was required of her. Her mother taught her to read at the age of three, and when she balked at words of more than three letters she was put over Maya's knee and slapped. From that point, she remembers, she had no difficulty with reading – but she did have difficulties with her mother.[19] Part of Maya's expectations was the assumption that her children, especially her daughter, would take on the mantle of patrician responsibility which was entrenched in her view of the world. Like the Haldanes, the Trotters were bred to a sense of duty. The political framework was very different, Tory rather than Liberal, but service was at the heart of both. Throughout Naomi Haldane's life a phrase recurs like a refrain: 'I wanted to do something to help.' She herself has located its origins with the liberal Haldanes. It is equally a product of the conservative Trotters.

Louisa Kathleen Trotter was a Tory and a passionate believer in the British Empire. 'The Stuarts and Scotland were things to dream about, but the Empire was here and now; what could one do for it?' she wrote in the memoir she produced late in life.[20] She was a moving spirit of the Victoria League in Oxford, and wrote and spoke on its behalf. Her political views were strongly expressed and she became politically active, canvassing in North Oxford when required. She invited like-minded men and women to the house, servants of the Empire, who assorted oddly with the students and academics who were her husband's associates. They had agreed to differ, and before their marriage, J. S. Haldane undertook not to attempt to dissuade his wife from her views or activities, but was always aware of what he had had to give up. As a training ground for their children, this *modus vivendi* had its merits. As a portrait of a marriage, it suggested the possibility of an at least amiable relationship between two people of very different interests and very different views, both having to deny something of themselves. A long time later, Naomi guessed that sexual relations faded in early middle age. There were only two children (though there may have been a miscarriage) and from the age of ten Naomi herself shared her mother's bedroom, an inhibition to both the mother's conjugal life and the daughter's sexual awakening which was presumably deliberate.

The Haldane's early Oxford years were spent in a small house in Crick Road, but with the birth of Naomi they bought a larger house in St Margaret's Road, a broad, leafy street off Woodstock Road. The interior was decorated in a style which a quarter of a century earlier would have been avant-garde, with William Morris wallpaper and William de Morgan tiles. Naomi thought it an ugly house, but there were compensations. She could amuse herself by walking on the wall that separated the Haldane's garden from the one next door. And, unlike today, Woodstock Road soon left urban Oxford behind. 'One walked into the country in a moment,' Naomi recalled.[21] In 1906, there was another move. Maya's father died and her mother came to live with them, with her maid, so again more space was needed. This time, a house was built for the Haldanes at the end of Linton Road, close to the river (now the site of Wolfson College). Just across the Banbury Road, it was still North Oxford, and close to the preparatory school which both children attended. The house was called Cherwell, and it brought more space both inside and outside. Naomi described it as a 'large and ugly house',[22] but for her mother it offered possibilities. She was an intelligent and energetic woman who needed activity.

Cherwell provided enough land for Naomi's mother to farm on a modest scale, and meant that chickens, Jersey cows and a pony entered her children's lives. Naomi developed an absorbed but unsentimental attachment to animals which grew partly out of scientific curiosity, partly out of her appreciation of their value as sources of comfort. When she needed solace, she would embrace her mother's 'little silk-necked' Jersey bull.[23] There were no strictures against hands-on involvement. She could play with her mice, so long as she wore her blue cotton pinafore. 'I spent hours with my back to the grown-up world and my nose to my mice.'[24] The smell of mice lingered on her pinafore, however often it was washed.

Even as a toddler, the Naomi who appears in photographs has a direct, confidently enquiring, almost challenging gaze. There is no hint of nightmare or uncertainty. This is a girl who, whatever the climate of the time, is looking for and expects to get answers. Certain aspects of being female she had to tolerate – being buttoned into uncomfortable and restrictive clothes, for instance, or having her long, thick hair brushed. But having a big brother was a hugely formative compensation. They share a sense of enquiry, a love of experiment and a significant measure of courage. Jack was a playmate and also a colleague. He was a mentor – Naomi clearly strove to bridge those five years and keep up with him – but in some areas she was more than his equal. Through Jack, she had access to worlds that would otherwise have been denied her through force of circumstance. With Jack she learned the science that was not formally available to her. With Jack, and sometimes his friends, she engaged in adventures and escapades that were closed territory to girls without brothers. Through Jack she met the boys and young men who became her closest friends, including the man she married.

Brother and sister were competitive, but fiercely protective of each other. When Jack fell off his father's bicycle and fractured his skull, he lay upstairs with absolute quiet prescribed. Naomi took this with total seriousness, and when she herself fell down the stairs did not utter a sound. Later, on her tenth birthday, Naomi was thrown from the pony on which she was reluctantly learning to ride (side-saddle) and broke her leg and two ribs, with a suspected dislocation of her neck. This initiated new dimensions of pain, discomfort – and determination. Like Jack, she was cared for at home. The leg was set and re-set. She entered a world of chloroform, ether, opium and intensified nightmares. The surgeon visited regularly, to check progress. There were nurses, who frightened her. When, after three months, the cast was removed from her leg, some of the skin came with it, but with the help of a physiotherapist she regained the use of the limb, fired by overhearing the surgeon saying to her mother that she would never run again. Although there was permanent damage and a legacy of sprained ankles, after additional surgery and weeks of exercises she proved the surgeon wrong. But for a long time she was confined to her bed, and then the sofa. Her mother recounted the entertainment provided by a brilliantly-coloured macaw which placidly walked about on Naomi's bed but screamed when visitors, including her father, came into the room. Only Naomi and her mother were tolerated.

Both Jack and Naomi viewed these accidents with considerable interest. What exactly had happened? What was the experience like? What would the doctors do and why? It is possible, too, that Naomi derived a certain satisfaction from the fact that she had not been outdone by Jack – she too had sustained and overcome serious injury. A current of rivalry ran through their relationship until well into adulthood, perhaps even to Jack's death in 1964.

Naomi was expected to grow up with an appropriate sense of status and responsibility, and to behave in a ladylike fashion. Underpinning this was a hierarchical framework which held the social classes in their place and uncompromisingly identified who belonged where. Her mother attempted to set her on a path which would absorb this, along with a commitment to Empire and the idea of British superiority. The inflexibility of Maya's views might seem to sit oddly with the fact that Naomi was sent to a boys' school, but Maya was also a feminist who, like so many women of her generation, struggled to find a role commensurate with her abilities. There were clearly contradictions in what she wanted for her daughter, but the wish to equip her for a purpose beyond marriage and motherhood was an important factor. She encouraged Naomi to think of medicine, a profession that fitted her own code of service and conduct. She herself had wanted to be a doctor, but for her generation of women it was almost impossible.

The contradictions were inherent in the environment and ethos of Naomi's childhood. She was wrapped in privilege. Servants were taken for granted, and so was a degree of freedom. There was little curiosity about the lives of these men and women who were the pillars of the Haldane lifestyle. At the same time, application and hard work were equally taken for granted. Naomi was expected to conduct herself with dignity and was taught that appearances were important. Yet she was a tomboy. She played wild games, communed with mice and guinea pigs, and spent much of her time in the company of boys, all with the apparent approbation of her mother. Later she claimed that 'as a child I was much protected';[25] the impression, however, is of an unusual acceptance of risk.

3

Naomi went to the Dragon School just along the river, which catered mainly for the sons of academics. She loved it. To her joy, she was treated by the boys as one of them. She felt she was accepted, a member of the group, and although she was sometimes teased and was not allowed to play rugby and cricket, this was offset by her excellent academic results. In many respects, the Dragon School gave her everything she needed. She enjoyed most of the lessons, and outdoing the boys: exams gave scope to her competitive instincts, and later she would miss the excitement this generated. She climbed trees, jumped off walls and joined in escapades with the best of the boys, though 'I was never good at the things that really mattered, like conkers'.[26] Most significantly, she was part of a community, a community of males (aside from teachers) in which she was an equal. She belonged to a gang, which marked out territory, built forts and invented rituals. To her fellow pupils she was 'just another boy' and she rose to that challenge: 'I had to prove I was as good as a boy at everything.'[27]

The Dragon School provided community. It may also have laid the foundations of Naomi's writing career. Each summer holiday, the pupils were expected to keep a diary of their activities. Naomi's efforts, even at the age of six, were detailed and sophisticated. Her diaries included not only accounts of what she did and where she went, but careful observations of what she saw. Detailed descriptions of plants, of shells collected on the beach, of processes witnessed - the pottery at Prestonpans, for example - and of knowledge absorbed from the adults around her went into these diaries. In some respects, she was emulating Jack. She was also encouraged in her interest in plants by Granniema, who herself made botanical drawings and paintings and expected to receive from Naomi meticulous records. By the age of eleven or twelve she was a member of the Wild Flower Society and taking a serious interest in botany.

Like all children, Naomi received mixed messages. Her mother seemed both to oppose and reinforce the social *status quo*. She was a feminist, a modern woman, but maintained a highly traditional code of behaviour. Naomi spent a significant amount of time in her company and they enjoyed expeditions together. Easter holidays were spent at Sennen Cove, where they went initially because J. S. Haldane was doing experimental work at Dolcoath mine near Penzance, the location of an outbreak of a mysterious disease. While Jack went off with his father, mother and daughter had their own adventures, exploring dangerous cliffs and rocks and going on sometimes risky boat trips. 'It *was* rather rough,' Maya commented on a voyage to the lighthouse, 'and I was glad to find that Naomi really enjoyed it and showed no symptom either of sea-sickness or fear.'[28] Maya clearly did not believe in cossetting her daughter. On another occasion, the local coastguards took them out to the Brissons, a notorious cluster of offshore rocks. When they were safely back the captain remarked, '"You two be the only women folk to come alive off the Brissons."'[29] Parallel with the rules of etiquette came a model of adventure and physical courage, and perhaps also of female comradeship. Naomi had all her mother's boldness. On an occasion when she was being taught to paddle on the Cherwell her canoe overturned. The young man who was teaching her called, "I'll rescue you", to which Naomi curtly replied, "No you won't."[30]

At this stage, Naomi - and Jack - absorbed and echoed their mother's political views, in spite of the Haldane liberal tradition. Their father kept his opinions to himself; it was part of the bargain. He seemed oblivious of class, and through him Naomi mingled with miners, students from various backgrounds, artisans, whom he invited to the house. He saw no conflict with the world of social and intellectual privilege which he himself inhabited. And it was some time before Naomi herself became aware of the contradictions accommodated in the household.

She shared an environment with boys who were destined to achieve, at the same time as breathing an atmosphere of denial to women which could not be dispelled by her mother's beliefs or the adventures mother and daughter shared. She was cushioned by privilege, at the same time as encountering deprivation. Then Jack went to Eton, entering territory where she could not follow. It was made clear that, though boarding school was not exactly ruled out, the parental preference was for her to stay at home. When the time came for Naomi to leave the Dragon School, alternative arrangements were made for her to continue her education. But the contrast with Jack was stark, and resentment was inevitable.

Jack's departure for Eton was a severe wrench, intensified by his experience of victimisation. Naomi was incensed when she learned from him that, arriving at the school with a broken arm, he had been mercilessly bullied, though he had said nothing of this in his letters home. She implored her parents to remove him forthwith, but the prevailing ethos insisted that the public schoolboy learned to endure. Jack stayed, and the situation improved when senior boys, one of whom was Julian Huxley, took his part. This was the beginning of a longstanding friendship with the intellectually-prestigious Huxley family. Later, Naomi would visit her brother at Eton and thoroughly enjoy her taste of his life there. By that time, he was integrated into the Eton community, and she briefly felt a part of it too. She suspected that as a senior pupil he probably participated in exactly the same kind of torturing of younger boys that had been meted out to him. Though outraged by what she felt was injustice, there was an acceptance that the world was a violent place, that to excel, even to survive, required a robust courage. 'In many ways I think I was a pretty violent child.'[31] Naomi's own children were all sent to boarding school, though not to Eton.

Like the Dragon School, Eton represented community. It may not have been an entirely right-minded community in Haldane eyes, but it clearly fitted many Haldane requirements and Naomi believed that Jack came to like it. Over the years Etonians were frequent visitors to Cherwell. In a sense, Naomi herself became a vicarious Etonian, not only joining in whatever was going, but often taking charge, initiating, providing the imaginative spark. She was, after all, used to bridging the five years between herself and her brother, and his fellow-Etonians gave her access to more 'brothers'.

Jack was her first and best companion and in some respects her

most lasting love. He was closer to her than either parent. He was
an intellectual partner, a teacher, a colleague. At the same time, he
represented much that was denied her, even as he was helping her
to some of it. She wanted to be a boy. She wanted fully to enter the
male world of science and intellectual exchange whose margins she
occupied. She wanted to be purposeful and to be acknowledged. She
wanted to ride a bicycle, forbidden by her mother because she
believed it would damage the female sexual organs: this, in spite of
- or perhaps because of - the fact that Aunty Bay celebrated the
bicycle as an enormously liberating factor in women's lives. Naomi
was observing a world in which all these things came to men as of
right. Although she was amongst remarkable women, it was obvious
that they were unusual, and perhaps equally obvious that, with the
exception of Aunt Bay, they were unfulfilled. (Aunt Bay, of course,
may have been perceived as unfulfilled: she never married.) And in
her mother's case, it was hard to disentangle achievement from
aspects of parental control that were less palatable.

There was another world, however, and this one was totally open
to her - the world of books. She was an indiscriminate devourer of
words. She had free access to the books in the house, and had her
favourite spot for reading, curled up in a window seat. Anything
attracted her, not only fiction. She was as likely to pick up
something connected with her father's work as the latest E. Nesbit.
At the age of eleven she began a continuing habit of writing to
authors she admired, with a letter to Sir Percy Fitzpatrick who had
written *Jock of the Bushveld*. She remembers driving the pony cart
- the same pony who caused her broken leg - into the centre of
Oxford and tying up outside Blackwell's bookshop for a browse.
Sampling the stock at Blackwell's was 'a very good way of getting
through literature that you might not get hold of otherwise'.[32] She
also admitted a longing to read the popular children's papers which
were forbidden by her mother. She never did, because, she said, 'I
was in many ways rather a good little girl, and this longing seemed
to me to be supremely naughty.'[33]

At what point reading expanded into writing - beyond the
obligatory diaries - is not clear, but while she was still at the

Dragon School Naomi was composing her first poems. She also embarked on her first experiment with drama, forming a partnership with a schoolfriend named Jack Slessor. 'We wrote a who-dunnit play with revolvers and detectives and carefully designed exits and entrances.'[34] Half the fun was in the 'exciting meetings and conversations'.[35] Jack was lame and excluded, like Naomi, from the more vigorous sports, but the two rowed on the river together. Naomi would always be a sociable writer, whether or not she was writing in collaboration. She liked to have people around her, a sense of life going on, and often chose to write in public places. Yet she adds, 'We could be so enviably single-minded about such things, not letting any other aspects of the world interrupt.'[36]

As a teenager, writing plays and organizing performances became a favourite activity. In a sense it can be seen as an extension of the gang life of the Dragon School. Both involved ritual, and ritual was a strand that ran vividly through Naomi's childhood years. She found it at Cloan with the family prayers and church-going, where she warmed to the comfort offered by ceremony and custom. Even when very young (though this may be hindsight), she seemed to have an instinctive understanding of the bonding effects of joint worship. The rituals of Christmas, of birthdays, of all celebratory occasions, held strong appeal. It was partly the excitement, the heightening of experience, partly the drawing together of lives which in ordinary circumstances perhaps hardly touched. Throughout her life, wherever she made her home she required an environment suitable for a ceremonial communality.

There were other kinds of rituals, of the gang or the group, the exchange of dares, the elaboration of codes of language and behaviour, a whole range of actions and ceremonies that bound the individual into something larger than herself. Granniema presided over such a ritual when, every New Year's Eve, she summoned Haldane children and grandchildren together to assess the year just past and the year ahead. In such a context, for Naomi to find for herself an occupation that embodied one of the world's oldest rituals, that of story-telling, was no surprise. She discovered it at an early age, and discovered also that through it she could channel most of her emotions and aspirations. Writing has served that function for her for more than nine decades.

4

Writing seems to have come instinctively to Naomi. It was a traditional route to female self-assertion, and she had the example of Aunt Bay as well as countless works of fiction written by women to support her. (Decades later she was attacked by a male writer for children, whose book she had criticized: he insisted that all good fiction for children had been, was being and would always be, written by men.[37]) She grew up in a household where, if her father had a profession, her mother had a role, and a room of her own in which to pursue it. Her mother's desk, with its books and papers and all the signs of purposeful work, may not have had the intrinsic interest of her father's laboratory, but it nevertheless signalled serious activity. Naomi's holiday diaries were also serious, not just because they were a school task but because she herself, and her family, took them seriously. In a letter to a young aspiring writer, probably dating from the 1980s, Naomi remembered being confined to bed by her broken leg. 'I think that was the time I began to think about telling myself stories.'[38]

But stories were already an integral part of her life, with its openness to make-believe and dressing-up, to pageantry and colour, to objects to be treasured and handled as icons of other lives. It was a natural step to put these currents of her life into words. She had always been encouraged to write, to observe with care and record what she saw. She grew up believing this was valuable. It was excellent training for the harnessing of the imagination required by story-telling. In her teenage years she was writing poetry, which was a way of constructing a narrative which reflected her own life. It was also a way of filling time in a purposeful fashion.

Although she loved the Dragon School, she recognized the

inadequacies of formal education, though that was probably not quite how they appeared at the time. She was frustrated by rules. There was too much that was not explained, too many questions that no attempts were made to answer. There were subjects that were a struggle, Latin verse and mathematics in particular. History and literature were a pleasure, but the books she 'had' to read at school never had the same magic as those she discovered for herself at home. And there was much else that she discovered at home in areas, science above all, that school did not tackle. Her education was, from a very early age, bipartite. At home there were currents of enquiry and investigation which taught her much of interest but, perhaps most importantly, also taught her to be resourceful and intellectually self-motivated. These lessons were to be crucial.

Her formal schooling came to an abrupt end when she entered puberty. No one had explained menstruation to her. She was baffled when she discovered blood and was whisked way from a male habitat. Growing up with boys, there had been no girl friends to learn from. Now everything was different, and she was hedged by reticence as to why. No one now could close their eyes to her gender, and the world of gangs and dares and shared adventures was snatched away. Or so it was thought.

Bewildered by her precipitate removal from the Dragon School, Naomi did not seem to have strong feelings about an alternative. It was likely that she was aware that no girls' school could be a substitute for the Dragon School, and her first vicarious experiences of Eton, through Jack, cannot have encouraged her to have positive thoughts of what public school might offer. What she got was a less than happy compromise. With four other girls, only one of whom became a real friend, she was taught by a governess, Miss Blockey, who stayed in Cherwell with all the ambivalence of status that still clung to that particular role. She was neither a servant nor one of the family, although when required she could be almost treated as the latter. Naomi learnt little from her, apart from a smattering of German. Deprived of the competitive ethos of the classroom, subjects which had once been challenging seemed dull. Literature and history lost their appeal. At the same time, the pressure to behave like a lady became more onerous.

Lessons took place in the schoolroom at the top of the house, still containing reminders of the games shared with Jack, the box of bricks, the model railway, the doll's house which had been a particularly absorbing plaything. Miss Blockey was amiable but much of the time Naomi was bored. She had extra lessons from others in Latin and arithmetic, which helped a little, but essentially formal education had become something to be tolerated. The Dragon School had helped to nourish the life of the imagination. One of the few ways in which Miss Blockey contributed to this essential aspect of Naomi's development was when, at her pupil's insistence, she played the piano while Naomi danced and recited.

Games of the imagination remained pre-eminent, and her four fellow-pupils were important here. 'We went to tea with one another and played versions of the games I had always played, with an element of make-believe, of being someone else, someone more interesting.'[39] Frances Parkinson, granddaughter of the Warden of Wadham College, was her most sympathetic companion, entering into the spirit of Naomi's more adventurous games. They played in the Fellows' Garden at Wadham. 'I do remember playing prisoners and captives under one of the dark, spreading yew trees and making Frances tie my wrists...'[40]

Naomi bought a jug at a jumble sale, inscribed with 'Adventure to the Adventurous'. She made up her mind that this would be her motto, yet was experiencing the increasing circumscription of her life. It was not just the closing of the door on the escapades of the Dragon School and the confinement to largely female territory. It was the discovery that the limitations of that territory were not only social, but physiological. Being female meant painful periods, embarrassment, curtailed activities, the awkwardness of dealing with menstrual blood in the days before sanitary towels or tampons. With the exception of Frances, her female companions were clearly disappointing, not the comrades in adventure she was wanting. For a girl who had been growing up a boy and encouraged by her spirited mother to be spirited herself, it was particularly hard. Both boyish activities and an acknowledgement of burgeoning sexuality were denied. Inevitably, the games in the Wadham Fellows' Garden suggested a way – only partly conscious – of flouting this denial.

Two factors clearly undermined restriction. One was the surviving vigour of the imagination, which like a river in spate carved out new channels if it met an obstruction. The other was a huge and cool curiosity, fostered by an environment of science and research which was always within reach even if not wholly welcoming. Such education in science as she received was self-motivated, and therefore particularly valued. It also stemmed from her closeness to her brother, a further enhancement.

Jack was nearing the end of his time at Eton. He recognized his sister's hunger for knowledge, and the deficiencies of what was being supplied. On occasion he gave Naomi lessons himself. He drew her attention to new books, and encouraged an interest in the theatre, an enthusiasm shared with their father. Pantomimes, Shakespeare, Gilbert and Sullivan, Shaw and Galsworthy were all experienced in Oxford. When she was fifteen, there began visits with Jack to London theatres, or sometimes the cinema – 'but I don't think we took that seriously'.[41] Visits to London included the experience of eating in restaurants, a rare treat. If at first it was the larger-than-life colour and action of the theatre that appealed, by this time Naomi was responding to the portrayal of modern life and problems found in Shaw and Galsworthy. A visit to Oxford by the Abbey Theatre introduced her to contemporary Irish playwrights, and the excitement of works such as *The Playboy of the Western World*. 'It wasn't acting; it was being,' she wrote later.[42] It was a distinction to be aware of, but also one that she herself learnt early to blur.

The world was changing, not only because Naomi was making the transition from schoolgirl to young woman and was encountering new experiences – though not as many as she craved – but because the everyday environment really was becoming substantively different. The overwhelming impact of the First World War tends to exaggerate the picture of Edwardian life and society retaining a quiet order and unhurried pace until shattered by the horrors of modern war. The shattering had already begun, and Naomi was growing up in the midst of it, however protected she was. Electricity, the telephone, the internal combustion engine were all challenging the fabric of existence. A telephone was installed at Cherwell, there were motor-buses and cars on Oxford's streets. The first flying machines were taking to the air. The Haldane household had never shut its doors to innovation, nor the consequences of industrial and technological success; even if it had wanted to, it was becoming less and less easy. If North Oxford sheltered the adolescent daughter of the Haldanes from many of life's less palatable realities, novels, plays and science penetrated that shelter, and provided plenty of glimpses of other worlds for the imagination to feed on.

However strong was Maya's needs for a vicarious career through her daughter, her requirement that Naomi recognize and conform to polite behaviour and traditional standards was stronger. The transition from girlhood to young ladyhood was explicit. The long hair was put up. The short dress and pinafore gave way to long skirts, and the behaviour that went with the pinafore, the tree-climbing and company of mice, was expected to be abandoned too. Naomi now joined the adults for dinner and was constrained to obey the rules of polite conversation. There were frequent formal dinner parties, to which students were often invited, and Naomi enjoyed them. Everyone dressed for dinner, a habit that Naomi has never given up, and if the food was plain, the table itself, with its silver, linen and flowers, was not, and neither were the manners that accompanied it.

There was a counterbalance to such elaborate formality. Sunday suppers, to which students were also invited, could be jolly affairs, especially when Jack was at home and had friends to stay. Their father's unconventionality flourished in spite of the pressures of an orthodox environment, and of course Oxford offered plenty of examples of eccentricity, enjoyed by Naomi and tolerated, it seemed, by the community. When Jack entered New College as a student, Naomi was able to have closer contact with university life. She did not like to be excluded. She was in a hurry to be admitted to the grown-up world. Asked in her nineties what it was she thought she would gain in adulthood, she replied, 'Power'.[43] She wanted to be able to control her own life in a way that was hardly possible for an Edwardian girl of privileged upbringing. She clearly also, from an early age, wanted to influence the lives of others.

Naomi could not move around the streets of Oxford or spend time in the company of the opposite sex without a chaperone, but she could observe and monitor the behaviour and breeding patterns of her guinea pigs. An interest that began as curiosity developed into serious experimentation, encouraged by Jack. They acquired large numbers of the animals, kept in hutches alongside the path that went past the tennis court to the boathouse where their canoes were kept. Naomi fed them and cleaned out the hutches. They kept stud books; every guinea pig had a name. Although Naomi's relationship with the animals was probably unhealthily close, it did not prevent her from doing post mortems on pregnant females that died, to find out the characteristics of the unborn litter. The combination of intense personalization and objective curiosity was well established; it would stay with her.

Jack took her scientific activities seriously and accepted her as a partner in experiment and enquiry. Her father was clearly less accepting, not, perhaps, because he did not value her but because there was Jack, male and older, as a natural colleague. He did not need Naomi, except to give an occasional hand with some of the more mundane tasks. Though not excluded from his lab, she was not included in the work or admitted to her father's thoughts and theories.

> Sometimes I did a bit of washing up, or watching what was happening in one of the large metal chambers where experiments on respiration were going on, occasionally I was left with the instruction that if the experimenter – usually my father – fell over unconscious, I was to undo the door, pull him out and do artificial respiration. But this never happened.[44]

Yet she absorbed information as well as a scientific habit of the mind. And even if she was not seen by her father as a fellow-scientist, in the way that Jack was, clearly he took it for granted that she would act reliably and sensibly if required. This sense of trust and assumption of responsibility must have helped to build confidence.

Her first scientific paper, written jointly with Jack, on colour inheritance in rats was published before she had received any formal education in science. But although at various times in her life Naomi has described herself as a scientist, and the scientific habit has never left her, there is no suggestion that she had a burning ambition to follow science as a career. She loved her guinea pigs and was fascinated by genetics. She admired her father enormously and had a huge respect for his commitment, his hard work and, perhaps most of all, for his often lonely position *vis-à-vis* the scientific establishment. Her interest and her instinct for experimentation came naturally and her lack of training did not seem to bother her. Jack himself, destined for a highly distinguished scientific career, did not take a degree in science. After a year at Oxford reading mathematics and biology, he switched to Greats and pursued his interest in Greek and Latin language and history. These interests would also rub off on Naomi; equally important was an assumption that formal training was not a prerequisite for a career. For Jack, there seems never to have been any doubt which direction he would take. For Naomi, science was not an irresistible call: 'Have I any reason to think I was a budding scientist? Not really.'[45]

5

The years between the Dragon School and marriage were in many ways a curious lull. If Naomi was not a budding scientist, neither was she, she writes, a 'budding anything else serious or tangible'.[46] At this stage, she disliked history and had no particular flair for languages. 'If I was anything, I was a good observer, not only of guinea pigs and wild plants, but also of people, and especially of

people in relation to myself, a not-uncommon teenage interest.'[47]
She was growing up physically. She was acquiring a patchy
knowledge of a few subjects in which she took no particular
interest. She was meeting interesting people - academics, her
father's co-researchers (especially Ted Boycott, who was one of the
team in Cornwall), friends of her brother, the Empire-builders her
mother invited to the house, politicians. There is no sense that she
was unhappy; rather that her life was pervaded with a vague
dissatisfaction. The main escape route was the imagination and its
stimulants. Fortunately, there were quite a lot of those, and people
featured prominently amongst them.

Friends were crucial, not so much the girls - except for Frances
- who shared her desultory education, but those who came to the
house as students or with Jack. Chief among these were the
Huxleys. Julian had championed Jack in his early, unhappy years
at Eton, and Aldous and Trevennan, his younger brothers, became
close friends. Aldous started at Eton a year after Jack, and when he
was recovering from an eye disease which had made him
temporarily but distressingly blind he came to stay at Cherwell. It
was 1913. He was given a room next to the schoolroom at the top of
the house 'where he played the piano for long hours by himself'.[48]
He became an influential friend of the fifteen-year-old Naomi, and
they remained close for many years.

In spite of the fact that Naomi proposed that Aldous should be
her lover, probably moved by curiosity rather than passion, their
relationship was essentially comradely. Aldous declined the
invitation, possibly rather shocked at the proposal: the seduction
of the daughter of his hosts would not have been out of place in the
fiction he would later be writing but clearly went against his
principles in reality. He was at this time tall and thin and
'dreadfully vulnerable looking, his long arms and legs dangling
across the back of chairs or sofas'.[49] He and Naomi spent a great
deal of time together, having picnics up the Cherwell, 'making fires
and boiling kettles'.[50] 'We were always laughing and scrapping.'[51]
But in amongst the laughter there was extensive and serious
discussion and debate, and education. Aldous introduced her to new

writers, encouraged her to read in areas she had not encountered, exciting her interest in literature and stimulated her urge to write.

Trev Huxley and Gervas Huxley, a cousin, were both at Oxford. They were frequent visitors to the house, along with Lewis Gielgud, another Old Etonian. Naomi had got herself a new gang. In a sense, the games they played were an extension of Dragon School adventures. There were charades and play-acting, suppers and picnics, walks and river expeditions. Naomi was surrounded by boys again, so accepted in the house they were almost like brothers. Bird and flower spotting walks with Trev were not considered improper or to require the safety of numbers. No one supplanted Jack, and Cloan still offered opportunities to have him to herself, when they set off on long walks in the hills, Naomi no longer having to be helped or carried. But even at Cloan she could not always have him to herself. There was an occasion, on an expedition to climb Ben Vorlich, when Jack chose another young woman as his climbing partner, and Naomi seethed with jealous rage.

In the early summer of 1914 they were in Oxford, Jack's undergraduate career was nearly at an end. Naomi was allowed to accompany Jack to two college Commem balls. Some dancing classes were necessary, and of course an appropriate dress – long and white, with a low neck and short sleeves, and long, white, close-fitting kid gloves with pearl buttons. Careful preparations, careful instructions as to behaviour, advice and warnings – yet, somehow Naomi managed to find herself with a young man to whom she was not related in Oxford's High in the early hours. He 'wandered down with me in my white dress to the empty High. A single motorbike came and went, passing Univ and Queen's and I saw for the first time, the shape, the exact, beautiful curve of the High, normally blotted by two-way traffic, but suddenly clear. We both saw it.'[52] A shared experience, a moment of dual consciousness: it was perhaps hindsight that gave that moment a particular significance, nevertheless, it was recalled and set down. Also set down in *All Change Here*, memoirs published in 1975, was a poem Naomi wrote at the time about the New College Commem ball. She and her partner are sitting out – the title of the poem:

Surely you heard, as we sat here –
It pierced right through the violins –
That foreman's whistle, shrill and clear?
They go to work; and we sit here.[53]

The partner would become her husband, but the poem, written in the summer of 1914, contrasting the privileged world of the dancers with that of everyday work, has a resonance less of romance than of premonition.

The academic year was coming to an end. Aldous and Gervas, both at Balliol, gravitated to the Haldane household where they, and all the young men who were drawn into Naomi's gang, were welcomed not only by Jack and Naomi, but by their mother. 'Short, square, energetic and vital, Mrs Haldane had a great love and understanding of young men and women,' Gervas wrote in his autobiography.[54] There was open house at Cherwell, and a rare opportunity to meet young women. Professor Haldane was a vague presence in the background, only visible at mealtimes and usually silent – perhaps something of him found its way into Aldous's portrayal of Lord Tantamount in *Point Counter Point* (1928). But if Uffer was silent and remote, Jack made up for it, 'looking like a great shaggy bear and matching his wit with the bawdiness of his repertory of songs'.[55] The latter were presumably kept out of mixed company.

In an atmosphere of relaxed good spirits, Naomi assembled her cast and directed their fictional actions. It was her second dramatic venture with the group. The first, the year before, was a performance of a play she wrote herself, *Saunes Bairos: A Study in Recurrence*. Clearly influenced by her current preoccupations, including genetic experiment, it is set in a mythical country and explores ideas of cultural engineering and repression. Significantly, the central characters are a brother and sister. With her next attempt, Naomi was clearly in her element, tasting something of the power of the adult world for which she had been so impatient. In the garden Naomi, Jack, Trev, Aldous, Gervas, Lewis Gielgud, a friend of Jack's called Dick Mitchison, and others performed scenes from Aristophanes' *The Frogs* and another play by Naomi called *Prisoners of War*. The prisoners are captive members of the Roman army. A sacrifice is required. Naomi herself played the king's daughter who wielded the knife: 'And now the sword. Look at the sun on it.'[56] The language is purplish. The strain of violence suggests that Naomi was already absorbed by the crueller aspects of human behaviour which would find powerful expression in her first fiction: violence, but no sex - which may explain the violence, the only channel available to an Edwardian teenager for passionate physical expression.

Naomi was sixteen years old, and with these plays was embarking on an exploration of the territory of her first published books. It was serious stuff, but, more important, it was enormous fun. The atmosphere was caught by Gervas, writing more than half a century later:

> In retrospect it seems as if the sun must always have been shining that summer so that our rehearsals were followed by gay picnics in punts on the river ... I fancied myself in love with Naomi; it was a pleasantly mild and undemanding form of love that was free from any pangs of jealousy or passionate desire and was satisfied by enjoying the presence of its object. An especially happy and hilarious farewell evening river picnic followed the play's final performance. It was the end of term, and poling our punts back in the warm moonlight we planned further play acting for the next summer and bade each other goodbye until we should meet again in October.[57]

For some it was a very long goodbye. That August, Trev committed suicide. And Britain declared war on Germany. All the young men except for Aldous, whose eyes made him unfit for service, joined the army.

But there was another evening picnic before that emphatic punctuation mark. Punts and canoes set off up the river. Naomi shared a canoe with Dick Mitchison, perhaps at his contrivance, for it was not only Gervas who was drawn to her. She was attractive, with vivid, commanding blue eyes, long light hair, and a look of almost imperious intelligence apparent in her photographs. Finding their canoe sufficiently apart from the others, Naomi impulsively began to talk to Mitch about the fears and nightmares that still plagued her. Everyday objects took on terrifying shapes. Sometimes in a state between sleeping and waking, she experienced currents of inexplicable sensations and trans-formations. 'In this state I was held, unable to move, while something rushed by or through me ... apparently taking with it some part of my thinking or will.'[58] There had been no one she felt she could talk to about the terror and distress of these experiences, not Jack, although she felt that he shared 'the irrational streak',[59] certainly not her parents, and none of her friends, until that evening on the river she suddenly found herself telling it all to Mitch. Until then she had felt 'no grown up would ever be able to understand why some things were frightening'.[60] It seemed in conflict with the scientific environment of Cherwell. To her surprise and relief, Mitch responded with sympathy and understanding.

Dick Mitchison, straightforward, honest and honourable, probably less prone to extremes of imagination, helped Naomi to break out of the grip of nightmare, although the nightmares did not end. If Naomi had a talent for the transcendental, Dick could counter with kindness and a steady decency. He did not laugh at her susceptibilities or attempt to diminish them with reductionist explanation. A relationship was founded which had little to do with the intellectual high spirits and competitiveness which marked so many of Naomi's Oxford friendships. Dick obtained a first class degree, and went on to read for the Bar. He too wrote verse, but he was not a volatile wit, like Jack, or an ironic observer of human fallibility, like Aldous. He did not challenge Naomi to compete and outdo. He did not drench himself in poetry or abandon himself in currents of the imagination. Perhaps that was the attraction.

With poetry as well as plays, the habit of putting into words her feelings and her attempts to get to grips with the physical and intellectual world was well entrenched. But she occupied a world where it was almost taken for granted that men, at least, of sensibility and education were steeped in literature and spoke and wrote accordingly. It did not necessarily mean that they would choose writing as a profession. Naomi could not avoid seeing Jack as a model, even if it was a model that she knew she could not imitate. Literature and science sat comfortably together in his environment. Aldous Huxley occupied similar territory, which was clearly one reason why he became so close a friend. In writing poems and plays Naomi was not necessarily implying a choice of one direction rather than another.

Life was not all drama and serendipity. She felt that her education was accidental and occasional but some of it, at least, had an element of formality. At sixteen, she sat 'Locals' in Oxford, examinations which were a staging post to university, which she took in her stride, and went on to be a home student at St Anne's College. But she never took a degree. There is no suggestion that she felt this to be important, rather that formal study and the taking of exams were a sideshow. Real science was experimenting with breeding guinea pigs or the frontier science of her father. It was observing, recording, if necessary putting oneself to the test. The example of Jack and Dick and Aldous encouraged a belief that the important areas of intellectual study were language, literature and history, whatever profession one was heading for. There was no lack of encouragement for Naomi to read for herself in these areas. Classical history and literature and James Frazer's *The Golden Bough*, all twelve volumes of which she read avidly - it gave credence to her own sensitivity towards magic and the irrational - were particularly stimulating nourishment for her imagination. They added to the raw material that was building into the foundations of much of her early writing.

Naomi's seventeenth summer may in retrospect appear to be a glorious and carefree holiday before the terrible realities following August 1914 assaulted her. But the constraints remained, the strictures as to what was acceptable behaviour, the inconvenience of confining clothes, her hair brushed by a maid, the disproportionate weight carried by the minutiae of life, the daily tasks and chores generally looked after by someone else but appearances counting for almost everything. Naomi was extraordinarily privileged in many ways, and had expectations, however ill-defined, that placed her worlds away from most of her contemporaries. That she was at least partially aware of this privilege is suggested by her poem 'Sitting out'. Her father's work and associates had opened doors to people and places outside the immediate territory of North Oxford. She was beginning to question her mother's assumptions about the British Imperial destiny.

In the meantime, it was obvious to everyone, though perhaps not to Naomi, that Dick Mitchison was in love with her. But love was overtaken – or perhaps accelerated – by war. No one realized the extent to which life would change after August 1914, but for Naomi, Jack and Dick and thousands of others the fact that it did change was evident at once. It seemed like an adventure, life imitating art, the real thing. Naomi fretted that she was excluded from the action. Jack joined the Black Watch. The Haldane cousins joined up, Patrick also in the Black Watch, Graeme in the navy. Pat would be killed. Dick initially joined the Inns of Court Officers Training Corps and then went on to become a Second Lieutenant in the Queen's Bays, a cavalry regiment. His younger brother volunteered as a dispatch rider; he, too, would be killed. Naomi started classes in first aid and home nursing.

Everyone thought it would soon be over. Nevertheless, it is probable that war shaped the process of love. Naomi was invited by Dick's parents to visit the family at Frolbury Manor in Surrey. She was nearly seventeen. She took the train from Oxford to Paddington with little or no experience of travelling by herself. To be invited solo to stay in a rather grander home than her own was also new. She did not guess that the invitation was laden with significance and that high-level exchanges had taken place between her mother and Dick's.

Dick appeared in uniform. 'I am inclined to think now,' she wrote many years later, 'that I might have said yes to the first man (I beg your pardon: officer) in uniform who asked me to marry him in

August 1914. It would have been 'war work'; it would have been involvement in the great excitement.'[61] The war would involve her, like many others, in ways she could not have anticipated. Its outbreak turned the tables on her life. That summer, she had been the leader of the gang. Now the gang was breaking up, its members entering territory where she could not follow. But she could, at least, marry a soldier.

She was fond of Dick, as she was of several of Jack's friends. She said 'yes' at once when he proposed, but then panicked. 'I was very frightened at having said yes ... the first time in my life I couldn't sleep all night. I thought, what have I done, what have I done?'[62] She rushed home to Oxford, ostensibly to take a nursing exam, but more urgently needing familiarity in order to digest what she had undertaken. In a notebook of 1981 Naomi reflects on the making of choices:

> When we make choices, that is not usually felt to be something irrevocable, or even deeply important. But one choice determines the next. And suddenly another river opens out and some of us feel we have just got to see what comes next.[63]

A series of small choices had led to a big choice – of Dick as her husband. The river opened out, and was alarming in its expanse and strangeness. Naomi wondered if she would not lose more than she gained. After all, life itself was opening out and offering more. The summer that was ending had demonstrated that. To step straight into marriage without exploring that growing freedom might be to deny opportunities that would never recur.

She did not back out. Her family approved. More important, Jack was pleased. It was perhaps inevitable that Naomi would marry a man who was already a close friend of Jack's. He wrote encouragingly from Nigg on the Cromarty Firth, where his battalion was stationed:

> So he has has he? It was plain that he was in love with you, but I didn't know how far you realized how much in love he was, and if so how far you reciprocated it. I also didn't know if he

would propose now in view of the war, though I think he was quite right to.

Dick, Jack felt, was 'a good egg' and in his view sixteen was not too young to marry: 'there is, I think, little question of your not knowing your own mind, because you have one to know'.[64]

Naomi and her parents visited Jack at Nigg, but the business of war still wasn't entirely real. Back in the south of England, Dick was practising cavalry charges.

Naomi began to visit Frolbury quite often. She enjoyed the countryside - it was new territory for botanizing. But it was the billiards room where the courtship between Naomi and Dick was acted out, in the months before Dick went to the front. It was a difficult time, the pressures of war inevitably intruding on their developing relationship. Naomi was still uncertain.

> I couldn't explain there were words and touches I didn't want. It had been something of a shock to find that someone whom I had considered as a brother, somebody who had understood about the nightmares and not laughed, had suddenly turned into something else. Perhaps if it had been possible to take the whole thing at a slower tempo I would have been able to respond. But there was a war on and nothing could wait.[65]

Jack wrote in March 1915 and asked, 'how do you like being kissed?'[66] The answer seems to have been, in spite of her bold suggestion to Aldous Huxley, not a great deal. In a poem called 'The proposal', published in her first collection *The Laburnum Branch* (1926), she expresses the intensity of her difficulty in accepting the transition of Dick from brother to lover:

> *Oh please, you're hurting me! Oh, let me go!*
> *You mustn't, mustn't, mustn't kiss me so!*

The poem reflects doubts and anxieties about more than physical intimacy and worries about the survival of friendship when the nature of a relationship changes.

> *We were such good friends.*
> *(When a thing's perfect, then of course it ends.)*

It then goes on to look at the effect on other friendships of having pledged herself to one man.

> *Will all my other friendships change as well?*
> *Will they think differently of me now*
> *Because I'm yours? One never does know how*
> *These things work out. And, oh, it's not a bit*
> *Like any book or poem talks of it!*[67]

The ambiance of friendship would certainly change, in fact had already, for nothing would bring back the summer of 1914, and it was not Naomi's impending marriage that brought that loss.

also brought a flood of advertising from department stores. From Jenners in Edinburgh, for example -- 'may we ask if we can be of any service at this time, in preparing a scheme for any furnishing that may be required'.[2] This was the world that beckoned, the world of running a home, of responsibilities, of being grown up. Society photographers also touted for business. Engagement photographs taken at this time show a serious but schoolgirlish young woman with a slightly hesitant expression.

The exploration of her relationship with Dick was hedged with constraints. It was not considered correct for them to be alone together in public. When Dick took her for lunch at Simpson's in Piccadilly, parental wrath descended. When they went north to Cloan to meet the family, they had to travel in separate trains. Naomi resented being treated as a child, although these restrictions limited the opportunities for the intimacies she found difficult. It is likely that part of her motive for marriage was precisely to escape parental rule, to reach a territory of her own. It would be some time before she achieved this.

At the front, Jack was quickly gaining a reputation as an officer of singular courage who took risks with a boldness that was nearer bravado. At first, life in Oxford continued peacefully, hardly touched by the war apart from the noticeable absence of men. The letters that came from the front tended to be determinedly cheerful. But gradually some perception of what was happening leaked through, as casualties returned and men came back on leave. When the first gas attacks began, Naomi's father suddenly found himself in the centre of the war effort, analysing the effects of gas and committed to developing a gas mask that worked. Jack was drafted in to help, as indeed was the entire household at Cherwell. The men experimented on each other. 'The house reeked of chlorine, the noise of coughing and retching was continuous from the study and beyond.'[3] When their frantic efforts were successful, Jack returned to the front to find the Third Battalion of the Black Watch engaged in an attack, at Richebourg L'Avoue, in which most of the officers were killed. He escaped the worst, for he never reached the front line, but nevertheless was himself wounded by a shellburst which left him with shrapnel lodged in his elbow. His niece Lois Godfrey would say decades later that he claimed to have enjoyed the war.[4]

Certainly, he was lucky. Some of their Oxford friends were already dead, and by this time the real nature of the war could not be denied. The unimaginably grim conditions of trench warfare became known to a public who had, with very few exceptions, only months before cheered their young men on to sort out the Germans. The realities of mud, lice, rats, disease hovered at the thresholds of homes accustomed to being able to mask or ignore dirt and pain. Above all, casualties began to touch every family of every class, even if their often appalling nature, and the appalling effects on those who survived, were not understood. The battles intended to break the deadlock of the trenches killed men by the thousand: 60,000 in a single day of the British offensive on the Somme. In the four years of war, half a million men under the age of thirty would be killed, including a quarter of the students at Oxford and Cambridge. The chances of both the men closest to Naomi surviving were slim. Dick did not leave for the front until the early summer of 1915, but each time he or Jack departed she felt she would never see them again.[5]

This was the environment in which Naomi, now seventeen, approached her marriage. And there were other factors affecting the ideas and attitudes which were beginning to take shape in her mind. Her Uncle Richard, Liberal MP for East Lothian since 1885, Secretary of State for War until 1912 and Lord Chancellor when war broke out, lost his post in 1915. He was suspect because he had been to a German university and openly admired German philosophy and culture. His brother was included in the suspicion, and J. S. Haldane's war work was never acknowledged or rewarded.

It was impossible for Naomi to step back from the contradictions. Increasingly, she questioned her mother's faith in the Empire. What was happening around her seemed to make nonsense of a belief in an inherent British superiority and all that imperialism implied. She was beginning to meet people of rather different views. With her friend Agnes, daughter of the Classical scholar Gilbert Murray (the Murrays had been neighbours in St Margaret's Road), she went to hear G. D. H. Cole speak – 'the dark and flashing Magdalen revolutionary'[6] – and a more radical politics began to rub off on her. She discovered that there were people who openly questioned the war. Agnes was herself 'very much the leader of the progressive women students'[7] and in her company Naomi began a process of radical politicization. Interestingly, it was not the vigorous activities of the suffragettes that attracted her, although these were much in the news. It was another brand of unorthodoxy, both more intellectual and, in a number of ways, more emotional. Cole, 'tall, thin, proud, black-haired and grey-eyed' was inspiring.

> I knew nothing at all of economics; I had no idea what Guild Socialism was about. I was simply carried away by the fire of the speaker. He was angry; what he hated we must hate. We had to look round the world we had taken for granted, but which had now collapsed into war and devastation and so must have had something wrong with it, even for us, the well-off.[8]

With Agnes, she went to more meetings in Cole's rooms in Magdalen, listening hard although too shy to ask questions. The gulf between mother and daughter was widening.

By the summer of 1915, Naomi was becoming increasingly impatient to contribute, whatever her doubts about the war itself. She passed her nursing exams, and after persistent nagging persuaded her parents to allow her to join the Voluntary Aid Detachment (VAD) as an auxiliary nurse at St Thomas's Hospital in London. The fact that she was going with an acquaintance from Oxford and they both stayed with the Hale Whites, closely family friends, must have helped her parents to accept this new development. The Hale Whites' son Leonard was one of Naomi's admirers. He was killed.

The VAD was started in 1909, and between 1914 and 1918 supplied 23,000 nurses and 15,000 orderlies, known as VADs, to service hospitals. The majority of them were, like Naomi, from comfortable backgrounds, hugely ignorant of the realities of practical medicine and general hospitals. Naomi at least had the advantage of some direct experience of the effects of disease and accident; nevertheless for her, as for millions of men and women, the war brought a sudden expansion of horizons. She left home to work, almost unthinkable for an upper-middle-class girl of seventeen, and to work in a huge public hospital in wartime, in an environment of horrific pain and mutilation but under a regime that was severely disciplined. This was no place for a restlessly independent young woman to spread her wings. Nevertheless, she managed to find ways to sidestep certain of the rules.

Much of the work was grindingly routine and most of it, even hemming sheets, meant being on her feet. VADs were at the bottom of the hospital hierarchy, a position Naomi was not used to occupying. There was a great deal of cleaning, bed-making, fetching and carrying, disinfecting: she had had no experience of even rudimentary housework. 'I was told to make tea but hadn't realized that tea must be made with boiling water.'[9] Only with experience was she allowed direct contact with the patients – bed-baths, changing dressings. She learned to take for granted the sight of naked male bodies; having an older brother, this was less of a shock for her than for some of her fellow volunteers. But the contact with pain was another matter. 'Hard to hold one's basin steady when a man is writhing about in his bed, white with pain and begging the nurse not to go on,' she wrote to Aunt Bay, who had, of course, worked in hospitals herself.[10] Naomi did not work only in the surgical wards, but it was there that the casualties flooding in from across the Channel were treated. Many of the men had appalling wounds and burns, and gangrene was common. The smell of rotting flesh and paraldehyde was overwhelming. Naomi recalled that she fainted only once.

Unlike her contemporary Vera Brittain, who also broke off an Oxford education to become a VAD and also saw her fiancé off to war, Naomi was able to escape the hospital when her work was done. She returned to the Hale Whites. Vera Brittain was miserable in an uncomfortable hostel. Naomi also managed to escape at dinner time. She had brought some of the guinea pigs with her as experiments were at a crucial stage. She kept them 'in the animal house at the far end of the terrace along the river'[11] and it was only by missing pudding at dinner that she could slip away to keep an eye on them. This was no doubt important for scientific reasons, but the guinea pigs were also a tangible link with home, with Jack and with childhood normalities. Jack's letters often contained instructions on which animals to mate and what to look out for.

This episode of Naomi's growing up did not last long. In August, there was an outbreak of scarlet fever caused by infected milk. Naomi succumbed and was rushed back to Oxford in an ambulance. When she recovered, she did not go back to St Thomas's but worked in the outpatients department at Radcliffe's Hospital in Oxford, helping to treat civilians. That autumn, she also returned to her studies, and began to help out at a soldier's club in Oxford.

Wartime lent an urgency to everything. There seemed little point in putting off the wedding, though Dick would have to get leave. Naomi still took little interest in clothes and was impatient of the assumption that she should be devoting her attentions to her trousseau. 'I was still wearing boys' clumpies and sandals.'[12] A note of defiance can be detected here, for Naomi liked nice things and over the years acquired objects and paintings and beautiful clothes which she refers to with pleasure and satisfaction. But in wartime a preoccupation with acquisition did not seem appropriate. Her mother insisted on underwear and nightdresses, to replace the flannel pyjamas of her childhood. Naomi shied away from her mother's attempts to prepare her for the wedding and share the excitement. Many years later, she acknowledged her inability to recognize the importance of the coming rite of passage for mother as well as for daughter. Part of the difficulty was Naomi's reluctance to think about the sexual implications of what she was about to undertake. Her education and background encouraged her to be cool and objective: she had observed her own guinea pigs and the activities of her mother's Jersey bull with interest and understanding. At the same time, it is clear that she was very unsure of her own feelings and inclinations: 'I was thinking with increasing uneasiness and even alarm about the coming event.'[13] She was not going to admit her ignorance. 'I knew extremely little about the physical side and I pretended to know more than I did.'[14] There was no question of her raising her anxieties with her mother, who made oblique and uneasy references to what lay in store, and Naomi was the first of the young women of her acquaintance to marry. There was no confidante more experienced than herself to turn to.

She resisted a trousseau. She also resisted Dick's parents' pressure to put the wedding off until the war was over. There seems to have been some conflict between the two mothers over this, as well as between Naomi and her prospective mother-in-law, who was not equipped to deal with the determined and opinionated teenager her son was going to marry. There was a certain unreality in preparing for a wedding while not so many miles away men were being killed in circumstances that still seemed almost beyond belief. Yet many aspects of life continued as before with no shortage of luxuries in the shops. Naomi was not going to submit to expectations and, characteristically, made every effort to take control of the situation. It was wartime. She would marry in an appropriately sober fashion, and not in a church. Now, in 1916, the war was about to enter its most murderous phase, with the German offensive at Verdun. Dick obtained leave for February. 'I am delighted to hear that Dick is getting back for leave and unholy matrimony,' Jack wrote in January.[15] Naomi made arrangements at the Oxford registry office. When the day came she wore a black skirt and waistcoat with a green silk shirt. Dick was in uniform. A small group of friends gathered at the registry office. Aldous was there; most of their male friends were not. They took the wedding cake to the soldiers' club where Naomi cut it with Dick's sabre. There were not many wedding presents.

The young couple had only a week together before Dick's return to the front. In sexual matters they were both novices, and the pressures and urgencies of war must have made it even less likely that the first attempts at lovemaking would be a success. There was little pleasure in them for Naomi. Dick had approached his regimental doctor for advice and received a dismissive answer. 'I think we would have had a much nicer sort of week together had we known a little bit about it.'[16] More than seventy years later Naomi would claim that their sexual relationship never recovered from their early difficulties. Another brief period of leave allowed them a short break at a hotel in Dalmally in Argyll. But the war dominated their lives and inevitably distorted the first months and years of their marriage.

2

Naomi continued to live at home and apart from the brief interludes with Dick, life did not seem much changed. Being a married woman did not bring the anticipated freedom. She was still not allowed to enjoy the company of men, however well known to the family, without a chaperone. Lewis Gielgud returned wounded from the front: when he invited Naomi to the May Day carols at Magdelen, her mother insisted on coming too. Inevitably, resentment seethed as Naomi's mother continued to supervise her life. It was only with Jack that Naomi was able to escape and she continued to depend on him for many years after her marriage.

The dreaded telegram came, to Dick's parents, when Naomi was in London with Jack. Dick had been wounded in the head and was dangerously ill. Sick with shock and crying with the certainty that Dick was dead, Naomi at once made preparations for going to France where Dick was in hospital. She and Mr Mitchison crossed the channel to Boulogne where they were met by an RAMC car and driven to Le Tréport.

Dick, now a lieutenant with a signals corps, had been carrying dispatches behind the lines when he was thrown off his motor bike by an exploding shell. As well as the injury to his head, there were burns. He had some leave due, and he and Naomi had been planning to meet in Paris for a few days. Now Naomi was indeed in France, but under rather different circumstances. When she and Mr Mitchison arrived at the hospital (converted from a hotel - Le

Tréport had been a resort) they were told by the doctor that Dick's condition was dangerous, and that he had probably 'only a couple of days to live'.[17]

Naomi kept a diary of this period, which she drew on when she wrote *All Change Here*:

> I wait outside, while Sister goes in, leaving the door ajar. Suddenly a voice, so strong and familiar I can hardly believe it. 'What, my wife? Bring her in at once, Sister.' I go in. It is a small white cheerful room, a bed with a silk quilt. Dick, looking very well and normal, but for a very unshaven chin: 'Hullo Nou!'[18]

This was reassuring, but misleading. Dick was in a great deal of pain, often delirious and confused, and his memory was affected. Sometimes he did not know Naomi, thinking her a nurse or a fellow officer. Naomi saw him every day and observed and recorded with her usual, almost clinical curiosity: 'five minutes normal though in pain, talking sensibly and not very restless; then a few minutes while the pain comes on, very restless, perhaps trying to get up, with his body and arms rigid, mouth open and eyes shut'.[19] The act of recording may have helped her to cope: writing as therapy would become an acknowledged activity.

Naomi and Dick's father stayed at the Hotel des Bains, and Naomi at first visited Dick twice a day. Then Sister Holbeach, whom Naomi found more helpful and sympathetic than the doctors, discovered she had nursing experience and it was arranged that Naomi should nurse Dick herself. 'I made them think I knew more than I did,' Naomi remembered.[20] Sister Holbeach was optimistic. 'I say with good nursing he'll be all right,' she said to Naomi.[21] The doctors were concerned about brain damage and permanent crippling. Naomi refused to accept these possibilities. It was a huge burden for an eighteen-year-old, but she summoned all her energies, emotional and practical, to sustain Dick and to write down what was going on. It seemed to work.

There was little that Dick's father could contribute, although he visited his son every day, and relations between him and Naomi were strained. There had always been an awkwardness between Naomi and her parents-in-law, which was not overcome by this proximity. When he was not at the hospital, Mr Mitchison sat in the hotel, reading the paper and writing letters. Naomi, on the other hand, was out and about. She struck up a friendship with another young woman, Miss Cripps, with whom she went swimming and walked on the beach. She talked with the other residents of the hotel – French soldiers on leave, other families like themselves with hospitalized relatives, including the parents of Siegfried Sassoon who was among the wounded. She kept her diary and read Guy de Maupassant. Meanwhile, they could hear the distant sound of shells exploding and were aware that preparations were being made for a 'big push' – presumably the Somme offensive.

Pressure of new casualties meant that patients were evacuated to England as soon as they were at all fit to travel. Dick was to be moved, although his condition was still disturbing.

> He gets violently angry with both me and the orderly … calling us dirty cads and damned liars; he also hits out like anything … But often I leave him to the orderly, particularly when he says '*Enlevez cette femme là, c'est la mienne, mais enlevez la*'. And then as a parting shot when I'm going out 'I don't ever want to see you again.' He forgets all about it by next time, but I'm so afraid it will stay in some sort of distorted image on his subconscious memory.[22]

It was in this state that Dick was shipped back to England, without Naomi as she and his father had to travel separately. On the hospital boat he hallucinated, seeing 'rather horrid creatures that had come out of the sea'.[23] Then 'quite suddenly they all went away and never came back and he felt rather tired, but he was himself again'.[24] When he and Naomi were reunited in London, he was 'back in the ordinary world',[25] needing rest and recuperation but no longer subject to delirium.

They stayed initially with Dick's parents. He seemed to recover quickly but Naomi was always on the look out for signs of relapse or derangement. His brain seemed undamaged - while still recuperating he passed his Bar examinations - but on one occasion he pretended to have gone mad and Naomi screamed with shock and terror. It was too close to her worst nightmare, which she probably was not able to confide to Dick. Convalescence gave them time together. They rented a country house in Scotland in the late autumn. Dick loved to shoot, and tried to teach Naomi who was ambivalent about the sport, although later she would pride herself on being able to handle a gun. It is clear that there was an element of strain in being dependent on each other. Naomi was used to having numbers of people around her. Dick had been over a year in France and had been on the threshold of death. There had been no opportunity to get accustomed to proximity or to become aware of their differences. Dick liked to play chess, Naomi preferred dressing-up games or hide-and-seek - the games of the 'gang' in Oxford. Her recollections of this period imply that she fretted uneasily in the larger house, trying to read improving books, writing poetry, and both of them still struggling with sexual difficulties. In another poem in *The Laburnum Branch*, 'Postscript to a conversation', are the lines:

> *What I mean to tell you*
> *Is I am partly a boy.*[26]

This suggests perhaps less an ambivalence about her sexuality, more her love of active and adventurous games, which both the Dragon School and the Oxford theatricals had fostered.

To Naomi's relief, Dick applied for a Staff job and was accepted. He had to go on a course, and early 1917 found them in digs near Dunstable. By this time their physical problems were having physiological manifestations. As well as feeling very unhappy, Naomi was running an unexplained temperature. Dick was out all day and Naomi was left to her own devices, and although she went for long walks it was winter with little opportunity for the botanizing which could have given her a purpose. She and Dick found it impossible to talk to each other about their problems. They had been married a year without any opportunity for a 'normal' married life, their future hedged with uncertainty. Yet they were forging a warm and valuable closeness. If they were unable to overcome the inhibitions which prevented them discussing sex, they communicated freely and committedly about almost everything else. Indeed, perhaps that disappointment at the centre of their marriage made other forms of communication even more important. Certainly, throughout their marriage, whenever they were separated, they wrote 'letters, letters, letters'.[27] Indeed, there were things that could be said more freely in letters than in conversation. Absence was a feature of their marriage from the beginning, and correspondence was a crucial part of the glue that bound them. Many of the letters survive, a consistent tribute to their love and concern for each other. There was, Naomi wrote in the 1970s, always 'the feeling that the other one was there: a permanent area of trust and confidence'. And she added, 'This kind of relationship has little to do with romantic love; it can develop just as strongly in an arranged marriage.'[28]

3

Spring 1917 brought news of the Russian Revolution, the collapse of a major power unable to sustain the demands and incursions of war. Few in the Haldane milieu were likely to have regretted the passing of the Russian monarchy, yet it was hard to know what effect events in Russia would have on the progress of the war. In the summer of 1917 Dick returned to France, in a Staff post which meant that he was less at risk. Once again, Naomi was back in the parental home. Once again, she needed a role, a purposeful existence. It was perhaps a relief that Dick had gone, given the unsatisfactory aspects of being only a wife. In September, news came that Dick's younger brother Willie had been killed. The family was devastated. Naomi had been very fond of Willie, a good-natured and easy-going young man, less serious than Dick.

By this time, the idea of the League of Nations, brainchild of America's President Wilson, was attracting attention and the League of Nations Society had been formed in Britain. Naomi was increasingly convinced that the way forward, politically, depended on a spirit of genuine international co-operation. A number of her friends shared her feelings. A letter to her from Julian Huxley, probably written in 1917, agreed with Naomi that the League of Nations offered the possibility of hope.[29] She contacted the Society: 'I came away convinced, and with masses of literature, and after that I had to do something about it.'[30] She took up her pen, and thus established a pattern of action that shaped her entire life.

She began by writing letters to the *Oxford Times* on the need for a 'supernational authority',[31] signed with a variety of pseudonyms. Very soon a full-scale correspondence was under way with a number of notable Oxford academics joining in, including Gilbert Murray. An Oxford branch of the Society was set up with Naomi as its first secretary: her first foray into active political involvement was a success. It brought a taste of power, a demonstration of an ability to influence events. Naomi already knew she could influence people around her, possibly already recognized a need for this. Now she knew she could reach beyond her own immediate circle, which strengthened her determination and single-mindedness.

By this time she was pregnant, and concerns for her health called a halt to her activities. The baby was expected in February; in December she had a slight haemorrhage, which alarmed her. There were worries because of the damage to her pelvis caused by her riding accident ten years earlier. She knew there were risks, and she prepared herself for pain. There had been no conscious choice to become pregnant – it was just something that happened. But since it had happened she approached the experience with a combination of scientific curiosity and apprehension. Pregnancy brought on hyperaesthesia, an intensification of her often already heightened senses.

Her mother and mother-in-law bustled with preparations for the coming event, acquiring all that the baby would need. As with her wedding, Naomi felt distanced from the activity, preoccupied instead with the uncertainty of her feelings: 'would I like the baby or at any rate would I like it as much as I was supposed to?'[32] Jack wrote to congratulate her, but clearly his feelings were ambivalent. 'Your approaching achievement fills me with envy,' he wrote in September 1917.[33] His younger sister was again beating him to it; he would be married twice, but never had children. In the event, Naomi's son's birth was 'worse than I had imagined possible',[34] in spite of chloroform. After the birth she contracted a complicating infection, but the baby was healthy and so were Naomi's responses to him. He was named Geoff, after Geoff Wardley, Dick's closest friend who had been killed in 1916. It was an important affirmation: one of the effects of Dick's head injury had been to blot out all memory of Geoff's death and Naomi had had to break the news to him all over again.

Dick was transferred from France to Italy, to liaise between the French and British armies. The war was moving into its closing stages. America had entered the fray, and although Germany and Russia concluded a separate peace, which freed German troops to concentrate on the Western front, the summer saw the Allied advance that brought the end in sight. That summer, Dick came home for leave with Spanish flu, which Naomi, but not the baby, caught from him. Dick was seeing his son for the first time and was not too sure how to respond. He returned to Italy and later that year the prospect of another few days' leave suggested the possibility of Naomi joining him there for a brief visit. By this time she was feeling trapped. Although she was breastfeeding Geoff, much of the routine work of caring for a baby was done by others – nurses, maids and her mother, who was in her element. 'If only I could get away,' Naomi wrote in 'Autumn', a poem of this period.[35] The idea of going to Italy, and without Geoff, was irresistible, yet it was nearly ruined when parents and parents-in-law insisted that she should not travel alone. A chaperone was duly found, and the two set off on the train from Victoria to catch the Channel ferry to Dieppe. On the boat, Naomi contrived to shake off her duenna and completed the rest of the journey by herself: a train to Paris, a change of station, then another to Italy, and finally Perugia, where she and Dick had arranged to meet. 'I felt suddenly and gorgeously free and grown-up. This time I'd really escaped and by my own wits.'[36] It was only the third time she had been abroad.

Earlier that year, 1918, a book had been published which would make a huge difference to many lives, *Married Love* by Marie Stopes. Naomi read it. It was a revelation, and she was hopeful that, if Dick would read it too, their difficulties would be solved. Part of her eagerness to see him in Italy was the result of this new knowledge. *Married Love* was a ground-breaking book, demonstrating that sexual fulfilment was a mutual need and explaining how that could be achieved for both women and men. It shocked many but helped more, selling over a million copies. The book did help Naomi and Dick, and the situation improved, but their problems were never fully overcome. There was still a communication difficulty. Nevertheless, they produced seven children.

Perhaps with Marie Stopes's help, Naomi had a wonderful time with Dick in Perugia. Italian pastries contributed too. Food shortages were biting in Britain, and Naomi was able to make up for a deprivation of sugar. Then Dick was recalled to join his division for the final push, and Naomi was summoned back to Oxford. Yet she was able to break her journey in Paris and spend a few days with Lewis Gielgud and Gervas Huxley, two of the survivors. There was an atmosphere of excitement and a sense of the war nearing its close. When she at last got back to Oxford she was no doubt greeted with reproach and criticism for having extended her absence. Little Geoff did not recognize her, but was healthy and crawling. Naomi was pleased to be reunited with him, although it did not seem to have been a problem for her to leave him. But then came the Armistice, and everything else became secondary.

The war was over, but it took time for life to change and it would never return to pre-war 'normality'. Whatever personal damage the war brought to Naomi, it had, as she put it eighty years after it started, left her with two very positive gains: 'there were two things – I got married and I got a typewriter'.[37] The typewriter was a present from her Uncle Richard, and from that time on she would never be without one. The gift was important, for it was in effect an acknowledgement of the fact that for her writing was a serious activity. She had had plays performed, albeit by amateurs, and was the pseudonymous author of letters to the press. By this time also she was beginning to get her poems published in magazines, including *The New Age*, a former Liberal journal which had been reshaped by the idiosyncratic editor A. R. Orage into a radical organ for experimental writing. She was entering new territory. Writing may not yet have occupied the forefront of her life, but it was an activity that would not be denied. Many of her male friends pursued it as a matter of course.

Naomi was still living in Oxford, her life presided over by her mother, although through her own efforts she was widening its dimensions. However much she fretted against the bounds imposed by her mother's undaunted Edwardian convictions, there were advantages. She avoided the responsibilities of running a home. She did not have to think about what to have for dinner or how to instruct the servants. She was not tied to her child; her mother seemed genuinely to enjoy having a new family to look after, with, of course, plenty of help. However, there was undoubtedly conflict between mother and daughter, not just in terms of political and ideological differences, but through two strong personalities living under one roof. Naomi was in many respects her mother's daughter, convinced, imperious and determined. But the pull of Cherwell and parents remained strong. Naomi's second and third children were both born in Oxford, although she and Dick had by then made their home in London.

Dick returned and the process of forging their marriage continued. Naomi became pregnant again. There seemed no question but that their life would be located in London, as Dick was eager to get back to the career that the war had interrupted. He had been called to the Bar in 1917. He shared a flat with his friend Bey Gillespie until he and Naomi found somewhere of their own, a house in Cheyne Walk in Chelsea. They moved in early in 1919. There were difficult adjustments to make. Now Naomi did have a house to run, and she did not take to it readily. Dick was having to bridge the huge gulf between war and peace, with continuing headaches and depressions that were the legacy of his fracture. There was a political legacy also, which cut across his background and upbringing. Like so many of his generation, conscience drove him towards a radical politics that was foreign territory to his parents' class and experience. Yet he did not want to alienate his parents, who were still shattered by the death of Willie. The pain of such contradictions, of loss and anger at the same time as an unwillingness to harbour thought that perhaps the conflict – and therefore the deaths – had been useless, runs through the next two decades, and haunted Naomi for much longer.

4

In 1919, Naomi had another son, Denis. Three years later, Murdoch was born. At the age of twenty-five Naomi had three young children. Having read *Married Love*, she was perfectly aware that frequent pregnancies were not necessary. It was choice, not ignorance, that motivated her, in spite of the difficulty that surrounded each birth. Writing some years later on the subject of birth control, she comments on the post-war trend towards larger families, to which she herself contributed. (By the time she wrote the piece she had produced another two children.) 'The general recklessness in the air shows itself ... in the larger families of those who were most directly affected by the war feeling, in so far as it was destructive, perhaps even in a fierce, remote way, hopeful, and not merely depressing.'[38] Having children was an affirmation of hope, a gesture against the destructiveness of war, as well as, in her case, a personal memorial to dead friends.

In the same article she reflects at some length on the character of married relationships, providing clues to what made her own marriage work and to what were probably continuing sources of friction. She acknowledged the importance of mutual kindness and warmth, and the satisfactions of shared parenthood. But there were also negative reasons for the survival of the relationships, with force of habit amongst the most powerful: 'because they are living in the same house, sleeping in the same bed, because it is very complicated practically and emotionally to do anything else … the couple still go on.'[39] Such a relationship, Naomi believed, could be valuable without necessarily being exclusive. Naomi writes with all the authority of a woman with more than ten years of marriage behind her, who is sure of her own needs and has worked out ways of fulfilling them. But in 1919 she had some way to go. Confident in some areas, including producing children, she was uncomfortable in others. Domestic life did not suit her, and she returned often to Oxford, to the familiar and safe environment which absolved her of certain kinds of responsibility.

Most difficult, though, was the effort to come to terms with absence. If Naomi had had some notion that marriage still allowed her the freedom to assemble and direct a group of friends, and to explore and experiment in the adult world without constraint, she was quickly disillusioned. The friends were gone.

> *My young, dear friends are dead,*
> *All my own generation.*[40]

Few of those who survived were in London. Lewis Gielgud was in Paris. Aldous was also often abroad while Jack was back in Oxford, later in Cambridge. It was not possible to transplant or recreate the pre-war Oxford days. 'I remember how lonely we were in the beginning, coming to live in London.'[41] The loneliness was probably more intensely felt by Naomi. Dick had his work, though it was slow to build up, and spent a lot of time with his parents, still devastated by the death of his brother. Although Naomi accompanied him on his visits, she did not like playing bridge, which was one of their favourite ways of passing the time, and her relations with her parents-in-law were no better. 'I don't think my mother-in-law ever really liked me and I didn't really like her.'[42] She would occupy the margins of the family, reading while they played cards, and a hint of truculent resentment is still apparent when she remembers it.

It is understandable why Oxford continued to exert a magnetic pull. Jack was a part of it, with Naomi's admiration and need for him as strong as ever, though relations with him could be strained. In some ways his war experience made more of an impact on her than Dick's, and the effect on his personality clearly disturbed her. Her poem 'The Reid Hackle' celebrates Jack's regiment, the Black Watch, not Dick's - 'nane fechts braver, an' nane fechts harder'.[43] She located Jack in a Scottish heroic tradition (which almost wiped out the Third Battalion). This excluded Dick, and had a romantic robustness which the Queens Bays lacked. She and Jack were both Haldanes, and however close Dick was to both he could not share that heritage.

What Naomi wrote about Jack later is a comment on the legacy of war for a whole generation, but it also highlights aspects of Jack's character which perhaps she was uniquely able to understand.

Jack had been killing people for several years, apart from the breaks which followed their attempts to kill him. That does something to shift one's personality on its base as happens with a knock on the head or a bad trip with some powerful drug. Return is slow. Nothing any more looks innocent. It is no use thinking it was simply the war. In this last war [World War II] you could fly over a city, drop bombs on what you knew must be families clinging to their children whom you were about to suck into a fire storm. But you had not seen them or heard them. You came back mission completed into the real world, lucky. Nobody knows the last moments of those who didn't come back. In trench warfare there was no coming back of that kind. You had to live among the smell and sight and thought of close death all the time; even a few miles back it was still there. Most of the officers and non-commissioned officers in the Black Watch were killed. In this kind of war they had to be leaders. But Bomber Haldane would creep out alone through the mudholes, throw his bombs and see bits of the men he had killed - arms and legs up in the air, perhaps hear shrieks of those he had mangled.[44]

Jack talked a little to Naomi about his experiences. From a perspective beyond the Second World War, when clearly this was written (it is not dated), Naomi saw the First World War as uniquely appalling in what it forced combatants to endure. Jack's experiences distanced him from his sister – here was something she could not possibly share – but at the same time she was impressed by, and possibly envied, Bomber Haldane's extraordinary, probably unnecessary courage. Dick seems to have been a competent and caring officer. Jack was in another league.

It is hard to know to what extent the complicated ingredients of the brother-sister relationship impinged on the Mitchison marriage. Naomi made no secret of her admiration of her brother and many were aware of it, including her children as they grew up, although her daughters found him a difficult and sometimes alarming man.[45] Dick clearly knew from the outset how important Jack was to Naomi; it seems likely that this did not make the early years of their marriage any easier.

Cheyne Walk was, however, a step to independence, even if there were aspects of it she did not relish. At last she had her own bank account and control of her own spending. There was furniture of her own choosing; she remembers a big table where she could sit and write.[46] She could, to some extent, arrange her life as she pleased, although this depended on coping with the existence of servants, something she did not find easy. Her months at St Thomas's had taught her a little about domestic chores, but she was far from confident about what was required, and servants could be difficult. There was a cook, housemaid, parlour maid and nurse. But Mrs Bell, the cook, was overfond of the bottle, and even when sober, domestic servants required instruction which Naomi often felt incompetent or uneasy about giving. Dick did not concern himself with daily practicalities, and there may not have been anyone with whom she could share her frustrations. In the early London years there were no close women friends.

She had seen marriage as a passport to the adult world, without giving much thought to adult responsibilities. Now she was faced with having to take control of at least some aspects of her life, while at the same time feeling that the adult world was oppressive: 'There still seemed to be a grown-up world on top of one.'[47] She wanted her own world, and at the same time a place in the real, adult world. She wanted authority herself, and also to be beyond the authority of conventional structures and arrangements. She was caught in contradictions, a situation that, though the details changed, remained with her all her life. Dick had a career and an identity. She seemed to have neither. In her story 'The Triumph of Faith' (*When the Bough Breaks*, 1924) she uses the character of Phoebe, reacting against an arranged marriage, to give vent to the frustration and sense of unfairness which had been with her ever since she was removed from the Dragon School.

> It's so hard being a girl! Here I am, just the same as a man really, and no worse than my brother anyway ... But just because of two or three silly little differences I have to be treated as if I was an animal, ordered about, not allowed to decide anything for myself! I'm shut up, I'm watched, I have to do what men tell me – nothing's my own, money or husband or religion – I have to take what they give me and say thankyou![48]

In the title story of the same collection the heroine Gersemi dresses as a man and sets forth with horse and weapons. Phoebe's complaint ends with 'Oh, I can't bear being a woman!'[49] No doubt that came from the heart of her creator, but so did the creation of the adventurous Gersemi. If there were times when Naomi could not bear being a woman, passive acceptance was not part of her make-up. She set about equipping herself for change. Gersemi fights alongside men, has her adventures and gets her man and marriage too.

Looking back from the perspective of the late 1970s, Naomi saw the twenties and thirties as a transitional period for women. There were opportunities, especially for women of her background, which would, paradoxically, become harder for women to take advantage of when another war had passed. There was a climate of experiment, of pushing out the frontiers. For women there was 'a new freedom to write, paint, do scientific or historical research, become doctors, lawyers'.[50] Even without the benefit of hindsight, Naomi instinctively knew herself to be one of these women and sought the company of others, just as she sought the means of making her mark. If she was lonely in her early years in London, it was not only because so many of the gang were dead, but because she had not really discovered the inspirations and rewards of friendship with women. This would soon change. The uneasy and fragmented early years of marriage were never entirely eclipsed, but friendship, not least with Dick, was a huge compensation.

having time to herself, the ivory tower had no attraction for her. Scribbling in a notebook while pushing a pram in Chelsea or lashed by wind and rain in Kilbrannan Sound made a statement that reveals an essential element of how Naomi saw herself.

It was almost inevitable that Naomi's apprenticeship in writing poetry and devising dramas would lead to fiction, as both forms were themselves conduits for story-telling, as were the earlier manifestations of her 'gang' activities. It was also harder now to assemble the personnel for dramatics, although the Cheyne Walk house was the scene of some theatrical activity, and therefore natural to produce stories in a form that could be read; natural, too, that she should hanker for a wider audience. She chose for her subject similar territory to that of her plays, territory that was partly shaped by her association with young men immersed in classical studies – the ancient world. Specifically, *The Conquered* is set in the time of the Roman invasion of Gaul, and examines issues of power, conquest and divided loyalties. It also reflects the present, for it was written partly in response to the contemporaneous situation in Ireland, to which Naomi reacted with considerable emotion but not a great deal of knowledge, as she herself admitted later. From 1921, Ireland was a divided country with a legacy of religious, political and cultural turmoil. To reinforce the nationalist point, Naomi headed her chapters with lines from 'The Irish volunteer' and 'The croppy boy', songs of the fight for Irish independence. The first political demonstration she took part in was a 'Peace with Ireland' procession in London which, she remembered in 1984, set off in the wrong direction.[2] Naomi had already shown in her plays her fascination with the impact of big events on people's lives. The struggles of Ireland and Gaul against their respective invaders were tempting subjects for her.

The choice of historical period owed something to Dick, for it was he who encouraged an interest in ancient history and suggested she read Gibbon's *Decline and Fall of the Roman Empire*. It was also Dick who saw the possibilities of using the ancient world to mirror current issues and helped Naomi to select the appropriate time and place for her purpose. Naomi has always made it clear that her novels reflected both the political and personal climate of the times they were written. 'For most of my life my love relationships affected my writing,' she wrote in *You May Well Ask*[3] and in an interview she talked of how the life she was living and the books she was writing 'tangled together'. 'All my life I have been very much in the hands of the books I was writing ... any of what I did was also part of a book.'[4] Bearing that in mind, it seems significant that *The Conquered* begins with a brother and sister, and that the sister is very quickly killed off. Fiommar and Meromic are a brother and sister of the Veneti tribe of Gaul, threatened by Roman invasion. They have a close and empathetic relationship. Fiommar has a fantasy in which her brother and herself are the only players. 'After the war, we'll run away together and find an island all by itself somewhere, and make a home out of stones, and thatch it with whin, and have a fire in the middle and heaps of fern to lie on and tell stories: and you'll be king and I'll be queen ...'[5]

The fantasy is short-lived. Rather than face slavery under the Romans, Fiommar chooses suicide. Meromic lives to endure defeat, slavery, and conflicting pressures of tribal and personal loyalties. None of these are resolved, except by myth, when, at the end of the novel Meromic becomes his totemic animal, a wolf, and passes into legend. Much of the novel is an exploration of the complex bonds of friendship and comradeship, a theme that endures throughout Naomi's work, in particular Meromic's relations with his Roman owner Titus and a fellow-captive Lerrys. It is clear that these relationships are only possible because the bond with Fiommar is broken. In other words, Meromic is liberated by his sister's death.

Sibling empathy and rivalry provide a pattern that runs through all Naomi's fiction. The enduring importance of her relationship with Jack is the key here, and the challenges it faced as their lives diverged and first she and then he married and formed new bonds and loyalties. 'The beginning [of *The Conquered*] is really me and my brother, romanticized, in a Sennen [Cornwall] background,' she wrote in *You May Well Ask*,[6] and the novel is dedicated to Jack. This relationship was written into many of her books. It is striking that her very first novel opens with siblings in an idealized relationship under threat, which does not survive. Naomi, of course, knew what she was doing. She also knew that she was borrowing from Jack's experience of the war. 'Once or twice he talked to me about pain and terror and love. I had begun to write *The Conquered* and began the transmutation of present into past, fears and feelings into writing.'[7] This transmutation, or fusion of past and present, is reflected in a rather different way in an unpublished piece she wrote in which she described herself returning home to find the characters of *The Conquered* ensconced in her drawing-room. She recognizes them at once and explains to them that they have moved out of time and out of her own head. It is a whimsical and entertaining little piece. Worried about what the servants will think of their somewhat unconventional dress, she lends them tweed suits of Dick's. A conspicuous aspect of this is the ease with which Naomi herself accommodates her transposed people: they are real, and have a place in her world. This suggests a clue as to her success as a historical novelist.[8]

However comfortable she felt with her characters, Naomi needed reassurance. As the chapters were written they were read to her mother. Naomi always sought a response to her writing; she could not operate in a vacuum. She wrote fast, working on 'the best bits' first, then filling in.[9] She sent the completed manuscript to the historian Rice Holmes for comment. When his response was unhelpful it went to Ernest Barker, who was impressed and wrote a foreword. She was then ready to try her luck with publishers. The first three turned it down. When each rejection came she wept, but soldiered on with the stories she was working on, which became the collection *When the Bough Breaks*. Then she sent *The Conquered* to Jonathan Cape, who summoned her to his office in Bloomsbury. She bought a new hat for the occasion, met Cape himself and Edward Garnett, one of Cape's editors who would become a close friend, and to her joy they accepted the novel. Unable to contain herself she ran all the way to Birrell and Garnett's bookshop in Tavistock Street where she shared the good news with Edward's brother David.

The book was published in the spring of 1923 and at once made an impact. It was recognized as something new, a novel set in the distant past that was emotionally as well as historically convincing. 'She makes the emotions of her characters actual and our own,' as the *New Statesman*'s reviewer put it.[10] There was a sense almost of excitement that a novelist had succeeded in writing about the past in language that was fresh and modern yet reinforced the credibility of time and place. Her intelligence and the striking quality of her imagination were recognized; 'a rare union of simplicity and insight', wrote *Outlook*'s reviewer, who went on, 'she is assured of an especial position among modern novelists.'[11] Friends and family were also enthusiastic. Aunt Bay liked it and Uncle Richard thought it 'a brilliant piece of work'.[12] E. M. Forster wrote, 'I found it so moving and beautiful and the character of Meromic holding it together from first to last,'[13] and a letter from Vincent Sheean praised its success in bringing to life a distant place and time.[14] In 1951, when Naomi's fiction had moved on to rather different areas of interest, Henry Treece wrote a piece for the magazine *Tomorrow* under the title 'My favourite forgotten book'. The book he chose was *The Conquered*. He praised its combination of romantic conviction and objectivity – 'her selection of incident is Romantic; her exploration of it as restrained as any classical writer could be' – and stated that the novel had become 'part of the permanent furniture of my mind'.[15] Treece's enthusiasm more than made up for the uncomfortable designation of the book as 'forgotten'. It was not forgotten quickly. It was recommended reading for Classics students at Oxford and Cambridge, and there was a school edition in 1926.

There could scarcely have been a better send-off for a first novel. She was already well into her next book, the collection of stories *When the Bough Breaks*, which was published a year later (some of the stories had already appeared in magazines). If Fiommar's suicide implied ambivalent and frustrated feelings about her own role – daughter, sister, wife, mother – there was now no denying that she had an acknowledged identity, as a novelist. The theme of blood sacrifice runs through much of Naomi's fiction. Fiommar's death not only liberated her brother; in a sense, it liberated her creator.

2

In the autumn of the year in which Naomi entered the world as a novelist, the Mitchisons moved from Cheyne Walk to a larger house, River Court, overlooking the Thames at Hammersmith. They needed more space for the growing family and also to accommodate their burgeoning social life. The days of isolation were gone. River Court quickly became a centre of all kinds of activity and constant comings and goings. With the physical move came the entry into a new phase of life.

River Court was an imposing house on Chiswick Mall, looking out on a broad curve of the river, which carried some of the same water that flowed past Cherwell. Whether Naomi consciously chose the situation for this reason she does not say, but the river and the green and leafy street have distinct echoes of the Oxford house. The garden was spacious enough for a loggia and a squash court. The house itself was on four floors, with a large drawing-room on the ground floor, stretching from front to back. Naomi had a desk at the window which faced into the room rather than out on to the garden, staking a space at the centre of things where the life of the house would not pass her by. She also had her own workroom specially built. Although professing a lack of interest in possessions – E. M. Forster believed her sympathetic to his own view that ownership was 'after fear, the wickedest thing in the universe'[16] – it was clear that Naomi enjoyed acquiring things for the house. She went to Sotheby's and Christie's, and brought things back from trips abroad. She did not see herself as a conventional home-maker, as a poem she wrote in 1940 indicates:

> *I wasn't exactly a home-bird, didn't fuss*
> *Over silk curtains and china and silver and all that,*
> *I never cared for possessions.*[17]

However, she did like to collect, and there was space now for furniture, objects, books, paintings – and people.

Running this establishment was a major charge, and Naomi did not relish it. She still felt she was being pushed into responsibilities she did not want to handle, whatever satisfaction there was in presiding over her own territory.[18] River Court depended on servants, and her attitude to that dependency was ambivalent. Servants continued to be an essential and accepted feature of middle- and upper-class households and the volume of hard, physical work was, in a house the size of River Court, extremely large. Cleaning, laundry, shopping and cooking were endless tasks. A nurse and nursery maid looked after the children. Meals were cooked, served and cleared away by servants. Naomi's chosen lifestyle was impossible without this, yet she seems to have been sometimes inept and impatient in her handling of the people who worked for her. She wrote in *You May Well Ask*, her last volume of memoirs, 'I am fairly sure my household staff were on the whole happy and felt they were doing a worthwhile job,'[19] but it clearly irritated her to have to be concerned with domestic trivia. (This emerges particularly in the diary she kept during the Second World War.) By the time of the River Court move she was at least more experienced in such matters than when she first set up house in Cheyne Walk, but there are still hints that she was not comfortable in all aspects of domestic responsibility, that this was an area of grown-up life which she did not care for. The incongruity of someone of her radical political views relying on 'service' also made her uneasy, at least publicly.

A solution seemed to offer itself when an ex-fellow officer of Dick's called Levinson appeared on the scene. In need of temporary employment, he and his wife were taken on by Dick and Naomi to run the house. It may have seemed like a way of 'breaking the old master-servant relationship',[20] but in practice it was fraught with difficulties, not the least of which were Mrs Levinson's alcoholic tendencies. What was embarked on as a few months' employment became a few years. Yet without substantial help not only would it have been very difficult for Naomi to write, her enthusiastic collecting of people would have been impossible.

As it was, parties became a feature of River Court, and there were guests sometimes several times a week. Dick's colleagues and increasingly his political associates were invited to dinner. Close friends came for less formal meals, although these were still cooked and served by staff and conversation was untrammelled by the practicalities of providing food. During the day, Naomi invited friends and fellow writers for lunch or tea. Every year the Mitchisons invited dozens of people to watch the Oxford–Cambridge Boat Race from their house, which provided an excellent view. It became a famous annual event, attended by an impressive mix of political and cultural figures of the time. The guest-list might include G. D. H. and Margaret Cole, John and Celia Strachey, E. M. Forster, W. H. Auden, Julian Huxley, Krishna Menon, Miss Nehru (Mrs Gandhi), Barbara Betts (Barbara Castle), J. D. Bernal, reflecting the extraordinary breadth of interest and activity of the two hosts.

Naomi loved to gather people around her, and any excuse would do. There were birthdays, fifth of November bonfires, midsummer parties. Later, she would write about agape, the love-feast, the sharing of food and drink in a way that was both informal and ceremonial, 'a breaking of barriers and setting free of resentments and complexes'.[21] This was a perpetuation of the Oxford gatherings, when Jack and his friends came for picnics and theatricals at Cherwell, but now it was on Naomi's own terms. Naomi tended to preside over River Court social life. Dick was genial but retiring. It was Naomi who was, if not literally the provider of the feast, the initiator of the idea. And it was an idea that ran through her whole life, perhaps best summed up in *The Blood of the Martyrs*, written in 1938 when the River Court heyday was coming to an end: '... they learnt how in the love-feast all those eating together could be sure of the temporary experience of the kingdom and got from it enough faith to go on in a world which seemed utterly against them.'[22] This is in the context of the early Christians. As always, Naomi wrote that book because it explored an analogy with her own time and experience.

The children were growing and moved with considerable freedom amongst the people who came and went. In 1926, Sonja Lois was born, Sonja after Naomi's Danish friend Sonja Carstensen, later

Meyer, who used to come to Cherwell and whom Naomi often visited in Denmark. Naomi breast-fed each baby, but as with most mothers in her circumstances, her involvement with her children was thereafter not necessarily close. With each baby she became less constrained by the prevailing child-reading orthodoxies of the time, notably the rigid views of Truby King. This relaxation meant more freedom. She enjoyed her children and was fascinated by them, but had not the upbringing, the patience or the inclination to be a full-time mother. Lois remembers her as preoccupied, working at her big desk by the drawing-room window and irritated by interruption. But Naomi read to the children in the evenings, and sat with them at the piano, picking out nursery rhymes although she had no ear and little interest in music.

She was, in Lois's words, 'a loved and important figure but not a vital centrepiece to one's life'.[23] Lois noticed her mother's absences, and worried when she was not at home, but nevertheless felt with hindsight that the children saw rather more of their mother than many upper-middle-class children would have done. To Val, her second daughter, she was a remote figure; nurse figured much more importantly.[24] Denis remembers her quick temper and fretfulness, and an occasion when a telephone directory was hurled across the floor.[25] A picture of a determined and dominating young woman emerges. She was ambitious, and impatient for action and results in all aspects of her life, whether personal or professional. Equivocators and draggers-of-the-feet were not suffered lightly.

At the same time it was a warm and positive family environment, with games and books and pets – cat, rabbit and Clym the Bedlington terrier. And if Naomi herself was irritable or absent, there were often other adults about who involved themselves in the Mitchison children's lives. This was an important dimension to their growing up. The upper-middle-class family of between the wars was less limited, less nuclear than the post-Second World War norm. There was a fluidity, dependent on space and money but nevertheless valuable. The Mitchison children may not have felt particularly close to their parents, but the sons, at least, did not feel deprived.

Holidays and travel were important features of life. Shortly after the war, Naomi and Dick had gone to Yugoslavia for their first holiday abroad and they continued to make trips together, without the children, to various parts of Europe. On occasion, Naomi went off on her own or with a friend. But there were also family holidays, usually shared with at least one other family. In the 1920s, they went regularly to Varengeville near Dieppe, with Dominick and Margery Spring Rice as their usual companions but with others often joining them. Naomi had met Margery Spring Rice through the Women's International League and the two couples rapidly became firm friends, spending a great deal of time together. Margy and Naomi had many shared interests, in particular the growing movement for birth control in which Margy Spring Rice, and to a lesser extent Naomi herself, played an important role.

Other close female friends of the time were Liz Belloc, daughter of Hilaire Belloc, a near neighbour, and Angela Blakeney Booth, on whom Naomi modelled one of the female characters in *The Conquered* and who also inspired a poem. Male friends were equally important. An affectionate relationship grew up between Naomi and Morgan Forster. When he wrote to her praising *The Conquered* she invited him to tea. In *You May Well Ask* she remembers him 'in the armchair on the right of the fireplace and I on a floor cushion, my favourite seat, looking up at him and feeding him with crumpets and chocolate cake'.[26] If there is something self-conscious about this image, the relationship with Forster illustrated an aspect of Naomi's need for encouragement and approval. Forster was eighteen years older than Naomi and had by 1923 written all the novels published in his lifetime, though *A Passage to India* did not appear until the following year. He was both established and respected as a writer. He was attentive and generous in his comments on Naomi's work.

It was important to Naomi to communicate with other writers, and she did not hesitate to write fan letters to those she admired. Her friendship with Stella Benson began with a letter congratulating Benson for *Pipers and a Dancer*, published in 1924. Stella Benson's independent and adventurous life clearly attracted

Naomi; her first novel was based on a trip to the West Indies, and later she taught in China, where she spent the last years of her life. Much of their friendship was conducted through correspondence.

Naomi herself was generous to other writers, and gave as much encouragement as she received. One of those she most enthusiastically promoted was the young Wystan Auden, some of whose unpublished poems were shown to her by Richard Crossman, at that time an aspiring Labour politician, whom Naomi knew first in Oxford and later invited to River Court. Having spotted Auden's talent, she quickly suggested they meet. She reviewed his *Poems* of 1930, quite certain that he would be a key figure in the younger generation of poets – he was ten years her junior. Whatever she contributed to establishing his reputation, he certainly turned to her for practical help on a number of occasions, as he struggled with uncongenial teaching jobs. For a while he tutored Murdoch in Latin, when he had fallen behind because of illness. On occasion, Auden criticized Naomi's own poetry, with a bluntness which she seemed to take in good part, although it probably contributed to her later disillusion with the younger generation of male, often homosexual, left-wing writers. Their friendship was eroded by his departure from Britain in 1939, although they sometimes met when he made return visits.

Another male and homosexual friend of this period was the philosopher Gerald Heard, one of the Huxley circle. (In 1937 he departed from California, at the same time as Aldous.) Naomi liked him personally, and much admired his books, *The Ascent of Humanity* (1929) and *The Source of Civilisation* (1935), which explored the losses and the gains brought by civilisation. Heard shared something of Naomi's experimental inquisitiveness. They both were members of an Engineers Study Group which was formed to discuss 'reaching out to group consciousness ... we would always and only speak the truth to one another'.[27] But for Heard, 'group consciousness' was not the politically creative tool that Naomi considered it, and she took issue with his later cynicism about the future.

3

When the Bough Breaks was published in 1924. The stories are concerned with cultural and political margins and meetings in the ancient world, the edges of the Roman empire, displacement, captivity. The reviews were again positive, although the book did not cause the ripples that came in the wake of *The Conquered*, and it was implied if not stated that it was not quite as good. Nevertheless, she was acknowledged as a skilled story-teller. She was no doubt irritated by the heading 'Second book by Lord Haldane's niece' which appeared in the *Daily Express* but this was a minor aggravation in the context of the acknowledged consolidation of her writing career. Many of the stories in the volume contain, like *The Conquered*, passages of bleak and brutal violence. The legacy of war drove the stories she was writing at this time as well as her first novel, and the compulsion to write about violence remained, 'to externalise it on to paper, in order to get it out of my mind: hence the blood and pain in *The Conquered* and my earlier stories'.[28] This was only part of the explanation, as her adolescent writing had also been preoccupied with violence, sudden death and sacrifice. It is as if she felt that recognizing human compulsions to violence was not enough. If she could not actually experience it, she had at least to confront it. From her earliest childhood, Naomi had courted experience, spurred to some extent by rivalry with Jack. Her exclusion from school and then from war made a lasting impression. She made up for it through language. She often expressed herself violently, in letters and in conversation. Fiction allowed her to get closer to forbidden territory.

In *The Conquered*, Fiommar commits the ultimate act of violence, turning the knife on herself. In some of the stories in *When the Bough Breaks*, Naomi allows her female characters more scope for expansive action. She writes about heroic women. In the title story, for example, Gersemi dresses as a man and becomes a soldier. This frees her from the conventional limitations of a woman's life, and allows her to develop comradely relations with men. But the stories also continue a preoccupation with the theme of divided loyalties, in 'The hostages' and 'The man from Alesia'. This is linked with an exploration of the experience of captivity. There are prisoners of war, and slaves, and the captives of custom and circumstances – Phoebe, for example, in 'The triumph of faith' who is faced with an arranged marriage. This consistent interest suggests that she still felt herself to be restricted, or perhaps that the feeling of restriction had become habitual. It certainly continued to feed her fiction.

These stories confirmed what *The Conquered* had already implied, that Naomi's fiction was entering emotional and psychological areas which would in many respects become her trademark. Her almost matter-of-fact tone and colloquial style, along with the distance in time and place, mask the genuinely experimental nature of what she was doing. If the freshness of her narratives and the immediacy of her characterization were seen as innovative, the challenge she offered to accepted social and sexual norms was not explicitly discussed. In *When the Bough Breaks* and the three books which followed, *Cloud Cuckoo Land* (1925), *Black Sparta* (1928) and *Barbarian Stories* (1929), she was not only delivering provocative ideas about the sexual identity of women, she was examining the structure and expression of human relations in a highly unconventional fashion. She described a world in which strong emotions, sexual or otherwise, were possible and natural between men, between siblings, and between tribes and races. She struck a chord with a post-war generation which was looking for ways of challenging tired values.

In six years there were eight books, and by 1925 she was also working on the novel that brought the first phase of her career to its peak, *The Corn King and the Spring Queen*. The writing was pursued in the context of an increasingly busy life. There were four children now. A complex network of literary and political life drew her in different directions. Above all, people made huge claims on her time, although this was a situation largely self-created. She wanted people around her, children, friends, fellow writers. The pre-war Oxford days could not, perhaps, be replicated, but they nevertheless represented the kind of community of living that she sought.

Jack's part in her life continued to be important if ambivalent, but when he left Oxford for Cambridge she saw less of him. They still competed, and Naomi's growing family was an implicit challenge, but her life had shifted into a different context and they no longer had shared enterprises. Jack's big-brotherly role as adviser and guide was diminished. In Cambridge he was involved in what was seen by the university authorities as a scandalous divorce case, in which he was cited as co-respondent. Initially he was deprived of his post by the university, though he successfully appealed against this, and in 1926 married Charlotte Burghes, the woman involved. There was a mutual coolness between Naomi and Charlotte; Jack's wife was critical of women who did not put motherhood first, and she condemned the use of contraception, a cause which by this time Naomi had strongly embraced. There may also have been an element of jealousy on Naomi's part. She, after all, had married a man who was already a close friend of Jack's. Jack did not return the compliment. The jealousy may have been mutual: Jack and Charlotte had no children of their own.

Before his marriage, Jack continued to spend time with Naomi and Dick, sometimes joining them on holidays. On at least one occasion he and Naomi went on holiday together, to France, walking in the Auvergne, recapturing the Cloan companionship. Naomi was working on *The Conquered*, so it was probably the summer of 1922, and it was hot, Naomi's fictional Fiommar and Meromic already existed. In *You May Well Ask*, she describes an incident which has a bearing on the book:

> Once we came down hungry to a village, ate well, washed it down with red wine and staggered into an old quarry full of wildflowers to sleep it off. And turned dizzily towards one another. And suddenly Jack was shocked to his respectable Haldane soul. I wasn't. But that was all.[29]

This passage is revealing in a number of ways. It highlights an undercurrent in the relationship between brother and sister that was much nearer the surface for Naomi than it was for Jack. It is impossible to say whether in this case experience fed the fiction or fiction the experience, but Naomi repeatedly emphasizes the closeness between the two. Just as on one occasion she slapped a friend's face so she could observe her reaction and use it in her fiction, so she may have wanted to act out something that was hinted at if not explicit in *The Conquered*. The experimental gene was powerful in both Naomi and Jack; they were both unorthodox; they both liked to shock. What is interesting in Naomi's recounting fifty years after the event is her interpretation of Jack's reaction. She coolly accepted the incident, examined it with interest, while he, it seems, was shaken. But it may have been another aspect of competitiveness, Naomi demonstrating that she could push out the frontier further than Jack.

Whatever the reasons – war, marriage, motherhood – brother and sister could not re-establish their former closeness. They had always had fiery rows from time to time. Now they were quarrelling almost whenever they met. The children found Jack difficult and alarming, although he was kind and encouraging, particularly to the boys when their interest in science was developing, Jack's marriage was a further inhibition; the dislike and disagreement between Naomi and Charlotte did not decline, although Naomi claimed she 'tried very hard to be pleasant'.[30] But even at a distance, physically and emotionally, Jack continued to be an enormously significant factor in Naomi's life.

It had taken two years and two books for Naomi to establish her position on the literary scene. In 1924, she was made an officer of the French Academy, a serious if not a glamorous acknowledgement. She had sufficient reputation to be invited to address the Heretics Society at Cambridge University, where she talked about the erosion of Christianity, the rise of science, and the instability of civilization, 'a mere water beetle skating over the deep floods of barbarism'.[31] The piece has a rather rambling message about the need to make the world a better place. A paper she gave to the English Club at Oxford five years later was more specific. 'What do we want most?' she asked. 'We want to get into a community. We are bored with being individuals and separate in our loves and hates and jealousies, our own overwhelming fears.'[32] This is in the context of a discussion of contemporary poetry which she believed to be straining to escape from the individual consciousness. Her ideas about community and communion were taking shape.

Naomi's hunger for new experience was as strong as ever, and her zest for travel was unabated despite literary success, children and domestic responsibilities. She and Dick went on a trip to Vienna, with Dick's parents paying for a hired car which enabled them to go on to Hungary and Czechoslovakia, experiencing problems at the border between the two countries. Naomi enjoyed the friendliness and spontaneity of the Hungarians who rescued them when they encountered Czech red tape. Summer visits to Cloan continued, and she was there when she finished *Cloud Cuckoo Land*, late at night; in a characteristic celebratory gesture she rushed out on to the hills to greet the early dawn. Again, her work was welcomed with favourable reviews. The *New Statesman* continued its strong support of her work. 'Mrs Mitchison ... not only succeeds, she has that ease, that definiteness of success, which shows that failure was not even thinkable: she does not *make* a book, it is there, real, solid, intimidating.'[33]

Cloud Cuckoo Land is set in Greece of the fifth century BC, with the title taken from Aristophanes' *The Birds*; Cloudcuckooland is the name given to the capital city. Its characters are caught up in the consequences of war between Sparta and Athens, and what is particularly striking about the book is that here the lives of women are especially constrained and hopeless. The book's heroine, Moiro, is gentle and well-meaning, and a victim. Caught in the political tensions between Athenian democracy – which excluded women – and Spartan oligarchical rigour, and in the more intimate tensions of emotional loyalties pulling in different directions, Moiro has no chance. She and her lover Alxenor escape when their island is raided, but the book's message is that in the context of war and large-scale political rivalries, it is always the women who suffer. Moiro has a son, then a daughter. The baby girl is exposed –

abandoned – in a manner sanctioned by Athenian tradition. When Moiro becomes pregnant again a crude abortion is attempted, and she dies.

The negative message, conveyed by women who submit, who accept that they cannot share the freedom or the political role of men, suggests that Naomi herself was finding the pressures and constraints of her roles as wife and mother hard to deal with. But an equally striking quality of the novel is the *ambiance*, the sense of place and period, all conjured before she had ever visited Greece. She had access to books, of course, and perhaps more importantly, access to the knowledge and scholarship of the Oxford classicist, Theodore Wade Gery. The book is, obliquely, dedicated to him.

The year 1925 was in many ways a watershed. As well as seeing the publication of her third book, Naomi began work on a huge enterprise which would occupy her for the next five years and into which she would write many aspects of her own life, *The Corn King and the Spring Queen*. She now had a daughter as well as three sons, a substantial family. Physical relations with Dick were obviously not a total failure, but at the same time neither of them were happy with the sexual dimension of their marriage. They were both, as Naomi put it, 'open to something better'.[34] It was in 1925 that they agreed they would accept relationships outside marriage and, according to Naomi, this agreement would not have worked if they had not both had someone in mind. For Dick, the 'someone' was Margery Spring Rice, already a friend of the family and well known to the children, who seemed to have experienced little disruption as the balance of their parents' marriage shifted. Neither did the changed relationship between Dick and Margy affect Naomi's friendship with her. The dedicatory poem, 'To Margery and Dominick Spring Rice', of Naomi's first collection of poetry *The Laburnum Branch* may have been written before the nature of Dick's relations with Margy changed, but the book was published in 1926.

> *But between us four*
> *Blossoms for ever the laburnum*[35]

Margy's personality was very different from Naomi's, according to one observer who visited at the time, Gabriel Carritt, an Oxford student who knew Auden and Richard Crossman. Also a visitor at River Court, a guest sometimes at the Boat Race parties, he found Naomi warm and accessible, easy to talk to. Young men were attracted to her, and she was friendly and sympathetic to them. Her unorthodoxy was a kind of magnet to the experimental young. Dick tended to remain in the background, less at ease with writers and artists and unconventional personalities. Margy herself was cool and commonsensical, with a tougher exterior than Naomi, whose emotions were always near the surface. Dick may have been drawn to her because she was less emotionally demanding than Naomi.[36]

Naomi turned to a man whom she had also known for several years. He had been drawn into the Cheyne Walk theatricals, one of the diminished Oxford crowd. It was probably in Oxford that she first met him; she was still often there. The university was familiar territory to Naomi, a constant source of stimulation and knowledge which she naturally tapped. Theodore Wade Gery was a part of this. He nourished and assisted Naomi's interest in classical Greece and his contribution to *Cloud Cuckoo Land* is acknowledged in the dedication, 'To my lover', and in her preface.

> ... the great thing is to find people who are just as interested, and better at a subject than oneself, and induce them to talk about it to one. If they are really good at it, they will probably like doing so. I have been extremely lucky about this.[37]

If Naomi's relationship with Wade Gery, or 'Widg' as she called him, began in shared intellectual interests, it eventually became passionately emotional. It was the first of her extra-marital affairs, and clearly the most lasting in impact. In her nineties she recalled it with a vivid sense of loss. But she also spoke of seeing him years after the affair was over, a 'shambling figure' in an Oxford street, her tone implying that it was hard to believe he was the man she had loved.[38]

This divergence between Dick and Naomi, based on their

continuing mutual love and respect, began the weaving of a web of emotional entanglements that was to be a salient feature of the rest of their life together. Perhaps a straining from the centre had always been present, for Naomi's need for both intellectual and emotional response was very evident from at least her teenage years. The lifting of the inhibition against giving this sexual expression did not affect the need. It did, of course, add a dimension to their married life which inevitably brought emotional and psychological complications. Their discussion of this step in their lives may well have been as cool and rational as Naomi would in later years imply. They were a 'modern' couple, unhampered by out-of-date ideas. Their essential loyalty to each other remained, their deep and sustaining friendship was unaffected. Their own sexual relationship did not end. And the availability of contraception meant that they could each safely embark on additional liaisons without the risk of pregnancy.

They moved in circles where unorthodox relationships were condoned, even encouraged. For Naomi, and perhaps for Dick, there was a feminist dimension to the decision, and it was also a way of making a political statement, of signalling the aspirations of women.[39] However, there are hints that this change in their lives was not as cool and straightforward, nor as mutually comfortable, as it appears in Naomi's later writings and interviews. Its political 'correctness' in the context of the radical milieu of the 1920s did not mean that it was emotionally either correct or painless. There is some evidence to suggest that Dick and Naomi each believed that the other was responsible for initiating the new arrangement.[40] The depth of their concern for each other was such that it mattered very much that they each benefited, that the situation was fair and equable. But it could not be guaranteed that new partners would be conveniently waiting in the wings when required. Naomi herself commented, looking back from the 1980s, that 'it did depend on having total trust in one another, and in not being possessive'.[41]

It certainly made life more complex. Margy Spring Rice and her children seemed to fit into the regime without too much difficulty, though her husband Dominick became a problem, if he was not already by the time the liaison with Dick began. By early 1928, Margy had told Dominick of her affair with Dick and a letter from Margy to Naomi implies that he reacted badly. But she had no regrets that she and Dick had not kept their involvement secret, and warmly professed her love for both Dick and Naomi in her letters to the latter.[42] Dominick's reaction can be judged from his attempt to prevent the Spring Rice children from seeing the Mitchison children, apparently on the grounds of Naomi's immoral behaviour - her affair with Wade Gery. Dominick and Margy eventually parted company in 1936, by which time other women had entered Dick's life.

The cultivation of these relationships, whether or not they involved sexual union, required time and space and little pressure to earn a living. The Mitchisons had both the former, and although Dick's legal work was slow to develop, his private income was substantial enough to contribute to the latter. (However, the slowness with which his career took shape appears to have caused unhappiness and frustration.) They were able to spend weekends at a cottage in Bledlow Ridge in Berkshire, often with the Spring Rices and Agnes Miller Parker and her husband William McCance, an avant-garde Scottish artist. Although Naomi grumbled at the expectation that the women looked after the house and garden while the men 'went for bracing intellectual walks', rural interludes played an important part in friendship.[43]

Naomi's relationship with Widg was rather different from the rather domestic ménage that accommodated Margery. He was single, in his thirties, and, it seems, had had no serious involvement with a woman before. It is not clear at exactly what point he made it clear to Naomi that he wanted them to become lovers, but her response to this does survive, though it is not dated. She proposed a form of contract, which included a preamble which discussed the nature of the relationship. She felt she would not suffer if it remained platonic. Deep friendship was what she valued most, and, in characteristic Haldane fashion, wanted to 'experiment on myself and you', to see if this was possible. She accepted that it was not, agreed that they would sleep together, but stipulated certain conditions. The conditions were designed to protect herself, Dick, the children and others closely involved with them. Naomi and Widg were not to be lovers in London or Oxford, for example, and nothing was to be allowed to interfere with her writing. They were not to become dependent on each other. They were free to fall in love with others, and jealousy was banned. She also addressed the practicalities of contraception, on which the whole thing depended.[44]

In an undated letter to a Mr Bird, Naomi refers to Wade Gery as 'my great friend with whom I went for unconventional and compromising, but quite virtuous walks'.[45] The platonic phase of the relationship may have lasted for some time. In a letter to Naomi, Margy expresses her view that Naomi deserves much more than Widg is giving her, which may imply that sex was missing.[46] But much more interesting than exactly when Naomi and Widg became lovers is the thought on her part that went into taking that step. This was no act of spontaneous abandon. She and Dick had almost certainly talked it through, as they talked through their initial decision to look elsewhere. Above all, Naomi wanted to ensure that no one got hurt. This, of course, was impossible.

4

The affair with Widg was conducted largely outwith the family circle; that was part of the agreement. Weekends away, walking trips in the West Country, were an important feature, always with Dick's knowledge and blessing. Margy, at least, rejoiced in the civilized openness of it all, although she cautioned Naomi against including some of her more personal poems in the forthcoming volume.[47] *The Laburnum Branch* was published to mixed reviews. To some, the poems, many of which had already appeared in magazines, seemed fresh and unconventional; to others they were too loose and colloquial. The poems do vary considerably, both in quality and subject matter, but there can be no doubt about their reflection of the personality and states of mind of their creator.

They express spontaneity, passion, impatience, a responsiveness to
the powerful currents of legend, a strong sense of Naomi's own
family and background. They also suggest a restlessness, a feeling
of confinement, which echoes the concern with captivity found in
the novels.

> *To-night, if I was free, I'd go*
> *Out of the house, into the rain...*
> *And get somewhere, away, away...*
> *If only I could get away!*[48]

In fact, physical confinement for Naomi was comparatively rare:
emotional and psychological restriction was something else. With
Wade Gery she did get away. Indeed, her need for him may have been
precisely as a point of departure, to prove to herself that she could
get 'out of the house', actually and metaphorically.

Theodore Wade Gery was not the only man to be drawn to the
magnetic Naomi at this time. By early 1927, she had met and greatly
impressed the radical essayist Llewlyn Powys. His vision of her
was heady and romantic and he wrote highly-charged letters to her
expressing his admiration. He was struck by what he saw as her
simplicity combined with a wild, generous spirit, and Naomi
enjoyed being depicted in this way.[49] Powys was married but
clearly attracted to Naomi (as he was to several other women) and
his letters suggest that friendship progressed to embraces.[50] The
Naomi that Powys portrays is charismatic and inspirational,
though at the same time there is a patronising note which is less
palatable. He detected in Naomi a melting femininity which does
not ring true. It was a rich mixture but it seems that, though
tempted, Naomi did not entirely melt. She may have been sceptical
of the extravagance of his address, or indeed known of his
reputation. In *You May Well Ask*, she regrets that she did not make
love to him.[51] They carried on a correspondence until at least 1937.
Powys died in 1939, aged fifty-four.

In 1927, Geoff, the eldest of the Mitchison children, now nine,
became ill with a mastoid infection. There was at first no

particular concern, but it soon became evident that the problem was serious, and then meningitis was diagnosed. Medically, there was little that could be done and his death was painful. It seems that Naomi was away, at least for some of the period of Geoff's illness. She was devastated, and her emotional equilibrium was deeply challenged. Inevitably, she felt guilty. She was living a complex professional and personal life, the well-known author of fiction, a collection of poetry, and articles and reviews. She had a husband and a lover and a wide circle of friends and associates. She gave time to people and causes in which she believed. Had she, perhaps, neglected her children? If she had behaved differently, been less ambitious, striven less for love and recognition, could she have protected Geoff from his fatal illness?

It was difficult for anyone to handle Naomi's distress. She turned to Jack, going to visit him and Charlotte in Cambridge, but the experience only fuelled her anguish as they both took the view that Naomi was to blame. Charlotte had written a book, *Motherhood and Its Enemies*, published in that same year, in which she condemned women who did not put their children first. Naomi did not put her children first. There were of course occasions when a child came before anything else, but it was uncommon for children to command the centre of upper-middle-class households. It was accepted that mothers would not necessarily be there. Charlotte and Jack, however, told Naomi that she carried at least some of the responsibility for Geoff's death. With Denis in the car, she drove from Cambridge to Oxford where the other children were with their grandmother. She was in black despair, suicidal, she says in *You May Well Ask*,[52] nearly crashed the car, and had to make a huge effort to continue the drive, mindful that her second child would be put at risk if she did not pull herself together. Dick, in the meantime, remained in London, comforted by Margy, who was with him when Geoff died and who dealt with many of the subsequent practicalities.

Denis (known as Denny) remembers the months following Geoff's death as a very tense period.[53] The effects lasted a long time. For a number of years, Naomi was subject to depressions, and her sudden outbursts of temper became even more erratic. When in

1928 her old and close friend Aldous Huxley published a novel in
which he describes a young boy becoming ill in his mother's
absence and later dying in an appallingly painful fashion, Naomi
was hurt and horrified. *Point Counter Point* drew on the social
circles in which Naomi moved, indeed some of the characterization
seems borrowed from her own family. But using the experience of
Geoff's death was going too far, especially as some of the details
Huxley included must have come directly from Naomi herself. He
describes Elinor Quarle's helplessness as her son is racked by pain
and convulsions. It was a long time before Naomi could forgive
him.

Dick did not find it easy to deal with strong emotion, especially
where children were involved. He is remembered as a nice but
distant father, kind but awkward. But he, too, had lost a son, and the
experience of losing his brother Willie and so many friends in the
war was not so very far away. Coping with the loss made huge
demands on both parents and the existence in both their lives of
others who were emotionally close probably helped. The year after
Geoff's death, 1928, there was a trip to Greece which included both
Margery Spring Rice and Theodore Wade Gery, as well as Liz
Belloc. (Liz and Naomi quarrelled later, over religion, literally
coming to blows, and never made it up.) This was an important trip
for Naomi. Aside from its therapeutic value, it was her first visit to
Greece, which she had already written about, and in the company
of the man who helped her to bring it to life.

They hired a yacht, the *Avrion*, and explored the islands. Naomi
and Dick each enjoyed spouse and lover, sunshine, and the
captivating interest of Greek antiquity, enhanced, for Naomi at
least, by Widg's knowledge. On the trip he discovered a new
inscription on the island of Thera. Naomi was pregnant, a
regenerative response to Geoff's death. Nicholas Avrion would be
born later that year. Naomi was working again on *The Corn King and
the Spring Queen*, and Greece, sea travel and pregnancy are all
present in the book. So is death, in particular the death of the
heroine's son. Avrion's birth seems to have been easier than the
earlier children's, and he was a good-natured baby. In the novel, the

description of Erif Der and her child surely catches the experience of Naomi herself:

> For the first moment of seeing him she thought he was exactly like her first baby; she thought it was her first baby come again. Then she knew that this was an appearance, and the new little creature was his own self already and the past was nothing to him.[54]

Naomi and Margy went on to Crete, where they stayed in the Hotel Minos, 'whose complete staff burst into fits of laughter' at the sight of two women on their own with rucksacks.[55] They absorbed the look and feel of the place, walking to Knossos where they examined the ruins of the Palace of Minos which had been uncovered by Sir Arthur Evans. 'Of course it is hard to reconstruct, hard to imagine the walls all lined with smooth and shining alabaster, now that the remains of it, exposed first to burning and three thousand years of burial, and then to sun and rain, have warped and crystallized into something unrecognizable.'[56] Naomi's description itself indicates the imaginative process involved in bringing to life what is ancient and distant. It was what she was doing all the time in her books.

Around this time, Widg met Vivian Whitfield, an archaeologist working in Athens. They quickly became seriously involved and she accepted his offer of marriage. It was very hard for Naomi to come to terms with this development. It seems that she and Widg had decided between them to give their relationship ten years and see where that took them. Naomi implies that the understanding was that they would then decide whether to make it permanent, in other words whether Naomi would leave Dick.[57] But it was recognized that there was always the possibility Widg might turn his attention elsewhere, and the solidity of the relationship between Naomi and Dick, added to the fact that she bore him another child while maintaining contact with Widg, must have put a strain on all concerned.

From the start Vivian knew about Naomi, indeed had said that she could not understand how, having been in love with Naomi,

Widg could love her. Naomi, she felt, was both very beautiful and had a great deal to give. She also intuitively sensed that Naomi would mind much more than Widg anticipated. He convinced himself that everyone would be happy.[58]

Naomi did mind. She struggled to keep things going. Hard as it was, she decided that the only thing to do was to draw Vivian into the circle. She accepted that sexual relations with Widg were at an end, but at first saw no reason why their friendship could not survive. She worked to establish a friendship with Vivian, with remarkable success. Vivian stayed with her, and an emotionally complex relationship evolved. Naomi wrote about it to Edward Garnett, by this time an important friend and adviser. 'What she wants of me is my intelligence and god knows she can have it, but I want her to have all of me...' Naomi made it clear that there was no hint of lesbianism in this statement; nevertheless it addresses the physical. 'I do doubt if people love me unless they assure me of it by word and touch.'[59]

Naomi's rational self argued that there was no reason at all why they should not all get on splendidly; after all, she and Dick had demonstrated that such arrangements could work. However, her emotional self was outraged, and could not be calmed by establishing a caring relationship with Vivian. Part of the problem was that this was something she could not control. Vivian and Widg were together an independent entity in a way that, for example, Dick and Margy were not. She discussed the situation with friends, and of course with Dick. Edward Garnett advised her not to attempt to compete with Vivian. In March 1929, she went to Norway for a visit, hoping that travel and distance would help. Writing to Dick from Oslo, she commented on the fact that Vivian had 'fallen for' her, and went on:

> But perhaps she, like he, will get over it. I think I am rather a wearing person. Probably she will find the same thing that both you and Widg found: i.e. that I look at her too hard and too close. I'm always pulling the plant up by the roots to see how it grows.[60]

In an undated letter to Wade Gery she wrote:

> I am not sure that the whole thing isn't just too straining and difficult and no good to anyone. Perhaps the best thing is to cut our losses while we can and start afresh, not seeing one another and not thinking of one another if possible.[61]

By early 1931, things had come to a head. Widg was not replying to letters, and there was little opportunity for face-to-face conversation. A carbon copy survives of a letter from Naomi to Wade Gery, dated 17 February 1931 and sent by registered post. The letter was copied to Margery Spring Rice and Edward Garnett, and was clearly intended as a formal statement of what Naomi saw as the options for the future. She offered three choices: that they should not see each other at all except when unavoidable at social occasions, and 'each of us shall endeavour to forgive and forget the other'; that they should avoid seeing each other totally for a year, and then 'take up our friendship by letter'; that they should meet as friends at least once a month for a minimum period of three hours. It is clear that it is this last that Naomi wanted; she did not want to lose Wade Gery's friendship, but above all she wanted to know exactly where she stood.

> I think you may feel that this is hard and cold. I doubt if it is really but a little toughness is necessary to get us out of the present state of affairs. I believe I love you in a rational and creative manner (if such terms can be applied to what is perhaps fundamentally irrational). I believe my love is good for you, although I cannot be sure and am certainly biassed. I believe your's [sic] is good for me. I strongly object to being made into a sentimental memory or to have my time and energy – and perhaps your's [sic] – wasted in questioning and yearnings. If the thing is over, let us realize that it is, tell one another that it is, and have done. If there is still good to be got from it, let us decide how the good is to be got.[62]

Naomi would have other love affairs, but this was the one that mattered most. The situation defeated all her efforts. She was good at manipulating, at getting what she wanted. This time she failed. The hurt that she experienced stayed with her for decades, still alive or at least dramatically vivid in her nineties when she exclaimed, 'It is still swords sticking into me.'[63] It is possible that she invested more emotionally in her relationship with Wade Gery than in that with any other individual, although there were causes that generated an equally intense emotional commitment.

Throughout this period the person she turned to for reassurance and advice was an old friend of her father who, when Naomi was a child, had taken on a godfatherly role towards her. Samuel Alexander, professor of philosophy at Manchester University, was a steadying fixed point in her life. She began to write to him when she was eleven or twelve and had maintained contact ever since. As a young woman she would go to see him in Manchester, seeking his support when life grew difficult. He listened sympathetically when she told him of her love affairs and gently countered her depressions. Part of the value of his response lay in his complete uninvolvement in Naomi's social and emotional world and the fact that he offered wisdom without judgement. She clearly regarded him with great affection, and found that he helped to unravel her emotional tangles. Confident as she was, the emotional risks she took often led her into uncharted territory. While she enjoyed the danger, there were times when it was important to know there was someone who would provide help without asking questions: the relationship with Widg was hard to explain, and in some eyes, harder to justify. Professor Alexander responded to that need.

5

In the meantime, two further collections of short stories had come out, *Black Sparta* in 1928 and *Barbarian Stories* in the following year, and a collection of plays for children, *Nix-Nought-Nothing*, in 1928. The stories were located in the same territory as her earlier work and explored similar themes: tension between personal and political, divided loyalties, the price of freedom, homosexual love. Sparta gave her the opportunity to examine the actions and implications of a narrowly-disciplined society at a time when Fascism had become a recognized force. (The insidious temptations of Fascism provide one of the themes in Huxley's *Point Counter Point*.) Although there are continuing preoccupations with war and cruelty, there are also lyrical celebrations of community and communion, for example in 'O lucky Thessaly!':

> They went into the feast; the curtains were pulled back now and the place filled with shallow level sunlight. But by the time everyone was wreathed and happy and settled down with food and drink, the sun had set and rapidly more and more stars came out over the apple trees and the dark river. There was a mixed smell of things to eat and drink, and people, and sweet herbs.[64]

The fact that this describes a gathering of men again suggests that Naomi was having difficulty finding a convincing, positive role for women, especially in a political arena. Relationships between men seem to offer more ways of operating outwith the conventional bounds of the state. Love and marriage confine and regulate women's lives, but neither limits men in the same way. The bonds between men, often accentuated by war and struggle, offer scope for comradely intimacy, with or without sexual expression. Many of these stories feature the exclusion of women, directly or implicitly.

Reviewers were a little less enthusiastic about these collections, although there were still those who were unequivocal in their praise. 'Mrs Mitchison can re-create the past with a skill that is extraordinary,' wrote the novelist L. P. Hartley of *Barbarian Stories*, in *Everyman*.[65] The *Times Literary Supplement* had reservations about *Black Sparta*: 'The sincerity of her intuition cannot be doubted, but it is so highly individualized that the reader may have some difficulty in following it.'[66] Jack felt that *Black Sparta* was uneven, 'some very good, some in my opinion, moderns in ancient chitons'.[67] This comment highlights a problem of Naomi's approach. Some readers were uncomfortable with the modernity of speech of her characters, and the fact that contemporary analogies shone through only too clearly. Jack was perhaps in a better position than many to recognize Naomi's current preoccupations. At the same time, it was precisely that freshness that had drawn readers to her in the first place, E. M. Forster felt that she handled this successfully. 'One of your problems in style happens to have been the same as mine and I see you are solving it; the problem of realism without facetiousness.'[68] Many felt that she succeeded in making her characters accessible to a twentieth-century readership at the same time as doing justice to historical context, but a few did not, including a reviewer in the *Cape Times* who criticized her 'maddening infantile lisp of a style'.[69]

There would always be those who considered that it was *gravitas* which gave historical fiction its authenticity. Not that Naomi was ever less than serious, but her tone implied that the past had no more weight than the present. And sometimes the urgency of focus on the here and now tinted the spectacles through which she regarded the past. All writers of fiction use their characters to experiment with their own ideas. Naomi did this quite shamelessly. It is understandable that some readers reacted against it, however deftly it was done.

With Sparta itself Naomi had a love–hate relationship, reflecting her ambivalence over the attractions of an ordered society which valued courage and comradeship. In 'The epiphany of Poiessa' Timas remembers Sparta as 'a lovely, free place, where one could be brave and generous and good-tempered quite simply, by oneself', in other words a society that created the ethical environment for individual fulfilment; but then he goes on, 'all as different ... from the real Sparta as a child's mind from a grown man's'.[70] In the title story Naomi celebrates both community and the individual, in particular Phylleidas who places personal loyalty above loyalty to the state. When challenged as to whether he considers himself a better judge than the state, he says yes, to which the response is, '"he is singing a song of his own, against ours.'"[71] Although the story ends with an upbeat communal ritual, there are sinister undertones. Ultimately, as Naomi herself demonstrates elsewhere, Spartan values destroy the individual.

Black Sparta is dedicated 'To two real historians, H. T. Wade Gery and Vivian Whitfield'. The dedication suggests both that Naomi did not consider herself a 'real' historian and that, although Vivian had clearly entered the scene, she was not yet a threat. Characteristically, Naomi was happy to signal her involvement with people important to her, just as she had with her earlier dedication 'To my lover', although not naming names. That hardly mattered when she was making it obvious that she, a married woman, was conducting an extra-marital relationship. Sending out signals of this kind was one way of attacking convention, and Naomi derived great satisfaction from being provocative in this way.

One of the poems interpolated between the stories in *Black Sparta*, 'Arrow-struck', is a reminder of what was involved in contending with the pain of Geoff's death:

> *How curious it is, one goes on with things in spite of heart ache:*
> *Gets up and washes, brushes teeth and hair, dresses,*
> *Noting the feel of buttons and laces...*

And in the final lines an echo of the drive from Cambridge which so nearly added to tragedy:

> *is it worth driving one's car*
> *Safely through streets full of buses at some careful pace*
> *With one's brakes ready to stop one from bumping things-as-they-are,*
> *Not all out and over some deep, desperate edge of time and space?*
> *How curious it is, one goes on with things in spite of heart ache.*[72]

It is characteristic that Naomi should have embedded an intensely personal poem in the midst of a collection of stories set over two thousand years earlier.

The four plays in *Nix-Nought-Nothing* were written specifically for non-professional performance, relying on resources that could normally be provided in the home, and that is part of their appeal. A legacy of Naomi's own amateur theatricals, they have a vigorous humour. Two of them, *Elfin Hill* and *My Ain Sel*, were performed by the Edinburgh Children's Theatre in December 1929. Naomi had now published poetry, drama, fiction and non-fiction, for 1928 also saw the publication of Naomi's first piece of extended non-fiction, *Anna Commena*, part of a series designed to bring forgotten women to the surface. With this book she is in the territory of late Byzantine Europe, telling the story of a woman who was herself an historian. If Anna Commena as a personality remains shadowy, Naomi tackled the Byzantine ambiance with her usual verve. She writes almost as if it were fiction, or as if she had been there, catching the colours, the styles, the action. She also comments on the role of the historian, who should, in her view, be 'more or less conscious of his own place in history'.[73] The interpretation of the past depends on where you are when you interpret it as well as affecting the way you see the present. Too much respect for precedents or for posterity are both dangerous, she argues. 'We, like the Byzantines, are living at the end of an epoch, and must beware of rules.'[74]

The decade was drawing to a close, and social and political change and challenge were impinging more and more on the Mitchison household. Dick and Naomi had embarked on their own personal rebellions and unorthodoxies; increasingly, the personal was moving them into the sphere of politics. It would become harder for Naomi to locate her creative self in the past, however much she used it as a way of writing about the present. 'I am writing a book on the Corn King and Spring Queen,' she scribbled on a postcard to Gabriel Carritt, 'really about modern politics.' She added, 'I'm sure all my friends will hate it.'[75] She finished *The Corn King and the Spring Queen* in 1930, the year in which her last surviving child was born and in which she herself had her thirty-third birthday. In the next decade, she began to write uncompromisingly and without disguise about the present. There was a growing sense of urgency which could no longer be contained by the past.

CHAPTER FOUR

Causes and Campaigns

I began to realize that politics was not a special kind of game for skilled players, but rather a whole aspect of life.

The Moral Basis of Politics

1

Naomi's sixth child, Valentine, was born in 1930. Val, like Avrion, may have been part of the legacy of Geoff's death. In any event, another child signalled a determination on Naomi's part to sustain all of her lives. She was in her thirty-third year. She was an accomplished writer of fiction, a recognised figure on the London literary scene, and an energetic hostess. She had an authoritative voice in print, quick to identify and encourage new talent, such as Auden, and often urging readers to tackle difficult but worthwhile books. 'Everyone should read it,' she insisted in her review of Wyndham Lewis's *The Diabolical Principle and the Dithyrambic Spectator.*[1] At the same time she did not hesitate to weave personal reflection through critical assessment. If from time to time she suffered a crisis of confidence, it was less because she had doubts about her convictions or abilities than the result of uncertainty about her audience, a not uncommon cause of insecurity among writers.

It was now twelve years since the end of the Great War. The initial shock and sense of loss had diminished, but the imperatives of action had not. Writing fiction was one way of articulating a commentary on social, political and personal relations, but for Naomi it did not take the place of practical involvement. Driving the urge to act, to be involved, was a strengthening belief in communality. It is expressed in the fiction. It is clearly stated in her review of Gerald Heard's *The Ascent of Humanity*, a book she welcomed with barely disguised excitement as 'a clarifying mirror of our hopes and intentions'. Heard, she said, was writing about the evolution of 'a new kind of consciousness' which would reach beyond selfish individuality. 'Then we shall no longer be troubled by our separateness – greed and revenge, and jealousy and terror and the need for a personal god and personal salvation – will show themselves for the unreal and unnecessary things that we already suspect them of being, and vanish.'[2] Naomi felt that Heard's book encapsulated the feelings and aspirations of her generation, the generation that had experienced the War and believed that a new direction was essential.

Her fiction allowed her to explore some of the problems and some of the possibilities. What happened to a defeated people? Could individuals survive when communities were conquered or shattered? Could democracy really work? Was the group more important than the individual? What kind of political and social environment allowed women's lives to flourish? The great advantage of fiction was that the telling of stories did not need to go beyond exploration. But that was a limitation also. There were some things that Naomi not only wanted to put into practice herself, but which she also wanted to promote. There was a need to propel others in the same direction. In her review of *The Ascent of Humanity* she wrote of the need for 'a great effort of understanding, by all shoulders to the skidding wheel of civilization'.[3] Her own shoulder was ready to help in the effort to get civilization back on the right road.

Sexual freedom was one element of what she wanted to put into practice. By 1930 she had learnt that its consequences could be both difficult and painful. But there was a practical aspect where she felt she had something to offer and, characteristically, did not hesitate to get involved. In the early years of marriage Naomi and Dick had benefited from the work of Marie Stopes who, in addition to publishing several books on sex and contraception, opened London's first birth control clinic in Holloway in 1921. In November 1924, the North Kensington Women's Welfare Centre was opened just off Ladbroke Grove, founded by a group of men and women inspired by Stopes's work. North Kensington was, like Holloway, a run-down, working-class part of London and a key aim of these clinics was to help working-class women limit the number of their pregnancies.

A leading light was Margery Spring Rice. Naomi and Dick were both on the committee, which had its inaugural meeting in the summer of 1924. At first, women were slow to come to the clinic but gradually this changed. Many of those who came for advice had had more than a dozen pregnancies and had lost several of their children: seven of a twenty-nine-year-old's nine children had survived, six of a forty-two-year-old's twelve children. Naomi regularly helped out at the clinic as well as serving on the committee. It brought her into direct contact with lives very distant from her own.

It was a kind of crusade. In February 1927, the Birth Control Research Committee (later the Birth Control Investigation Committee) was set up, again with Margery Spring Rice in a key role and Naomi and Dick as members. This group sprang directly out of the North Kensington Centre's work. Its aim was to promote the scientific investigation of contraceptive methods and their side effects, and to make knowledge and information available. The committee was also concerned with the ethical implications of the use of contraception and tried to bring together a diversity of views. Naomi herself volunteered for tests: 'this could be embarrassing,' she wrote in *You May Well Ask*, 'but somebody had to do it'.[4] She was following the tradition of her father and brother: it brought science and experiment back into her life. The Centre needed more than time and participation: it needed money.

Money-raising entailed activities that were right up Naomi's street. A fancy-dress ball gave her the opportunity to wear medieval costume. In January 1932, two theatre performances of her own children's play *Kate Crackernuts* featured three-year-old Avrion dressed up in tinsel as the fairy baby.

Inevitably, the result of this involvement was a commitment to print, and in 1930 Naomi's long article, 'Comments on birth control', was published. It is a wide-ranging and very personal piece, much more than an expression of views on a narrowly-defined topic. Birth control was an issue that involved an examination of the nature of marriage and of social expectations, and the article is full of clues to understanding Naomi's own personal circumstances. 'It must be fairly obvious to everyone who considers it that there is something profoundly wrong with the sexual life of people in general,' she states early on, 'and particularly perhaps of married people, in our present urban civilizations. Ordinary life, as most of us have to live it, is a compromise between what we need and what is allowed us by modern conditions. Sexual life is, of course, a compromise too.'[5]

One of the things that Naomi thought was profoundly wrong was the notion of marriage as possession, usually the ownership of the woman by the man. Naomi called this 'domestic prostitution', commenting that it was 'in a way, fair, so long as most married women are economically dependent on their husbands'. Even 'very nice men' were pleased by 'this pretty habit of dependence', and many women, she pointed out, colluded in it.[6] Many accepted an unsatisfactory sexual relationship in exchange for economic security. It is a pattern that had been in existence for a very long time.

Another feature of marriage that was also long-lived was how, inevitably, in Naomi's view, married sexual relations became a matter of habit rather than passion. Her description has the ring of experience.

There is kindness, friendliness, some mutual excitement, partly spontaneous, partly worked up by both to put a little brightness and gaiety into plain ordinary life. There is force of habit, the knowledge that nerves will be soothed and pleasant sleep come, the marking of actual possession, if not of one another at least of a relationship, a little world, a certainty amongst much chaos. There is tenderness and gratitude towards the other parent of present and future babies.[7]

The interpretation of this passage as a portrait of the marriage of Naomi and Dick is reinforced by her assertion that such a relationship is not incompatible with being in love with someone else. Indeed, she argues that in some circumstances a temporary change of partners could be of benefit to all concerned. The traditional marriage was beset by the pressures of urban life, the fragmentation of communities, the demands of work. 'Adequate love-making is hard for tired people.'[8] For women this presented particular difficulties:

Intelligent and truly feminist women want two things: they want to live as women, to have masses of children by the men they love and leisure to be tender and aware of both lovers and children; and they want to do their own work, whatever it might be … They insist – as I think they should – on having both worlds, not specializing like bees or machines; but they must give up something of both, not necessarily all the time, but sometimes the work and sometimes the full sex life. It is very unfortunate, but there seems to be no way out of it.[9]

Naomi is clearly speaking for herself here, and perhaps for those of her associates who had expressed similar views. Compromise was not easy for her, and elsewhere she complained of its demands, but she had learnt to acknowledge the need. She had had several years of pushing life to the limits, of attempting to have both worlds, to live several lives. She knew what the cost was, and she also knew that it was all very much easier for someone in her position. There was little chance of the women attending the North Kensington Centre successfully balancing marriage, children and lovers, with or without the assistance of contraception. But contraception at least gave women a measure of control over their bodies and their lives, and that is the point with which the article ends.

'Comments on birth control' attracted attention, at least among the intelligentsia who debated the ethics of contraception and were concerned with alternative moralities. *Time and Tide* felt that the particular value of her writing was its 'undistorted steadiness' and a 'clear matter-of-factness, of mind as well as of style'.[10] Stella Browne in *The New Generation* also praised her directness, but felt that some of her comments were 'highly disputable'.[11] Not everyone involved in promoting birth control approved of her more radical conclusions.

Naomi wrote several articles about birth control and its consequences for women's lives, and also lectured on the subject, but this article was her most important and extensive statement on a subject that was, inevitably, deeply personal. Hints of contradiction are never far from the surface, reflecting her struggles with the necessity of compromise. While aware of the personal benefits for thousands of women, and the economic benefits for society as a whole, part of her resisted the idea of contraception. She used it herself, but acknowledged the argument for letting nature take its course. 'There are still many women for whom it is right and part of the way of Nature to have this continuous flow of life passing through them. But in great cities there is now no clear way of Nature left: worse luck for us: perhaps we have gone past that; we are individuals, out of communion with ourselves and nature. In our own very different way of Civilization we must do the best we can.'[12] The temptation to submit to nature in tension with the drive to take responsible control, to avoid passivity, runs through much of Naomi's writing.

This period of her life, its adventurousness and its pain, is contained in the heroine of what was to become her best-known novel, *The Corn King and the Spring Queen* (1931). In Erif Der she creates a character who moves across a wide canvas, experiences constriction as well as frightening independence, and is enmeshed in an intensity of emotional relations which reflect Naomi's own. She is also a symbol, carrying the weight of a community's traditions and expectations and, unlike Naomi's 'civilized' generation, is in communion with nature. In the five years over which Naomi worked on the book she bore two children, lost one, had a passionate love affair, travelled widely alone and with companions, and was generally exposed to challenging ideas and encounters. Throughout those years she was working on other fiction, and writing articles and reviews. And a considerable amount of research went into the book, on both written records and artefacts.

The novel absorbed and accommodated the life she was living. It travelled with her, in practice and in her head. She wrote it while on holiday in France and Cornwall and on trips to Scandinavia as well as in Oxford and London. There were periods of stagnation, after Geoff's death for example, but being on the move was no deterrent; indeed, it seemed to be a stimulus. The novel's scope was wider than anything Naomi had attempted before, and it has a boldness and an ambition of a different quality from her earlier work. In *The Corn King and the Spring Queen* she gathers together many of the threads that run through earlier stories and allows Erif Der to experiment with life on a scale denied by the circumstances of previous heroines. It is significant that Erif Der not only has the power that goes with being queen, she is also a symbol of fertility and has supernatural gifts: nature, super-nature and responsibility. Naomi was fascinated by witchcraft, by implication, at least, a reserve of female power quite separate from physical strength. Erif's shamanistic role takes her beyond normal limits.

The novel invents a country, Marob, on the edge of the Black Sea, shaped both by the nomadic culture of the horsemen of the Asian steppes and the urban flowering of the Greek city states which established trading footholds on the Black Sea margins. Elemental forces of cycles of growth, of the clash of male and female principles, are confronted by the defining precepts of rational philosophy. This fictional territory had a particular emotional resonance for Naomi. It represented an environment created for herself to occupy. Erif Der - or Red Fire in reverse - has a role, several roles, recognized and acknowledged, however difficult to fulfil. It was clearly important for Naomi herself to have a role, and to have that role valued. Like all her locations, Marob, the Black Sea and the Mediterranean through which Erif travels, are much more than geography. They come with a social and cultural apparatus which has a psychological as well as historical authenticity. This is a key aspect of Naomi's achievement.

Erif is part of a tangle of relationships, involving her father, her husband Tarrik, the Corn King, and her brother Berris, an artist craftsman. Her father, who manipulates her life for his own ends, is killed by her own hand. This leaves the remaining three held in an uneasy balance. The complementariness of Corn King and Spring Queen is clear: the Corn King has power, but it cannot be released without the Spring Queen. Erif is the essential catalyst of fertility. She also has that unpredictable tool of magic. The position of Berris is more ambivalent. In different ways both Erif and Tarrik inspire and need his creativity, but he never quite achieves an independent role. It suggests an uncertainty in Naomi's mind as to the artist's role - is the artist perhaps a parasite? However much she wanted the artist to be powerful, it was clear that political authority rarely came with that particular territory.

There is a sacrificial element, picking up a theme that was present in Naomi's work from her earliest writing. Erif is a successor to *The Conquered*'s Fiommar; sacrifice runs through all her roles, as the memorable passage describing the spring fertility rites makes clear. Erif, in a white dress sewn with coloured wool flowers, waits passively in the centre of a field while Tarrik moves with plough and oxen round and round the field, the plough digging into the earth an obvious sexual metaphor. As he draws nearer to Erif the surrounding crowd begs her to be 'kind', to submit to the plough. Finally, when the plough is almost on her, Erif 'leapt to her feet, ran under the horns of the oxen, between their panting flanks, and leapt the plowshare itself as it made the last furrow right through the centre of the fallow field, tearing apart the warmed, flattened grass where she had been sitting.'[13] There follows the collective 'dance of courting', which underlines the intensely sexual nature of the episode. Erif represents fertility, of women and of the earth, but this goes hand in hand with submission. The earth submits to the plough. Tarrik leaps at her; 'she gave at the knees and all along her body'.[14] She cannot, as Erif Der or as Spring Queen, choose not to receive the plough or Tarrik. Later she has to lie still as the people of Marob pull the woollen flowers from her dress. 'The Corn King turned her over for them to pluck the flowers from her back ... she was the sacrifice.'[15]

The message is that there is power as well as submission in sacrifice. It is a way of strengthening the woman's role. In other words, it is not only by entering a male arena that women can have influence. This is the climax of the first phase of the novel. Later it opens out. Erif becomes a voyager, and moves in a mode which is much more 'male' in its conventions. The narrative examines different kinds of sacrifice. Philylla, the Spartan girl, is confined by the state. When she challenges the definition of her life she is challenging the patriarchal authority that controls it, and is destroyed. Erif's journeyings expand her self-knowledge and allow her to return to Marob and accept her role, recognizing both its power and its constraint.

Given Naomi's own claim that her fiction directly reflected her life, it is fair to see a parallel with Naomi herself in Erif's quest for some kind of fusion of identity and action, of creative and political fulfilment, of the spiritual and the practical. On occasion Naomi uses the word 'priestess' to describe what she saw as an essentially womanly function of provider and intermediary. Erif as Spring Queen is a priestess, acting for her people. Naomi's own aspirations to act in a similar fashion were becoming clearer, and the compass of *The Corn King and the Spring Queen* is indicative. Its vividness and tension and the extraordinary confidence with which her players move from territory to territory, from culture to culture, are equally pointers to Naomi's aspirations. And, like some of her other books, it acted as a kind of harbinger. In the next few years Naomi would travel further than she had before, and encounter new cultures and new experiences. She would go to the Black Sea, and encounter the source of Marob after she had created her fictional country.

The Corn King and the Spring Queen was recognized by reviewers as a book of great importance. W. W. Hadley in the *Sunday Times* called it 'a remarkable book', 'a great story told in heroic strain'.[16] 'A triumph of the historical imagination,' claimed the *Birmingham Post*.[17] In the *News Chronicle* the novelist Winifred Holtby was so impressed that she felt the author was 'of the calibre of which Nobel prize-winners are made'.[18] More recently, Neil Ascherson praised 'the sheer force of her imperious, empathetic imagination'.[19] The book appeared in 1931 'books of the year' lists and was shortlisted for the *Femina Vie Heureuse* prize. Stella Browne wrote in *The New Generation*, 'It is a world, this book',[20] and in a sense it is Naomi's own world, for it shows every important facet of her life. Her personal involvements, the causes she embraced, her growing political commitment, the never-ending tension between different responsibilities and loyalties, are all present. It was not the last time Naomi wrote about the ancient world, but it was undoubtedly the climax of the first phase of her writing and took her to the threshold of new ventures.

2

Naomi was now a well-known figure, attracting considerable respect from her peers although perhaps less from some quarters of the press which at times adopted a condescending tone: 'a very interesting, pretty, and aggressive little person' was how *The Star* described her.[21] In the *Yorkshire Observer* she was 'pale and earnest', and compared to an Oxford don;[22] in the *Herald* she was 'one of the most handsome and vivacious of our younger women novelists'.[23] She was a guest at a Foyles literary luncheon, a regular literary event presided over by Christina Foyle of the Charing Cross Road bookshop. In January 1932, she was speaking at a Burns supper run by the Scottish Women's Club in Glasgow, along with novelist and

Burns biographer Catherine Carswell. A piece in *The Weekly Scotswoman* described how, when challenged to prove her Scottish identity, she took part in a reel 'with such enthusiasm … that it brought her beautiful hair streaming around her shoulders'.[24] She had become a public figure.

Politics was moving into the foreground. Dick's legal career was not going particularly well and he hankered after more purposeful activity. The notion of a career in politics had been with him for some time: shortly after the war, Naomi's Uncle Richard had advised him to go into Liberal politics. It might have been seen as a way of channelling post-war unease, but political liberalism was tainted with the barbarism of war, and, for many, no longer seemed sufficient for the task in hand. By the early thirties, that task had acquired a sense of urgency.

Dick's background, founded on new wealth (his grandfather had made money in New Zealand) and money management, hardly seemed compatible with radical politics, but he and Naomi had remained in contact with Douglas Cole, and invited him and his wife Margaret Postgate to River Court. As leading lights of the Fabian Society, they were an influential pair in left-wing circles. Cole had published in 1913 the first of his many books promoting socialism, and although in the twenties neither Naomi nor Dick were members of a political party, they were attuned to socialist thinking. The backlash against what Margaret Cole termed 'the atmosphere of euphoria'[25] which characterized 1920s Oxford, where Douglas Cole still taught, made itself felt as the economic situation worsened. The General Strike of 1926 had not made any particular political impact on Naomi and Dick – 'Neither Dick nor I was clear about where we stood,' Naomi recalled,[26] and a poem, 'Remembering 1926', is quite savage about remaining on the sidelines[27] – but their social and economic awareness was expanding all the time. It was beginning to look as if capitalism was indeed collapsing, as the Communists had predicted. The great slump of 1929 sent shock waves through America and Europe. In the words of Eric Hobsbawn it 'confirmed intellectuals, activists and ordinary citizens in the belief that something was fundamentally wrong with the world they lived in'.[28] That belief had been lodged in Naomi's mind since at least 1916. She now began to see political action as a way of responding to it.

The Coles cultivated Dick. In 1930, legal work took him to South Africa for several months and his letters to Naomi reveal his sense of personal commitment to the Coles and a growing political conviction. In the climate of the time and in the circles in which the Mitchisons moved, neutrality was scarcely an option. Social occasions at River Court took on an increasingly political tone, with the young Hugh Gaitskell as well as Richard Crossman, both destined for senior positions in the Labour Party, among the group who visited regularly. Naomi was attracted to Gaitskell, who joined one of the Mitchisons' Scottish family holidays, but he was not interested and nothing more than flirtation came of it. Naomi's interest may have had more to do with difficulties with Wade Gery than with Gaitskell himself.

Dick's background even more than Naomi's warred against his developing socialist inclinations, but was vanquished, with Naomi and the Coles urging him on, Dick wanted to be 'effective' and 'to get out of my shell'[29] and saw an involvement with politics as a way of achieving this. But there was an added complication. By this time Dick was emotionally involved with Margaret Cole, adding another twist to the network of relationships that radiated out from the Mitchison household. Margy Spring Rice was still a close friend of both Dick and Naomi, and Tish Rokeling was by now also part of the scene. Naomi's emotional entanglement with Wade Gery was still unresolved.

In her autobiographical *Growing Up into Revolution* (1949), Margaret Cole described the impact of getting to know the Mitchisons. She encountered Dick first as 'a large and curiously shy object at parties, who managed somehow to give the impression of always standing on one leg'. But, 'Shortly afterwards I found myself from time to time going out to dine and dance with Dick.'[30] Dick introduced her to a different world, of good food and wine and a relaxed generosity with money. There was 'an oysters-and-champagne element in the new association' which she was not used to, but which she enjoyed.[31] She was more extrovert than Douglas, who perhaps did not recognize that she had been suppressing that aspect of her personality. In any event, Margaret's sense of confidence flourished under Dick's attention, though it seems that the relationship meant more to her than it did to him. Naomi was a part of the generosity, welcoming Margaret and Douglas and their children, absorbing them within the Mitchison circle with apparent ease. 'I tried to look after them both,' she said in a letter to Margaret Cole's biographer, Betty Vernon.[32] On her part, Margaret greatly admired Naomi, who was, she said, 'one of the most original and gifted people I have ever known'.[33]

All the parties concerned were aware of the involvement. In 1930 and '31, the Coles joined the Mitchisons on holiday in Scotland, at Craignish Castle on the west coast south of Oban. Dick and Naomi had rented Craignish, partly to allow Dick to indulge his passion for shooting, which he shared with Naomi's cousin Archie Haldane. The entertainment was lavish - Margaret was particularly impressed by a party at which a piper performed. On at least one occasion Margy was also there. She was clearly unhappy at Dick's involvement with Margaret, and he worried that Margaret would give him up. He also worried that the situation would distress Douglas, although, initially at least, he and Margaret avoided sex. Margaret apparently commented to her son Humphrey, 'I was made monogamous, but not faithful,' which implies that the relationship was eventually consummated.[34] Not all the Mitchison children liked the Coles or their children, and there were ripples of tension.

At the heart of it all remained the union of Dick and Naomi. In a letter from South Africa in which Dick agonizes over Margy and Margaret and possible hurt to Douglas, he is supportive over the Widg dilemma and reasserts the centrality of his marriage. There is also a hint that he and Naomi had talked of maintaining a celibate relationship. 'I feel I am going back to court you,' he wrote to his wife, ' - with chastity and the intellectual affections, if you like it so - but to court you more deeply that I'd court anyone else. I don't know that that's conventional marriage, but it means more to me than anything else.'[35] It would be hard to describe the Mitchison's marriage as conventional, not only because of its accommodation of others, but also because of its remarkable strength. It is expressed in an undated letter from Dick, possibly also written around this time:

> It does run very deep, this business of you and me – and not merely a matter of having lived together so long. We don't talk quite the same language but we do understand one another pretty well – and at the end of it all, I suppose I laugh at you a little sometimes and, more often, I'm rather jealous of you for being so successful – but I do think you're fine stuff and generous beyond measure and, though you may laugh, rather a great woman.[36]

Margaret Cole believed that she and Douglas were responsible for drawing Dick into politics; indeed Naomi said that Margaret was largely responsible for 'converting' Dick to socialism.[37] Douglas was Labour candidate for the Birmingham constituency of King's Norton, but in 1931 he was diagnosed as having diabetes. He felt he could not stand, and asked Dick to take his place. Dick agreed, was adopted as candidate and was precipitated from the political sidelines into electioneering, and Naomi with him. It was not the easiest political baptism, as the 1931 general election brought three years of Labour government to an end with the unhappy compromise of the National Government under the leadership of Labour's Ramsay MacDonald. Dick did not win the seat, and thus escaped association with a government which introduced the Means Test, substantially reducing benefit to the growing numbers of unemployed.

Naomi joined the Labour Party in 1931. She was ambivalent about the experience of being a Labour candidate's wife, a response which was sharpened when, in 1945, she finally became the wife of a Member of Parliament. Keen to participate, she discovered that the expected wifely role was in the background, taking on the unexciting committee room work, addressing envelopes and making tea. However, she wrote a 'message to the women voters' (only in 1928 had the vote been extended to all women) which was distributed as a leaflet, and she attended and sometimes spoke at political meetings. There was an exhilaration in the election atmosphere, and the campaign also brought a long-lasting friendship with Dick's election agent Tom Baxter and his wife Bettie. Dick and Naomi often stayed with the Baxters who played an important part in their practical political education.

There was a lot to learn and, in customary fashion, Naomi threw herself into getting to know the place and its people. She had no intention of experiencing King's Norton on Dick's coat-tails. She came to face to face with extreme poverty and appalling housing, with women struggling with numerous, often ailing, children: the need for something like the North Kensington Centre was clear. The frustrations were multi-stranded. Naomi was never comfortable in a supportive role, and when something needed doing she wanted to do it, which was often not possible. Her political energies were fired, but there seemed little scope for action. And she had continually to be aware of local sensitivities; the omission of a hat or her wedding ring could prejudice Dick's chances.

Her political initiation coincided with the launch of a new writing project. She was approached by the publisher Victor Gollancz to edit a volume of essays for young readers, covering 'the foundations of knowledge' in social and cultural subjects and science.[38] Naomi agreed, and embarked on harnessing appropriate contributors. Inevitably, she turned to people she knew to edit the different sections, and roped in, among others, Gerald Heard for the history of ideas, Margaret Cole for the organization of society, Dick for law and government, Hugh Gaitskell for economics and Auden for writing. To deal with science she approached a young lecturer in the history of science at Bristol University called John Pilley. It was hard work, as she readily acknowledged. She had to chivy and persuade, and the actual editorial work was considerable.

This was to be a book for the next generation, reflecting the best of the leading liberal thinkers of the day, challenging many of the more conventional social and cultural assumptions. Its ethos is reflected in a review Naomi wrote in 1930, of Freud's *Civilization and its Discontent* and *A Propos of Lady Chatterley's Lover* by D. H. Lawrence. In it she talked of the need for 'communion': 'Our new communions must be in some way compatible with the good part of our civilization, with science, with consciousness of our own psychology, with the freedom which knowledge brings.'[39] This echoed the theme of her talk to the Oxford English Club, although the context is different. *The Outline for Boys and Girls and their Parents* was attempting to draw attention to what were, in Naomi's view, 'the good parts of civilization' and how they could be built on. Both she and Gollancz had high hopes of the book, and put a lot of work into preparing the ground for its reception. Naomi was cheerfully optimistic, and produced a skit on *The Outline* in the form of a programme for a children's variety show: 'Hugh Gaitskell and his performing elephant ... Naomi Mitchison, comedy dancer, gracefully puts her foot in it every time.'[40]

The *Outline* was published in 1932. All involved knew the book would be controversial; it was intended to be. But they underestimated the force of the establishment. The Anglican establishment was the most outspoken, with several pillars of the church lending their names to an open letter to the press denouncing the book on the grounds that it not only undermined traditional Christian values but also approved developments in communist Russia. A public debate followed. Although some notable figures supported the book, including George Bernard Shaw, Rebecca West and C. E. M. Joad, the response to the *The Outline* remained nervous and it never achieved sufficient sales to make it viable.

One of the champions of the book was Margaret Haig Thomas, Lady Rhondda, founder in 1920 of the periodical *Time and Tide* in which Naomi (and Rebecca West) regularly wrote. *Time and Tide* had always had a left-wing and feminist inclination and encouraged women writers, and it was in its pages that Lady Rhondda leant her voice in support of *The Outline.* She stressed that there was much to admire in the infrastructure that the Soviet Union had put in place to support working women and suggested that sweeping condemnation of Communist Russia was unwise. This was hardly an argument to appease an orthodoxy disturbed at the prospect of women moving beyond the home: even some left opinion was uncomfortable with a book for the young which questioned patriarchy and advocated borrowing from Communism.

The experience reinforced Naomi's socialism and her feminism. It also reinforced her impatience with the liberal establishment; her divergence from those who had at one time been thought of as natural allies was under way. Early in the 1930s Naomi had planned to write a book on feminism. A piece in the *Lancashire Daily Post* shows that such issues were in the forefront of her mind:

> The feminist problem must be solved, and fairly soon, before the confidence and courage which women got during the war and during the few years of prosperity immediately after it are broken down and wasted. It is, I think, up to the community, if it really wants to grow into a whole, straight, healthy entity, to fit, not the women to the jobs – by pruning and forcing women out of their natural way of life – but the jobs to the women.[41]

In a letter to Stella Benson, Naomi wonders if she can handle the kind of book she feels it should be. 'Goodness knows if I shall ever get it written because I want it to be history and philosophy and political discussion and that may be more than I can do…I am quite sure the feminist position wants to be restated every few years.'[42] Naomi did not see feminist issues contributing to a war against men, however much she resented patriarchal values, but as an essential part of an integrated society. So far in her own writing career she had had little difficulty in getting published. Jonathan Cape were happy with her books. *Time and Tide* had, since 1928, provided a regular outlet for reviews of fiction, poetry and non-fiction, and occasional short stories and travel pieces. She reviewed many of the most prominent writers of the day, including D. H. Lawrence, Freud, Laurence Housman, Julian Huxley; also

French and American fiction, and children's books, always with the directness of approach, intelligence and style which had become her trademark. Perhaps because she did not have to fight for outlets and from the beginning wrote from a secure social and economic base, she was never associated with the avant-garde feminist writing of an older generation of women writers, such as Dorothy Richardson or Catherine Carswell.

Feminism was an issue she discussed with Lewis Gielgud, still based in Paris, but with whom she maintained a sporadic yet productive playwriting partnership. He understood her pre-occupation, indeed perhaps helped to fuel it. Feminism, he felt, was about modifying social and political structures to allow people, men and women, to operate according to their actual talents and abilities, very much what Naomi expressed when she wrote of fitting jobs to the women, rather than women to the jobs.[43] However, he also teased, and told her that according to a French colleague, feminism was not having to offer a woman a seat on the Métro.[44]

The political world which Naomi was now entering was overwhelmingly dominated by men. There was still only a handful of women MPs. By 1931, there had only been one woman cabinet minister (Margaret Bondfield) and it was 1945 before a second woman, Ellen Wilkinson, gained that rank. Of the River Court social circle, the only woman to have a political role in her own right was Ellen Wilkinson, and she lost her seat, temporarily, in the 1931 election. Naomi recognized the importance to Dick of the King's Norton candidacy, and was determined to support him. But it was not always easy.

Her political education was also being pursued in other quarters. Part of his attraction of John Pilley, the contributor on science to *The Outline*, was his intellect and his socialism. He was a member of the Communist Party, and inclined to put the political before the personal, or to interpret the personal in political terms. Naomi was responsive to ideas of the collective good and respected Pilley's disciplined commitment. They became lovers, and Naomi wrote several poems which expressed their physical intimacy, celebrating *al fresco* sexual congress, and in one comparing her lover to a bull. The poem 'Plowing Eve', written in March 1932, directly echoes *The Corn King* and suggests that Naomi saw her relationship with John in symbolic as well as emotional terms: 'We are mixed, warm in the melting, tossed up and foaming.'[45] Another poem, one of a series of songs probably written in the early 1930s, is also indicative. Called 'Land of Freedom', it begins:

> *Yes, it is a good name, 'Comrade'.*
> *It means kindness,*
> *The love of neighbour for neighbour,*
> *You had that.*[46]

The songs interweave Soviet and Scottish themes. There was an emotional appeal in the ideals of socialism; the idea of comradeship, which Naomi had already explored in her fiction, was an important part of it. John Pilley was a comrade. Comradeship meant sharing bodies as well as ideals. It meant not being selfish with sex. It meant being kind, the word Naomi often uses to describe the woman's experience of sex. John Pilley appears in his letters as confident and assertive, and is remembered by Gabriel Carritt, who knew him in the thirties, as 'aggressive'.[47] He was clearly very different from Dick.

There was no question of the liaison being secret. John met Dick and in a letter to Naomi wrote perceptively about her marriage:

> ... what a contrast you are, you two. You are confident and he is shy; you believe that the mind has only to work to transform Nature, while he has a kind of fatalism which makes him dislike analysis and believe that emotional facts have to be accepted as final and unalterable. You think I minimize all the difficulties, whereas he despairs of them.[48]

He also met Margaret Cole, whom he liked and felt to be good for Dick. He was aware, presumably from Naomi, that there were as yet unresolved problems in the relationship between Dick and Margaret. He responded sympathetically to Dick, commenting that he seemed resigned to the impossibility of having a better relationship with Naomi. This does not suggest a man who had happily adjusted to the realities of 'open marriage'. John saw that Dick might 'drift further and further away' from Naomi without her being aware of what was happening.[49] Margaret and Naomi also confided in one another, Margaret reassuring Naomi that she thought Dick was coping, though they – Dick and Margaret – were envious of the physical intimacy of Naomi and John.[50] At the same time she felt that Dick and Naomi were 'as matched a couple as I know'.[51]

John Pilley's letters to Naomi, though supportive and admiring, tend to be cool and slightly impersonal. Whatever his feelings for her, he did not express strong emotion or appear vulnerable, unlike Widg. Their correspondence is full of debate, covering the moral and social fundamentals of political ideas as well as questions of ideology. John was a determinist, Naomi much more fluid in her belief that human relating was at the heart of political aspiration. Their liaison underlined what was for Naomi the essential dilemma: the tension between individual and group needs and interests. She refused to acknowledge that she was in love with him, as if there might be something 'un-socialist' about such an admission. She would not cling possessively to his affection, but would see it as part of the potential for a better society.

An aspect of John Pilley's socialism was his disbelief in sexual intimacy as possession, and he accepted with apparent ease the web of attachments and friendships of which he became a part. The web admitted yet another figure at about this time. Naomi was fond of her cousin Graeme Haldane, a childhood companion at Cloan, but with a rather more restricted upbringing than Naomi's – although Naomi herself felt that her growing-up was equally hedged with rules, albeit not the same rules. Graeme, who had been in the navy and was trained as an engineer, was now in London and re-entered Naomi's life. He talked to his cousin about his problems with women, the result, he and Naomi agreed, of his Calvinist upbringing. She, in turn, talking of her own circumstances, of the nature of her marriage. Their shared Haldane background sustained a mutual sympathy.

3

In the summer of 1932 Naomi had the opportunity to travel to the Soviet Union with a Fabian Society group which included Hugh Dalton (to become a prominent Labour politician), Frederick Pethick-Lawrence (socialist and campaigner for women's suffrage), Kitty Muggeridge (a journalist, Malcolm Muggeridge's wife, 'a restless creature, probably a good deal unhappier than she has any business to be'[52]) and Christina Foyle (with whom Naomi shared a cabin on the voyage). Graeme Haldane was also one of the group. Naomi was ambivalent about the Communist Party but enormously curious about the Soviet Union and prepared to be impressed. She was encouraged by John Pilley, who had already been there. He wrote to her from Bristol shortly before she left, saying that she would probably find that personal preoccupations would be seen in a very different perspective and 'seem more trivial and unimportant than you would have thought possible'. In the Soviet Union, he felt, individual concerns were overshadowed by 'the great work of the Five Year Plan'.[53]

Each member of the group had a particular area of interest to investigate. Naomi, who felt slightly out of place in the company of people with specialist training and knowledge, elected to look at the way archaeology and museum work were organized. She was also interested in birth control practices and in particular what seemed to be an enlightened attitude towards abortion. The Soviet Union was the only country in the world where it was legal.

In Soviet Russia, Naomi was hoping to find not only fairer political and social structures, but better human relations. 'I felt that in a fairer world people would become automatically nicer, all social intercourse would be happier and easier.'[54] Yet she was ambivalent. She reflected as the journey began:

I am in such a state of compromise! Sometimes lately London has seemed quite unreal, going about among the advertisements and little shops and people hurrying each on their own errand, each trying to outdo what another has done, and this thing I am going to see alone seems real. And sometimes I find I believe intensely still in certain values.[55]

She could not honestly say she believed that all individualism, all choice, was bad, or that she was ready to give it up. She was prepared to be impressed by what she would find; whether she would be convinced was another matter. The voyage from the Thames to Leningrad came to an end on 7 July. There began a packed itinerary of organized visits and, whenever Naomi could manage although it was not easy, independent exploration. In Leningrad, Moscow and Kharkov there were visits to factories, rest homes, schools and hospitals. After a few days in Leningrad, her impressions, recorded in a detailed diary she kept of the visit, began to crystallize. There was much that she liked – the confidence of the women, for example. But she felt that Soviet Russia had yet to grow up.

> At present Russia is just like a big school, and there's a lot of public school mentality; possibly that's inevitable with Socialism; one's bound to think of the honour of the school, and perhaps it's not as bad as one thinks, perhaps one only really dislikes the school because it cuts across this other sort of group. Yet it is rather annoying and seems childish, and I can't help thinking that if you have a majority of people feeling like school-boys you will have a minority feeling like school-masters and mistresses. I believe Stalin is really THE supreme head master and the man that Auden is always writing about in his poems, the terrifying hero that most people want – something between head master and head boy, I suppose really.[56]

At the same time, she was encouraged by the position of women, and detected no conflict between socialism and feminism. 'The way women have reacted to economic equality is the best advertisement for Marxism, and convinces me more than anything else.' And she went on:

> When women have become great in spite of economic
> inequality and the social conditions which it has imposed,
> they have been strained and torn almost beyond endurance,
> and they have had to use a lot of their working energies in
> making themselves into personalities: here that is not
> necessary.[57]

Letters came from home, and she found it reassuring to hear about
what Dick had been doing. Most of all, she missed Valentine. At the
same time, that world seemed remote and not quite real, 'all bright
and coloured like the small aquariums in the Zoo'.[58] Soon Dick too,
with a separate group, would be on his way to Russia. He wrote from
Moscow expressing a mixture of enthusiasm and caution.

She found Moscow more cheerful than Leningrad, although her
experiences there were mixed. As well as going to hospitals and
birth control clinics, Naomi visited one of the city's thirteen
abortion clinics. It was made relatively easy for a woman to have
an abortion, and the scale of the demand was indicated by the fact
that this one clinic carried out 20,000 terminations a year. At
the clinic, Naomi witnessed an abortion performed without
anaesthetic, which was normal practice. The woman was clearly in
acute pain. Naomi described the episode in cool yet excruciating
detail, but made no comment.[59]

She was determined to get to the Black Sea, Corn King and Spring
Queen country, to see the place and the artefacts which she had
absorbed into her fiction. In particular, she wanted to get to Kerch
on the eastern edge of the Crimea, where archaeological digs were
in progress. At first Intourist, who handled all arrangements for
foreign travellers, were resistant, but Naomi finally persuaded
them to allow her to go, though she had misgivings. 'I confess I feel
rather frightened, though it is silly of me ... But I have seldom been
on my own. I feel I've jolly well got to now.'[60]

The first stage of the journey took her by train to Kharkov. She
found herself sharing a sleeping compartment with an amorous
Russian, whom she managed to fend off. After a few days in
Kharkov, with a series of organized visits, she was on her way again

and finally arrived in Kerch on 29 July. She was met by Professor Marti, the archaeologist in charge of the digs. By this time Naomi was not well, suffering from a sore throat, but that did not prevent her from energetic expeditions to look at the archaeology, under the concerned guidance of the professor.

She left Kerch by boat on 1 August, bound first for Yalta, then Sevastapol. It was hot, there was swimming in the Black Sea, and Naomi became sunburnt. She spent a few days in Odessa, the round of visits continuing – to clinics, factories, museums. In Odessa, there was news from home that Murdoch was ill, then another telegram saying he was better. 'I begin to feel the pull of my ordinary life again,'[61] Naomi wrote in her diary, and later she reflected on what it was going to be like when she returned to her old life:

> I suppose I shall sink into it all again when I get back. Or perhaps one is never quite the same after being in this other world. I feel very much more grown-up, very much more serious, and definitely very determined to see, as far as it lies in my power, that this place and this thing and idea shall not get smashed.[62]

Crossing the Black Sea, she experienced what she had already described in her novel. She sat alone on a coil of rope, watching the land and the dark blue sea, feeling calm and peaceful. Yet at the same time she felt troubled: 'this place has changed me; I can never be the same as I was a month ago. Surely here, surely now, in this calm, I can come to some judgment about Russia.'[63] Yet she felt as divided as she had when she left England. Communist Russia had got things 'half-right'. She recognized in theory the values encapsulated in the primacy of work, the rejection of possession, but there she was 'dirty with coal dust, bitten by insects', longing for a bath at River Court, to wash her hair in scented shampoo and to put on clean linen. 'To have values and to be free from possessions and being possessed, to have values and yet to be alone. Is that the thing one wants?'[64] Russia had perhaps furnished the right question, but where was the answer?

From Odessa she headed north again, by train to Kiev. The journey home was overland: Warsaw, Berlin, then into Holland, which seemed 'unbelievably peaceful and clean; even the towns look as though they had no factories, no workers' tenements.'[65] From this perspective she could reflect on her visit rather more constructively. She made a conscious effort to be objective. Material conditions were worse than first impressions suggested. 'Things are hard for anyone who is not definitely in some kind of organization,' she wrote.[66] Women without jobs, people who had once worked but whose jobs had been rendered valueless by a changed society, old people without pensions – there were some who were starving. There were shortages, overcrowding, and many people were living in worse conditions than before the revolution. To balance this, there was job security, free education and health care, facilities for sport and entertainment were either free or very inexpensive.

These reflections helped her to work out her own attitude to Communism. She was not converted, but she could understand the appeal.

For those who believe in it, it appears to be completely satisfying; through this system of belief, death and hardship lose their terrors, there is no such thing as boredom or individual fear, general love is made possible and happiness such as is very rare in other countries becomes a matter of course. A good Communist at work on something with Communist value cannot be bothered by individual preoccupations, as an ordinary, unco-ordinated individual is.[67]

A letter from Aldous Huxley to Naomi echoes this perception. He agreed that people in Russia were probably happy, because 'happiness ... is a by-product of something else and they've got a Cause.'[68] Yet Naomi was aware that this was countered by the fact that there was no choice, no room for individualism, that a rigid and essentially religious doctrine combined with a heavyweight bureaucracy was wasteful and repressive. The only thing she could be sure about was that the position of women was more nearly equal than in capitalist societies, and that this equality 'solved, or nearly solved, the sex question which has preoccupied us for so many years.'[69] By the 'sex question' she meant the superficialities of sexual attraction, sexual games and sexual battles, and the tensions caused by guilt and hypocrisy. In the USSR, relations between the sexes were straightforward, down-to-earth; that appealed to Naomi.

On the channel ferry they ran into fog. Naomi got into conversation with people who knew of her, had read her books – 'I was made to feel a personality again.' The inevitable reassertion of individualism had begun.

> And how English the train was! – the stiff women in the corners reading shilling magazines, the chill in the air ... Then the Liverpool Street and the car and this terrible feeling of time suddenly telescoping, so that one was back where one had been before the beginning and it was all perhaps a dream.[70]

It was not a dream, but it was the stuff of fiction. The visit to Russia fed importantly into the novel that Naomi would soon begin to write, *We Have Been Warned* (1935), her first novel with a contemporary and overtly political setting.

One aspect of her visit to the Soviet Union did not find its way into her diary, nor, at least directly, into the novel. It emerges in letters to John Pilley. Concerned about what she perceived as the sexual repressions of one of the male members of the group, she undertook to make herself responsible for overcoming them. There was considerable awkwardness, nervousness and anxiety on the part of both protagonists in this episode, but Naomi convinced herself that this was something she had to do, that she was putting socialism into practice, and she used arguments that John had put to her to justify her actions to herself. At the same time, she was clearly anxious about the possible consequences: it had to be understood that there was no commitment on either side. The letters in which she described the situation to John, who seems to have encouraged her, reveal the contradictory forces at work.

> John, I am really rather frightened; you have landed me with being a priestess, when my individual self wants to be your lover and nothing else. I am very inexperienced and I am so afraid of doing something which will leave a bad memory for him (and, for that matter, for me).[71]

Yet 'priestess' was one of the roles to which Naomi aspired. Perhaps she wanted to prove to herself that she could do this thing. The deed was done on board ship, as they made their way through the Kiel Canal. It was not an act of passion, but of kindness; it was not easy to come to terms with, and it clearly left Naomi in an emotionally raw and confused state. Yet at the end of the fourth in the series of letters to John in which she described the situation in some detail, she is able to pull back. 'Damn it all, I'm the best if not the only English historical novelist [*sic*] and this is a really interesting piece of writing. Think what your heirs will be able to sell it to America for!'[72]

At first she could not tell Dick about it, although eventually she did. She was worried that the episode would affect her relationships with both him and John. She felt vulnerable, out of her depth. At the same time, something – probably her adventurous love of experiment – drove her on. This was no thoughtless or spontaneous response, although impulse may have been the initial trigger. It is characteristic that the episode was documented and wrestled with in letters to a third party.

Every effort was made to keep the Mitchison network free of tangles. Though John eschewed a sense of possession, he cautioned Naomi to be circumspect as far as Dick was concerned. After all, although John did not find it difficult to be selfless, Naomi was not his to bestow. He felt that Margaret Cole's influence would support Dick and ensure that Dick's affection for Naomi did not diminish. They were all concerned not to hurt each other; for Naomi, the repercussions of sexual and emotional liberality involved the realization that perhaps hurt was inevitable. But the kaleidoscope of relationships was constantly changing. Naomi made no emotional claims on the partner of her Russian experiment, and expressed a hope that he would find a permanent relationship, for her sake as much as for his. Soon, she was without John, who himself married. They had agreed that their relationship was not compatible with his married state. Margaret Cole remained in the picture, a good friend to both Naomi and Dick, and Dick had another female companion, Tish Rokeling. With Widg and John both in the past, no one else took their place, at least not in the same way.

There may have been brief encounters. Naomi remembered one such which took place in an apple orchard, though she did not name her partner. It is probably the episode commemorated in the poem 'Midsummer eve 1933'.[73] There were certainly close friendships with many different men in many different circumstances. And through it all Dick remained central, as she did for him, and their virtually daily letters to each other when apart did not falter. She did not seem particularly distressed at parting from John Pilley, and remained friendly with him and his wife, and later with his children. A poem, included in *The Delicate Fire*, conveys the pain of parting and a determination to put a brave face on loss. The tone suggests it is more likely to have been about Wade Gery than John Pilley.

> *I take it this means, practically, goodbye;*
> *And that's all right, of course. I'm not going to cry.*
> *O, I shall have plenty left, all earth and sea and sky,*
> *Why should I cry for you?*[74]

The following year, 1933, a volume edited by Margaret Cole, *Twelve Studies in Soviet Russia*, was published by Gollancz in association with the New Fabian Research Bureau. With an introduction by Douglas Cole and Clement Atlee, it contained pieces by both Naomi and Dick. He wrote on 'The Russian worker' while Naomi covered museums and archaeology in an article entitled 'Archaeology and the intellectual worker'. Graeme had a piece on 'Power and industrial developments'. Naomi had liked what she had seen in Russian museums, the efforts to present and interpret material in the context of the environment, natural and economic. She approved the provision of practical information, 'the sort of things one has always wanted in museums', even if the labels were often written on the backs of used sheets of papers.[75] She had always been a committed museum-goer, had haunted the British Museum to brood over the artefacts that related to whichever novel was in hand at the time. If the Russian museums had a tendency to over-simplify, to leave out religion, for example, their approach was nevertheless stimulating: 'history is always being interpreted from one point of view or another, and any new point of view throws fresh light and sets alight trains of thought between historians and historical fact.'[76] In other words, whether or not one agreed with the approach, there was room for creative argument.

4

From time to time Naomi was able to get to Paris to continue her playwriting partnership with Lewis Gielgud. Lewis had stayed on in Paris, where he had been a member of the British Military Mission in the last years of the war, working for the International League of Red Cross Societies. His better-known brother John was by this time attracting attention on the stage. Lewis and Naomi wrote several plays together. Most were unpublished. A few were performed or broadcast. Whatever their fate, there was a great deal of pleasure in the writing, and a reminder of Oxford days. The plays evolved through letters, and took final shape in frantic writing sessions in Paris, with breaks in the local lesbian café, Chez Louise. They explored the early Christian period which had initially fascinated them. *As it Was in the Beginning*, probably the best known, was broadcast by the BBC in September 1940, and was quite well received. At least one other play, *The Key of the Garden*, was also broadcast, in April 1955. *The Price of Freedom* was performed by the Sheffield Repertory Company in 1938. *Full Fathom Five* moved to a contemporaneous topic, being about the murder of a man shell-shocked in the First World War. It was performed in Birmingham in 1932. Although Naomi never became really established as a playwright, the theatre remained an abiding love. Several plays and parts of plays, written without Lewis Gielgud as a partner, survive in typescript.

The trips to Paris were interludes. Throughout the thirties fiction was the driving force. Nineteen thirty-three saw the publication of *The Delicate Fire*, a collection of stories and poems, and several articles and further short stories. *The Delicate Fire* took her back to Greece for the last time, exploring themes she had touched on before. There is a starkness about some of the stories, one of the most interesting of which is 'The wife of Aglaos', which concerns a woman who experiences violence and captivity yet whose identity as wife and mother survives and strengthens. Kleta is above all a maternal figure, offering 'kindness' to many men, which is sexual, maternal and comradely. As a member of a group of runaways, she feels this is something sustaining she can share, without eroding her feelings for her husband, who eventually comes back into her life. In another story, 'Lovely Mantinea', Kleta appears again, offering help to slaves: 'What she could do for them was to make them feel they were people.' Through comfort and contact 'she could try to get them in a better relationship with one another, so that they could feel a little solid and strong, not just each for herself and what she could get.'[77] Through Kleta, Naomi expressed some of her own aspirations towards helping others.

Naomi felt that the present was increasingly intruding on her fiction and that this was beginning to show. Of two stories in *The Delicate Fire* – she doesn't specify which – she said, 'These people were half out of the past.' She felt she was being pulled towards writing about the present – 'I'm sick of the past really' – but was not confident about writing about the present. 'When I write about modern things people will find out I don't know anything really … the thing I can do is put descriptions of ordinary things into vivid words, so they stand out and make people jump, but that's not good enough.'[78] Although the book's context is ostensibly ancient Greece, a contemporary note is also struck. In a poem, 'Two men at the salmon nets', Naomi reflects on her exclusion from the male world. It was probably written in August 1932 when she was staying at Paxton House in Berwick-on-Tweed. The men are netting salmon at the mouth of the Tweed while 'I stay in with the children and books'.[79] It is a nostalgic poem, as if the author were cut off from a world she once belonged to. In reality, Naomi was determined not to lose her participative life, nor was there any need for her to be excluded.

Her experiences in the Soviet Union inevitably widened and sharpened her political perspective. In her introduction to her book *The Moral Basis of Politics* (1938) she said, 'I began to realize that politics was not a special kind of game for skilled players, but rather a whole aspect of life.'[80] Something of that was expressed in the novel she was now working on, *We Have Been Warned*, in which she drew directly on her own recent experience. The novel has a rawness, a lack of authorial mediation, which makes it uneven and unsatisfactory in many ways. The lengthy dedication, containing the names of many, perhaps most of the people who were crowding her own political scene (several of her friends appear in the narrative itself) signals the book as 'a story of our time', and it is revealing, both of aspects of Naomi's life and of the way she was thinking and feeling. Her heroine, Dione, a well-off middle-class woman, is married to a Labour candidate. Her roots are in Scotland, interestingly the Argyll coast of Naomi's recent visits rather than the Perthshire of antecedents and childhood. Dione is restless, ambivalent about politics, though wanting to make a contribution. Part of the book concerns a trip to Russia. Dione and her husband Tom both have affairs, Tom with a Russian woman, Dione with a shy, working-class Scot, Donald, a Communist whose political convictions have led him to murder. The melodramatic strains of the plot sit uneasily with the near-naïvety with which Tom and Dione discuss their marriage and their feelings for others. They try to pretend that there is no anxiety, no jealousy, but without success. Dione reflects that 'perhaps these things would have an easier convention in a hundred years. Little comfort now!'[81]

Tom goes to Russia to find 'socialism in action'.[82] Dione feels pressured by her socialist beliefs to 'be kind' to men. The consequences are not happy. The novel highlights the difficulty of being female in a movement which, whatever the theory, was deeply coloured by prejudicial attitudes towards women. Clearly this was something with which Naomi was struggling at the time. Simultaneously, the novel articulates quite precisely some of Naomi's own ideas. Dione reflects 'We can only imagine a few years from now, we can only imagine easy things – tidying up the world, making it all as good as the best now.' But there is no vision of a radically different world. The Labour Party's strength, Dione goes on to say, is that it confines itself to the things it can do. But that is also its weakness. Dione – and Naomi – are dispirited by the reduction of everything, even idealism, to the level of a transaction.

> Goodwill, that curious product of consciousness, of leisure and energy to spare and share. That thing we put out against the forces of interest. That extra thing. Religions and nations and political parties have taken it and used it as coinage, have said you must only give it in exchange for value ... We will give you goodwill, but you must give us in fair exchange your soul, your body, or your mind. And lately, since goodwill has been spoken of more freely, since we have given lip-service to universal goodwill, distributed free as a kind of advertisement for humanity, we have asked instead that we should be given something to show for it, peace, prosperity, happiness even. If we don't get it we are angry about our bargain and say we have been done.[83]

It is not a good novel, but it is an extremely interesting one, for a number of reasons. As well as the articulation of some of Naomi's own thinking and the reflections of the difficulties of her marriage, it illustrates the relation between Naomi as observer and Naomi as story-teller. As observer, Naomi records in her Russian diary a cool, objective account of a woman having an abortion in a Moscow clinic. In *We Have Been Warned*, this same event is witnessed by the fictional Dione: 'the smell of blood in her nostrils, the look of the woman, so terribly uncovered, branded into her imagination.'[84] It prompts Dione to reflect, 'There is no freedom here ... What was the good of putting so much pain and effort into exchanging one bondage for another?'[85] Naomi felt she was not cut out to be a scientist, because the story-teller in her always moved in to rearrange and interpret. It is never possible to know how much rearrangement takes place in the translation from 'fact' to 'fiction' – in the case of *We Have Been Warned* perhaps not enough – but in Naomi's writing it is sometimes possible to see the process at work.

Although this was Naomi's first full-length contemporary novel, she was confident about it, which was somewhat defiantly expressed when she ran into problems with her publishers. Both Jonathan Cape himself and Edward Garnett, Naomi's old friend and ally, were critical. 'I am more sure about this book than I've ever been about any of the other books,' she wrote to Garnett, explaining why she could not accept his criticism.[86] The main problem Cape and Garnett had was with sexual explicitness, in particular a scene in which Dione feels pressured to sleep with a working-class Communist Party member she does not like in order to avoid being branded bourgeois. The circumstances of the scene, the bed-sit permeated with the smell of gas and tea-leaves, the blind insistence of the man and the fastidious reluctance of the woman, contribute as much to its effect as the specific details of sexual union.

Naomi vigorously argued her case, insisting, 'I must finally go my own way.' She acknowledged Edward Garnett as her literary godfather, but nevertheless felt that this was something she had to do on her own, despite his advice. 'After all, I'm 36, and must be able to judge for myself.'[87] Her angry refusal to make the changes Cape asked for may have had as much to do with a wish to be treated as grown-up as with literary conviction. But whatever the reason, it ended a publishing relationship which had continued for a dozen years. Victor Gollancz liked the book but would not publish. He was worried about repercussions which might prejudice his effectiveness in running a socialist press. The book, he felt, would be 'widely described as "filthy"'.[88] Sex could detract from the broader and bigger political ideas that it was his concern to promote. Ironically, the book itself is not only about politics and sexual politics, but about sex as politics. John Lane also turned it down. It was finally published by Constable, but there was more upset when, initially happy with the book, they insisted on changing the offending passages when it was already in proof. In *You May Well Ask*, Naomi explains that part of the reason why she bowed to pressure was her concern about affecting Dick's political career. She had overtly borrowed from the experience of King's Norton, where Dick was expecting to stand again at the next general election. 'I would not compromise at all if I had not to think of my husband's political career and the mud that's likely to be thrown.'[89] Publishers were sensitive. It had been considered too great a risk to publish an unexpurgated edition of *Lady Chatterley's Lover* in Britain, though an expurgated version came out in 1931. Radclyffe Hall's *The Well of Loneliness*, though published in 1928, was banned after a trial for obscenity. Naomi would no doubt have relished doing battle in the courts over her book, but her publishers made sure she did not get the opportunity.

Sixty years later, Naomi remembered, 'Yes, they pulled the book about but what a bad book it is, as far as I have looked at it again.' With hindsight she felt her people were 'not possible' and was uncomfortably aware of the novel's self-reflective nature: 'the book seems to have a lot of photos about myself'.[90] She did not like the picture of herself that the book revealed. The difficulties surrounding *We Have Been Warned* left Naomi with a growing scepticism about publishers and critics. It was probably no accident that, although she wrote non-fiction about political issues, she returned to the ancient world as a way of writing political fiction.

5

The political scene enveloped Naomi. It was personal and local, and it was international. 'I think I'm getting increasingly red, and increasingly frightened of what I'm being driven to think,' she wrote to Edward Garnett.[91] She turned her attention to social conditions in her own country and planned a book on slum life. The book was never written, but early in 1934 she went to Glasgow and Salford, and later that year to Leeds and Birmingham, to investigate slum conditions. She recorded these visits in a 'Housing Diary', describing the overcrowding, the dirt, the gas lighting still common in Glasgow, and the deeply depressing, though in a way admirable, passive stoicism exhibited by people who had little or no control over their own lives, who were 'always having things done to them'.[92] In Glasgow, she visited the notorious slums of Calton near Glasgow Green, determined to make first-hand contact with extreme deprivation. In Salford, she was escorted by Walter Greenwood, author of *Love on the Dole* which had come out the previous year and another of Naomi's adopted authors. A flat in Leeds was fairly typical of what she encountered:

> Here in a cramped and filthy living-room, furnished with a table, a few rags, a few bits of broken stuff and a fierce smell, were four people, a fat slattern putting margarine onto bread, a powerful and talkative cripple who hurled himself about the room, a trim, patient-looking woman putting grey washing through a wringer, and a boy who said nothing.[93]

Three years later, Victor Gollancz published George Orwell's *The Road to Wigan Pier* as one of his Left Book Club titles. It covered similar ground.

There was no book by Naomi, but, as always, fact fed into fiction. She worked on short stories and a novel, the latter set in a fictional town called Sallington and looking at the experience of different levels of society, with a focus on working-class socialists. It appears to be unfinished; it was certainly never published. In it Naomi explores some of the implications of revolutionary action and what she saw as a need to reach beyond normal humanity. "'You can't let yourself just be human,'" her working-class activist says, "'That'll come after. But maybe not in our time.'"[94] It is the notion of sacrifice again.

She attended Fabian weekend schools, but did not take them over-seriously, risking disapproval by slipping away from the earnest atmosphere of meetings to swim. With the intellectual and political high-flyers she often felt both uneasy and guilty. But during one Fabian weekend she found a kindred spirit in Rudolph Messel, a journalist who helped with Dick's canvassing in King's Norton, and he quickly became a close friend. When he asked her to take part in a propaganda film he was making, she cheerfully consented. She played the mother of a young man on the dole. The film was never completed and, with hindsight, Naomi felt it was really no more than playing 'the old acting games'.[95] It did not affect the friendship, however, and it was to Rudi's home in Devon that she went when in need of care after a miscarriage. She was unconcerned by Rudi's sexual proclivities, and responded with interest when he asked her to tie and beat him.

The international scene also demanded attention. One after another, the milestones that marked the advance of Fascism were passed. In 1929, Mussolini introduced Frascism to Italy; in 1933, Hitler came to power in Germany; in 1934, a civil war in Austria resulted in defeat for democracy and brought an oppressive right-wing regime; in 1936 in Spain, a right-wing coup precipitated the decade's – and perhaps the century's – most resonant political contest. Naomi and Dick, like thousands of others with similar views, were appalled but resisted Marxism. Naomi, however, was excited by the prospect of revolution, of standing society on its head. 'I know it's going to be hell,' she said, picturing a post-revolution socialist society, 'and I know I shall hate it really and it will be damned uncomfortable, and I shall never any more have any of the things I like, hot baths and silk clothes and quiet and leisure and a good typewriter of my own.'[96] Nevertheless, socialism was right, and revolution was perhaps the only way to get there.

Lois remembers her own bafflement when, brought up with the idea that revolutions were good, she could not understand why her parents were depressed at the news of revolution in Spain in 1936.

Naomi had no illusions that revolution could be non-violent, yet she refused to accept the inevitability of war. Nevertheless, she was by instinct a fighter. Shortly after news of the defeat of the socialists in Austria, she volunteered to go to Vienna, informally representing the Fabian Society. She could afford both the time and the money to go. Victor Gollancz commissioned a book. She carried money and papers, on a mission to contact and help the defeated socialists. As always, there were personal as well as political motives: her affair with John Pilley had come to an end with his marriage and there was no chance now of sustaining with Wade Gery even a 'mutually profitable friendship, with a pretty vivid kind of affection through it', which was what she wanted.[97] It suited her to get away; it was her customary response to emotional upset.

She set off alone on 24 February: 'I think I rather like the idea of going by myself, but I'm not sure,' she wrote early on in what became *Naomi Mitchison's Vienna Diary*, to be published by Gollancz.[98] She thought about what sort of a diary it would be, and decided to be quite open about her political views and her background. She felt she could be a good and useful observer, but added:

> I'm also a Socialist, and my observations will be the observations of a Socialist, just as they'll be the observations of a woman of thirty-six, of someone brought up before the war, partly scientist, partly historian, nothing complete, the usual set of odds and ends that my social class and circumstance are likely to produce.[99]

She admitted that she was not brave, was bad at languages and organization, and was easily excited. For Naomi, it was as important to establish the personal context as the political, and part of the former was the fact that she had set off independently of her husband. She returned again to the importance of men and women as comrades, of women not being owned by their men, and went on to say that if she and Dick 'didn't like living together as much as we do, there'd be no value in going away from one another'.[100]

The prospect before her was daunting. She felt she could not be alone so long as she had her typewriter, and had travelled alone in Russia; in Vienna she would be meeting people she knew. Yet there was a manifest anxiety. She was aware of the contradictions. In England, there were those who regarded her as a wild revolutionary, 'a bad and dangerous woman',[101] while in reality she was uneasy at having meals by herself. But most important was her feeling that what she was doing was worthwhile. She was going to be involved, she was going to help, she would be in the thick of things.

Her two contacts in Vienna - unnamed in the published diary - were Hugh Gaitskell, who was spending a year studying there, and Frederick Elwyn Jones, a future Lord Chancellor but at that time a young journalist. Through them she met the families of socialists who had been killed and of survivors who were outlawed and deprived of employment. There was a desperate need for money as many were without any source of income. She visited the showpiece workers' flats which had been bombarded by the Dollfus regime. Everywhere there was an atmosphere of conspiracy and threat, and a tension between belief in the necessity of resistance and despair at the grip of dictatorship.

What Naomi encountered in Austria was not just deprivation, of which she had some experience, but overt political oppression, which was new to her.

> She stood there by her kitchen stove - and it didn't look as if she had much to cook on it. And she was going to be turned out of her house, and she had no money, and she could do nothing. Nothing at all. She had to stand there with her neck bowed. I don't think I've ever understood about oppression before. I've written about it, and imagined it, but here it was.[102]

She listened to accounts of arrest, imprisonment and torture. She slipped money and whispered messages of solidarity to those who struggled on. Her anger strengthened her sense of mission. She wrote articles for the *New Statesman* and *Time and Tide* which they would not publish: 'these dear little papers that are willing to call one a genius when one's writing fiction … won't have anything to do with one when one's writing about something that matters!'[103] She and Elwyn Jones went to Graz to find out what they could about the arrest and execution of Koloman Wallisch, the socialist leader. They talked to his widow. It was an experience both painful and inspiring, given an added frisson by the fact that because there was a shortage of rooms at the hotel, Naomi and Elwyn Jones had to share a bed, sleeping together only literally: comradeship was more important than sex.

Naomi hated the thought of abandoning Austria to return to England and talk about it, but accepted that this was part of what she had to do. She would be expected to relate her experiences, address public meetings, and indeed she was whisked off to do that as soon as she stepped off the train in London. It was the first of a series of public speeches which taught her, she said many years later, how to address a large audience without nervousness and without notes.[104] Her *Vienna Diary* ends on a hopeful note. Her contact with the realities of revolution, albeit a defeated revolution, had been a source of personal inspiration, perhaps because she felt that she had genuinely helped. The experience had been much more than vicarious standing on the sidelines and taking notes, which had characterized the Russian visit. This time, Naomi had been involved, and it was perhaps that which more than anything underwrote her optimism.

In Wallisch she had found a hero, wholly committed to the socialist cause, who had faced his trial and execution with dignity. She was moved to write a book about him, but never did, perhaps because events were moving so quickly. In July of that year, there was a Nazi coup in Austria, and although it did not succeed, Dollfuss was murdered. Right-wing Austria was pinned between Nazi Germany and Fascist Italy until the *Anschluss* of 1938 when Hitler moved in. There was little British socialists could do. Naomi's *Vienna Diary* is a vivid and immediate piece of writing. It is a highly personal account, charged with a sense of urgency and excitement. The experience added another dimension to her political education. Her visit also made an impression on the Austrians. A letter to her from Julius Deutsch, one of the socialist leaders, told her that she was remembered for the help she brought at a dangerous and difficult time.[105] With hindsight, the optimism implied here seems extraordinary, but it was a driving force in European politics, colouring efforts and ideas in Britain as elsewhere.

Another general election approached. Dick was standing again for King's Norton, having nursed the constituency conscientiously in the intervening years. His work with the New Fabian Research Bureau, of which he was treasurer, gave him a solid grasp of social policy. Unemployment was a key issue, its consequences evident everywhere. Dick did his share of travelling round the country, addressing meetings, talking to individuals. He spoke in the Midlands and Lancashire. In January 1935, he was in a snow-bound Tyneside, talking to the unemployed in Jarrow, one of the areas worst affected by economic decline. He was approaching his forty-fifth birthday (Margaret Cole would organize a birthday party for him) and had not really made his mark professionally. Nevertheless, he was optimistic. 'As to the [Labour] Party, there really is a wind blowing to the left,' he wrote to Naomi in February, 'and I believe they'll do things if they get in.'[106] Naomi was less convinced. 'I do not think we shall see our Promised Land,' she wrote to John Pilley; 'at best we can learn to die decently.'[107]

Nothing was achieved without fierce debate, and Naomi and Dick were both to the left of mainstream Labour Party opinion, to the detriment of Dick's future political career. River Court rang with argument. 'Looking back on it all,' Naomi wrote in *You May Well Ask*, 'what was so strange and striking was the feeling we all had that, if we tried hard enough, the millennium ... would come into being.'[108] Harry Pollitt, leader of the British Communist Party, was convinced that Dick and Naomi would soon be members of the CP.[109] That was never likely, but what is clear is that, for Naomi at least, political involvement was a matter of compulsion as much as conviction. Russia and Vienna had both demonstrated her need to be involved, and not just on a local level. But did it make any difference, other than to herself?

> And what about my own life as a political person? Would the world have lost anything if I hadn't made these journeys and had these doubtless mind-stretching adventures? If I had stayed at home and really studied local problems of politics, education and administration? If I had even finished my own broken education? Or if I'd been a whole-time mother with perhaps more children? or less?

She concluded that hindsight offered no answers. 'We go with the wave of our time, getting whatever is to be got out of it.'[110]

In the 1935 general election, Naomi was more than a candidate's wife – she was a candidate herself. She was asked to stand for the Scottish Universities, which at that time returned their own MP. In agreeing to stand, she had to bring into her political thinking issues of nationalism as well as socialism. She did so by insisting that the aims of Scottish nationalism could only be 'attained through Socialism', and her election address asserted the belief that only socialism would prevent 'a complete break-up of Western civilization' and provide a bastion against war.[111] Interestingly, she also stressed her role as mother of five children as a shaping factor in her thinking. She enjoyed the election campaign, but neither Naomi nor Dick was successful. There was a Conservative victory, with Stanley Baldwin as the new prime minister. Lois remembers that at River Court political conversations 'made everyone extremely sad'.[112]

In the midst of all this political activity, the household at River Court was maintained and Naomi found time to write. From the age of eight or nine the boys were sent to the Dragon School. They stayed with their grandmother, with whom they got on well. Denny had hated the school, but went on to Abbotsholme where he was much happier. Murdoch enjoyed it. Lois was going through a difficult period and a child psychologist recommended that she should be sent away to school, which she did not like. Avrion, easy-going and self-reliant, went off to prep school at seven, while Val, the child most mentioned by Naomi at this time, was still very young. When the children were at home they mingled with the adults, although their base remained the nursery. As they grew older, Lois and Val in particular became aware of tensions, of the presence or absence of key figures in their parents' lives, although they never felt that the marriage itself was under threat. Denny liked Margy Spring Rice, and at times found her more patient and sympathetic than his mother. Lois was less tolerant of Margaret Cole, and at times resented the intrusion of her father's other women.

With all Naomi's expeditions, there was still time for family holidays. In the 1920s France was the usual holiday destination, and they went several times to Varengeville near Dieppe. In 1934, they went to Zarauz in northern Spain, with the Coles. Murdoch remembers a churros-eating competition with Humphrey Cole. Denny won but was sick afterwards.[113] The next year they went to Madeira, to stay at Reid's Hotel, where tea on the veranda was a feature. There was a scare when Lois was swept out to sea, but she was a good swimmer and was rescued. There were regular visits to Cloan, as well as the holidays at Craignish Castle. Later, Scottish holidays took them to Vallay on North Uist. At Vallay, the older boys were taught to shoot, but there was not a great deal to do, and never enough books. On one occasion they found diversion through feeding seagulls bread soaked in whisky and then watching them fall down.

These holidays were almost always shared with other families. Naomi continued to gather people around her, and to write, regardless of where she was or who was with her. She also had her own expeditions, without the family. In 1934, after a period of illness when she was at a low ebb, she went to the Canary Islands with Agnes Miller Parker and then on her own by cargo boat to Morocco, where she was besieged by men who saw her as fair game. In Ouarzazat she spent an interesting evening drinking sherry with a group of lorry drivers, who then expected something in return. She had to barricade her door. She wrote about it in a piece called 'Why do the boys run after me?'[114] She may have found such attentions unwelcome, but she clearly also rather enjoyed it.

On the way back from Morocco she had an enforced stay in Gibraltar, waiting for a boat to take her on the next stage of her journey. She wrote about it twenty years later, highlighting the curious combination of Mediterranean and British cultures. It was a solitary time, and shortage of money curtailed her activities. 'I walked and walked and wrote whatever book I was writing then and came back to boiled mutton and tea.'[115]

Her output of fiction had slowed down a little, and she was writing more non-fiction. Although she never wrote her book on feminism, her views on the role of women found other outlets, in her fiction of course, but also in *The Home and a Changing Civilization* which came out in 1934. In it she discussed women's 'struggle to escape being owned',[116] echoing many of the comments that emerged in her Russian diary and in correspondence of the time. The home, she felt, kept women out of the world, was an 'impediment to women achieving, being creative'. There continued to be a pressure on women 'to spend their time … in greasing the wheels of life for the men who drive it'.[117] She argues for a more open approach to marriage and the home. The issues were the elimination of patriarchy, and the balancing of personal and social needs, both of which required a more equal society. One of the obstacles to this scenario was men's ignorance of and lack of interest in women's real feelings. In the course of the discussion she attacks D. H. Lawrence for promoting the ownership of women by men – the result, in her view, of his own fear and hatred of women.

Naomi herself had escaped being 'owned', though she would fret at being hampered by domestic responsibilities, by having to organize other people. Yet, in the eyes of others, including her children, she liked organizing. It gave her a dominant role. She liked to tell people what to do, and was quick to lose her temper if things did not work out as required. However, even with all the influence she had, there was frustration, and some of her fictional characters enact the owned woman, the powerless woman. *Beyond This Limit* (1935, illustrated by Wyndham Lewis) is an allegory, tinged with irony, of a woman artist breaking the bounds of convention, but in *The Fourth Pig* (1936), a collection of re-worked fairy stories, there is an example of powerlessness taken to the point of disappearance. In 'The snow maiden', Mary Snow grows up in Birmingham and marries the virile George Higginson, and 'then, she just seemed to melt away, to fade right out somehow. Like an ice-cream sundae on a hot afternoon.' Mary is destroyed, the author explains, by the sun-god, male and jealous, 'the god of life and potency'.[118] The reference to Lawrence is obvious, and the message of the stories is if anything too overt. When Naomi's mentor Professor Alexander read them, he suggested that they would make better poetry than fiction; a more subtle, less didactic medium could have made them more powerful.

Beyond This Limit is a tantalizing story, playful and ambivalent. The experience of working with Wyndham Lewis was invigorating, 'a total delight'.[119] Naomi believed she had never written better, partly because Lewis himself 'jumped on me like a tiger if I got a word wrong.'[120] She enjoyed Lewis's theatricality; it matched her own, and both are reflected in the story. Phoebe, her heroine, rises to the challenge of restraint, ventures to the end of the line and beyond. But although she is spirited and determined, we never find out if she makes it back.

6

The urge to organize was just one strand of Naomi's ambition. Her competitive nature had not been quelled by marriage, children or disappointment in love. Indeed, all of these things may have intensified the need to achieve more, in spite of her awareness of Dick's less rewarding existence which was at times a source of worry. It was not Dick she was competing with, but a shifting cast of all those who put her on her mettle, among whom was always Jack. She worked hard to support Dick in his political endeavours. She did not, or could not, disguise her ambition, but the contradictions raised by principles and privilege nagged. In

August 1932, she was writing to Victor Gollancz:

> I have had this devil of personal ambition biting at me, and I
> know I haven't got him down yet. I like power, and I know only
> too well that while I am using it I am apt to forget that I must
> not use it for my own satisfaction. Everything is against one
> – the whole structure of society is individualist and approving
> of personal ambition and the attainment of power. We have to
> be aware of the fakeness of our environment all the time, and
> we are in jeopardy of our souls.[121]

Ambition continued to bite – ambition to do more, to be in a position
where she could influence events, to be taken seriously as a
provider of ideas as well as of fiction. Her enthusiasm for *The
Outline* suggested how important it was for her to be read for her
intellectual and political contribution as well as for her
story-telling gifts. She wanted to be a story-teller in the traditional
sense, to keep the past alive and to shape the future. She
collaborated with Richard Crossman to produce a short book on
Socrates (1937) where, in her customary relaxed, almost chatty style,
they discuss democracy and political philosophy, including, of
course, the position of women. *The Moral Basis of Politics* (1938)
covers some of the same territory. At its centre is Naomi's focus on
what she called 'the right relationship between people and groups
of people'.[122] She is still preoccupied with the question of how to
achieve that balance between the group and the individual, and
explores it in her main work of fiction of this time, *Blood of the
Martyrs* (1939). In both these books Naomi is suggesting that in
order for the individual to transcend the limits of self, some kind
of transforming experience is required. People need to think and
feel collectively before they can act collectively. But without 'the
new kind of society' is this possible? And will there ever be a new
society if it is not? It was the classic dilemma, brought into sharper
focus by the political events of the time.

In 1935, the international arena claimed her again. This time it
was the United States. There was another cause to embrace, of the

sharecroppers of the southern states. On this occasion Naomi did not travel alone but in the company of her friend of some years Zita Baker. Zita was part of the Oxford left-wing circle, married to John Baker, a zoologist, and linked with several prominent left-wing figures of the thirties. In 1933, she had accompanied her husband and Tom Harrisson, social anthropologist and later one of the founders of Mass-Observation, on an expedition to the New Hebrides. Zita was having an affair with Tom, and her letters to Naomi agonized over her conflicting instincts. She felt she was in a muddle. Naomi knew all too well what was involved, but Zita nevertheless felt that Naomi's attitude to her predicament was disapproving. Part of the problem was that Zita no longer wanted to be married: she wanted to be more than a 'Mrs', and to do more than being a 'Mrs' implied.[123] Tom also wrote to Naomi, feeling equally mixed up.

Zita's life became more complex. By 1934 Richard Crossman was also a contender for her affections, about which Naomi was not happy, perhaps because she and Crossman had often crossed swords in political debate. She encouraged Zita to think of getting away for a while, and eventually, in February 1935, the two of them set off for America. It was the first time Naomi had crossed the Atlantic and there were aspects of the United States that she took to immediately, such as drugstore breakfasts and the general friendliness. Zita was an unconventional and flamboyant character and Naomi enjoyed her company immensely. They bought a second-hand Ford and headed south. By 21 February, they were in Memphis, Tennessee, making contact with the sharecroppers' union. They visited the Tennessee Valley Authority, an instrument of President Roosevelt's New Deal scheme to reactivate the economy.

The two women were conspicuous, attracting attention and curiosity, and this may have given them a certain immunity as they made their way deeper into the south and the tensions of racial antagonism. They had been warned not to give lifts, especially to blacks, but soon ignored the advice and cheerfully picked up whoever needed a ride. They especially enjoyed the company of passengers who played or sang as they travelled. Naomi was appalled at the poverty she saw, among both black and white sharecroppers (famously recorded in the powerful photographs of Walker Evans). She saw children 'rotten with malnutrition & disease; hardly any are at school'.[124] It was a system that was inherently unjust, tying families to working the land in return for their homes and minimal wages: 'this sinister and terrible country,' Naomi was prompted to write.[125] But there was much to impress as well and, as usual, no sooner had Naomi spotted an opportunity for involvement than she and Zita were in the thick of it. In Marked Tree, Alabama, the Southern Tenant Farmers' Union was planning a demonstration. 'The share croppers ... are organizing & *for the first time in American history*, white and coloured are working side by side in real equality,' she wrote to Dick.[126] Among those addressing the meeting was Jennie Lee, Labour MP for North Lanark and wife of Aneurin Bevan, a Labour Party rising star. Naomi, too, spoke to the crowd, alluding to the Tolpuddle Martyrs and the early labour movement in England, and was deeply affected when they sang 'I shall not be moved' in harmony, followed by the Lord's Prayer. Many of the leaders had been in jail and beaten up. The emotional intensity of the experience was heightened by the crowd's reception of Naomi and Zita: "'You'uns, you're fine girls!'", with handshakes and arms around their shoulders. 'Oh Dick, it was damned nice being on their side.'[127] But there were repurcussions. The black leader who had introduced Naomi to the crowd had put his hand on her shoulder. He was later attacked by angry whites.

From Alabama, Naomi and Zita headed west. Wherever they stopped they shared a hotel room and talked half-way through the night. There was a strong sense of a shared adventure: they were both spirited and unconventional women with families at home, eager to make more of their lives. They went to New Orleans, then to New Mexico, where they stayed with Mabel Dodge Luhan, the literary luminary who had made her home in Taos. Before returning to Britain, Naomi spent a few days in Washington and attempted to tackle government bureaucracy on behalf of the sharecroppers. She got nowhere. 'If I were a citizen of this country,' she wrote to Dick, 'I would join the Communist Party at once.'[128] Dick was feeling depressed. There was little legal work coming in and his political future was uncertain. Naomi wrote that she was feeling it was time she was home, back with Dick.

Whatever the rewards of the trip, and they were personal rather than politically constructive, it did not succeed in bringing Zita's relationship with Richard Crossman to an end – they married in 1937. At home, political optimism was hard to sustain: the Labour Party defeat in the general election was followed by rapid worsening of the international situation. Whatever encouragement the Spanish Republican resistance to the generals provided, it was short-lived. There was increasing and bitter argument among socialists as the Moscow 'show trials' of those who had not adapted their views to Stalin's unfolded. Naomi openly aligned herself with those who felt bound to criticize Russian Communism, and thus made herself unpopular with sections of left-wing opinion. Her 'comrades' were beginning to fall away. The Spanish Civil War added fuel to dissension, with uncomfortable accusations of Communist betrayal, most notably in Orwell's *Homage to Catalonia* (1938). In June 1938, Orwell wrote to Naomi, who had told him how much she liked the book, and summed up the dilemma. 'It is harder than ever before to make sure of the political line. If one allows a free hand to the Communists and their friends one is, I am certain, allowing the whole socialist movement to be perverted, whereas if one opposes them there is always the chance that one is, objectively if not intentionally, aiding the FASCISTS.'[129] Jack had been a member of the Communist Party for some years by this time and there seemed little prospect of healing the painful gulf between brother and sister.

Like many others, Naomi was deeply resistant to the belief that war was the only way to halt the progress of dictatorship. The scars of the last war were still raw, and her own sons were approaching the age when they would be expected to fight. She soldiered on with her own vision of communitarian values, propounded in plays, stories and novels as well as in articles and *The Moral Basis of Politics*. She continued to believe that revolution was necessary and violence probably unavoidable, but dwelt on the individual sacrifice rather than wholesale slaughter. However, the prognosis was not good. It was going to take more than the actions of a few heroic individuals to turn the tide, however vivid was Naomi's own vision of martyrdom.

In 1936 her father died. He had been unwell for some time, no longer striding over the Perthshire hills but walking slowly with the aid of a stick and his daughter's arm. A poignant poem, 'The Glen Path', written when she herself could no longer tramp the hills, recalls walking with her father at Cloan, riding on his shoulders.[130] His lifelong habit of experimenting on himself almost certainly hastened his death, which came quickly when he contracted pneumonia. Naomi and Jack rushed to Oxford, only to have their now customary fight, physical as well as verbal. In *You May Well Ask*, Naomi described her father dying 'with a look of intense interest on his face as though he were taking part in some crucial experiment which had to be carefully monitored.'[131] The gift for experimental self-observation was inherited by his daughter.

Granniema had died some years before, just after her one hundredth birthday. Then Naomi had also made the journey to Cloan, to take her place beside the coffin as it was taken from Auchterarder for burial in Edinburgh. This time, they were taking John Scott Haldane's ashes to Cloan. Jack and Naomi continued to quarrel, Jack refusing to travel first class with his sister and Aunt Bay, who had come to Oxford for the funeral and now travelled back north. Condemning their capitalist habits, he travelled third, with the ashes. Aunt Bay herself died the next year, leaving Naomi a modest legacy. She shared it with her brother, but was upset when he handed his part over to the Communist Party. The rift widened.

Naomi's mother was now alone in Oxford, elderly and unwell, but Naomi found it no easier to get on with her. They still quarrelled, and she still felt guilty. Their relationship never achieved an equilibrium. Both were committed to their own views; both were determined. The death of Geoff had if anything made things more difficult, but there seemed to have been no problem with entrusting Denny and Murdoch to Maya's care in Oxford. On Naomi's part, there was an inclination to accept that friction between mother and daughter was inevitable, and that anything else would need compromise on both their parts. When Maya wrote her volume of memoirs, she included a barbed acknowledgment of her daughter's assistance, which suggests that Naomi appropriated the project.[132]

There was less to take Naomi to Oxford, with Denny and Murdoch no longer at school there and fewer friends to tempt her to visit. But friends still came to River Court, new as well as old. A valued neighbour and fellow-writer who shared her love for the Thames was A. P. Herbert, and Naomi continued her habit of spontaneously getting in touch with authors she had never met whose books she admired. One of these was Olaf Stapledon, whom she enlisted to contribute to *The Outline*. She met him and Gerald Heard regularly for lunch at the Café Royal.

Literary friends of this period included Stevie Smith, some of whose warm, quirky and entertaining letters to Naomi survive. Members of the Bloomsbury Group were sometimes a presence. Elizabeth Longford, herself a close friend, remembers Adrian Stephen, Virginia Woolf's brother, with whom she discussed Freudian psychology sitting under a table at River Court. "He's a shy creature," said Naomi, "not often seen above ground."[133] Aldous was back in London in 1935 and Naomi visited him in his Albany flat. Wyndham Lewis came to Rivert court in his black hat and sweeping cloak, eccentric, paranoid, perhaps at times a little ridiculous. She visited him in his Percy Street studio. He made several drawings of her, and painted a striking portrait in 1938, when she was working on *The Blood of the Martyrs*. In spite of the frown of concentration, she looks younger than her forty-one years. He also drew Val and the boys.

By 1938, London life seemed to be crumbling. Naomi was out of favour, or felt that she was. There was a tension that affected literary as well as political life. She could not assume that her work would be published. Over the decade the balance of her life had changed, with the political sphere commanding much more attention. Although she had no strong ambition to be a party politician, she did feel that she had a political contribution to

make, and there were those who agreed with her. Frank Pakenham
(later Lord Longford) told his wife that in his view Naomi should be
in Parliament, and wished that she were standing for King's Norton
instead of Dick.[134] Naomi would not have wanted Dick to hear that.
He himself was fretting at his lack of occupation. Naomi had spent
most of the decade trying to do too much. 'Don't you go the pace too
much in everything you do?' Olaf Stapledon had written in 1935.

> It's so tempting sometimes because it gives one the sense of
> being effective. But its' dangerous for people whose real
> function is to use their minds because it blots out all the more
> delicate reactions and makes for bad work ... You must be
> yourself as precisely as possible otherwise you're no good for
> the community. You are different, 'special', and you must not
> funk the fact and try to bury yourself in the herd.[135]

Not only did Naomi have great expectations of herself, others had
too, and they did not always coincide.

CHAPTER FIVE

Another War

How can we think of our neighbours
except in a neighbourly way?
The Alban *goes out: 1939*

1

FROM CRAIGNISH Castle there is a view down Loch Beag, a small
finger of sea loch, out towards Jura; from the ridge behind the
castle a cluster of islands, the Firth of Lorn, then Mull. The relative
remoteness, the sea and the lochs, the lingering summer light on the
western horizon, the style of life which the castle itself invited – all
these contributed to the atmosphere of the Mitchisons' summer
visits. After Craignish came Valley off the island of North Uist,
further north and west and much harder to get to, and distinctly
less grand accommodation – there was no electricity. But there was
the Atlantic opening out beyond the island and the expanse of the
western horizon. Naomi and Dick began to think about acquiring a
place of their own in Scotland.

They spent part of the summers of 1936 and 1937 at Valley. In 1937
Aunt Bay died and, at Cloan for the funeral, Naomi went with her
uncle Sir William Haldane and cousin Archie to look at a house for
sale at the edge of a fishing village on the eastern shore of the

Kintyre peninsula. Carradale at that time operated twenty-two
fishing boats. The surrounding farms and crofts were mostly run by
tenants, who raised cattle and black-faced sheep. Much of the land
was rough hill country, not suitable for cultivation. The Forestry
Commission would shortly become a major presence, and was soon
the largest landowner and employer in the area. There were a few
summer visitors each year, but most of Carradale made a living
through fishing or farming.

Carradale House seemed promising. The original house had
been rebuilt in the nineteenth century by the architect David
Bryce, who made something of a speciality of redesigning old
houses and adding Scottish baronial features. On the ground floor
there was a large drawing-room, library, dining-room and kitchen
as well as smaller rooms. An impressive staircase led to the main
bedrooms, with an attic of more bedrooms reached by a back stair.
There was plenty of space for family and friends. An extensive
garden included a walled area, greenhouses and some impressive
rhododendrons. The estate included a farm and several cottages,
plenty of rough ground for shooting, a stretch of shore, salmon in
the river, and fields which had been largely neglected for some
years. Other farms and parcels of land that had belonged to the
estate had been sold off. Dick and Naomi decided to buy Carradale
House. It offered Dick and the boys land to shoot over. It offered
Naomi – whether or not this was what she was looking for – potential
for another role.

Carradale's location on the narrow, unpaved road that followed
the coast from Skipness to Campbeltown did not seem a problem.
It was accessible from Glasgow on the other side of the Firth of
Clyde, with two steamers, the *Davaar* and the *Dalriada*, operating
from Gourock and calling at Carradale. It was also possible to fly
from Glasgow to the airfield at Machrihanish. London was only
hours away.

The following Easter, the Mitchisons settled in and began to
carry out some improvements. There was no electricity, so a
generator was installed. The kitchen was altered and an Esse stove,
which burnt anthracite, was put in. Inexpensive furniture was

acquired in London and brought north. There were improvements to the cottages too, putting in damp courses and bathrooms. It was a new challenge for Naomi, not only another home to think about but a fresh environment, a traditional fishing and farming community with no pubs, two shops, two post offices and two congregations - Church of Scotland and Free Church. Naomi decided to farm the estate herself, rather than leave this to the tenant at the Mains, the estate farm. She persuaded Lachlan MacLean and his wife Mary to come from North Uist to work for her and took on local help for indoor as well as outdoor work, though not as large a staff as the house had been accustomed to. That summer, she was back again. With her customary vigorous conviction Naomi set about forging her new role and, in effect, a new identity.

London life continued, however. Naomi was working on *The Moral Basis of Politics* and *The Blood of the Martyrs*, both responses to the current political situation. The themes that absorbed her at this time concerned the moral and emotional imperative to resist oppression, and the potential for collective action. Both books are essentially about the difficulty of being a socialist in a non-socialist world. The way forward, she believed, lay in learning how to think and act as a group. It was a theme she had explored before. Her stories had portrayed individuals who had challenged the majority, and suffered for it. In the case of Erif Der, she dealt with a woman who represented the collective will and had to accept the constraints which that imposed. In *The Blood of the Martyrs*, a tale of early Christians in Rome, individuals derive strength from the collective to challenge a more powerful consensus. Their martyrdom is not without purpose. It is a reworking of the theme of sacrifice but with an additional edge, which certainly owed something to Naomi's experiences in Vienna and the inspiration she took from Wallisch.

Some of the thinking behind the novel is spelt out in *The Moral Basis of Politics*, where she emphasized the need for 'good and fitting relations between people'.[1] She looked for a moral and social environment where individuals could be themselves without harming the collective good, but got caught in the familiar dilemma: how could people be good if there was no good society? People 'cannot really be the material for the new society, which must on the whole build its own good individuals; yet they can if they will help to bring it about'.[2] It came down to an act of faith, the subject of *The Blood of the Martyrs*. *The Moral Basis of Politics* did not receive much attention and did not sell well, only 900 copies. Recognition as a novelist did not necessarily pave the way to being taken seriously as a political thinker, but Naomi had things to say, and fiction did not always seem the appropriate medium, however flexibly and imaginatively she was able to use it.

Not surprisingly, *The Blood of the Martyrs* was critically received in some quarters. The *Catholic Herald* accused her of being 'unhistorical',[3] and Frank Swinnerton in the *Observer* commented on her 'deplorable vulgarity of manner',[4] but elsewhere she was again being described as a major historical novelist. 'Mrs Mitchison has no superior in the historical novelists' art of recreating the past,' said the *Manchester Guardian*[5] and in the view of the *Christian World*, 'the whole political, social and religious life of the time is described with fine historical imagination based on careful study'.[6] The considerable praise did not compensate for the snide tone of John Mair's review in the *New Statesman*, which likened her Christians to 'a Fabian summer school captured by white slavers'.[7] The antagonism and the jibes hurt Naomi and strengthened her feeling that London was hostile to her. Her rapid adoption of a Scottish context and Scottish subjects for her writing did not help. Her stories were being rejected, for example by John Lehmann of *New Writing*. In an exchange of correspondence between them, Naomi's tone is almost defensive as she sends him material, describing her Highland stories as of 'quite low-brow interest'.[8] Lehmann did not like them; a pencilled comment on one letter from Naomi to him reads, 'It's well done, but awful I think. Fearful romantic-sexual suggestiveness.'[9] It is not clear to which story he is referring, but it may be 'Five men and a swan' which was published in a volume of short stories, under that title, in 1957. It was clearly not what *New Writing*, with its interest in documentary realism and giving space to working-class writers, was looking for. Neil Gunn, however, liked the story. A leading figure in Scotland's cultural renaissance who had got to know Naomi in the early 1940s, he commiserated with her. The *New Statesman* reviewers, he wrote in a letter of June 1941, were 'cleverish, liverish superior lads of the new intellectual world, pansy-pink complexions an' all'.[10]

Reinforcing Naomi's sense that she was out of favour was an exchange in the pages of the *New Statesman*, C.E.M. Joad wrote a piece entitled 'Complaint against lady novelists' in which he was highly dismissive of novels by women, accusing them of being 'moved by a curiosity to savour and appraise individual relationships as a woman handles stuffs on a much-littered counter'.[11] Naomi's response identified a political motive in Joad's comment. A time of recession, when men were unemployed and feeling threatened, encouraged anti-feminism. It fuelled the views of men 'who wanted to remove women in economic competition with themselves'.[12] She was aware of the challenge posed by the lack of work, a keystone of male identity. She had seen what happened after the First World War, when women had had to abandon the roles they had taken up in the absence of men. Whether or not Joad's comments were relevant to her own writing, it was galling to find this attack on an activity which was relatively unobstructed for women. It was perhaps just as well, she felt, that she had left the London literary scene and its highbrow, chauvinist prejudices. In the context of the reception of *The Blood of the Martyrs*, a diary entry snapped, 'after taking up the cudgels for women novelists, I didn't expect a fair deal from the buggers' union.'[13] The 'buggers' union' was a phrase she applied to a particular brand of socialist literary activity, some of whose adherents were homosexual. Her own English identity depended very much on her status as a writer, but in Scotland she saw the possibilities of re-fashioning herself.

Christmas 1938 was spent in London. It was much more than a family festival. Cards alone were a major effort: a hundred to the constituency, which Dick was still assiduously nursing, and five hundred to friends. Naomi organized presents for 52 people. There was a Christmas party for children, and guests for dinner on

Christmas Day included refugees from Europe. After Christmas, the family went north to spend New Year at Carradale.

Among early visitors to Carradale were the Coles. Douglas Cole described arriving at the village's rotting pier, which was perhaps an emblem of the economic decay affecting the community. Although the herring fishing was doing well that season – the summer of 1939 – it was, Cole said, 'getting harder and harder for those who dwell in the remoter parts of the British Isles to live at all ... The people here are the victims of a large-scale capitalism which regards their ways of living as obsolete.'[14] Local government could not be expected to afford the services and amenities that would revive the community, to build a surface road or a good harbour. National initiatives and funds were required. Cole claimed that Carradale people wanted 'a public authority to take over and maintain their rotting harbours and defective ferries, a public body to put capital into conserving and developing the potential value of their country for the production of wealth and welfare.'[15] That Cole should champion the cause of isolated areas of the Scottish Highlands was entirely due to the Mitchisons. It was the subject of conversations in the large-windowed drawing-room; it was to be a dominant theme in Naomi's life for two decades.

But the prospects for socialism, which is what Cole was talking about, were overshadowed by the prospect of war. Hitler's incursions across one after another of Germany's borders appalled Naomi, yet she was profoundly reluctant to admit the inevitability of war. And in Carradale the international political arena seemed that much further away. There were other, more immediate problems, and a whole range of tasks to command her attention. She lost no time in making her presence felt in the community. She and Dick were the new lairds, but things were going to be different. The traditional distance between Tigh Mhor, the Big House, and the village was no longer going to dominate the lairds' relations with the rest. People were welcome to walk on Mitchison land and take a share of Mitchison salmon from the river. They were welcome at the house. Naomi was ready to roll up her sleeves and work in the fields or take her place in a fishing boat. She and Dick got a local

The young Naomi with her parents, 1897

Naomi and Jack, 1898

Naomi with her mother, Louisa Kathleen Haldane

Naomi at the age of ten

Naomi and Jack, captain of the school, 1910

Naomi in 1913

Naomi and Aldous Huxley at Cherwell, c.1914

Naomi with Jack (right) and Dick, 1916

Naomi as a young wife, c.1918

Naomi in the 1920s

The Mitchison family in 1930

Carradale House in Kintyre, bought by Naomi and Dick in 1937 and still Naomi's home

Naomi in 1938

Naomi at Carradale with Margaret Cole (left) and Elizabeth Longford, August 1939

At Carradale with Naomi driving the tractor bringing in the hay

Naomi, c.1940s

A Matter Between MacDonalds, performed in Carradale village hall in 1940. Denis Macintosh is standing second from left

Naomi in the USSR with Pioneer Camp children, 1952

Naomi dancing at the Pioneer Camp with Arnold Kettle (far left), Richard Mason (far back), Doris Lessing (centre, dark dress), and Douglas Young (in hat)

Dick in the drawing room of Carradale House

Naomi making notes at
Mochudi, 1960s

Naomi in the 1960s

Naomi with Linchwe, after the pre-Independence Kgotla at Mochudi, September 1966

Naomi and Dick at their Golden Wedding Anniversary, with an entourage of grandchildren

Naomi signing one of her books, Botswana 1966

branch of the Labour Party going, though she felt a little uneasy about it: were the Carradale folk joining just to please the laird? She was also going to write her way into Scotland. She could not do otherwise.

In the summer of 1939, the Mitchisons spent their time at Carradale 'doing the usual things, swimming, picnicking, shooting and fishing, picking flowers and fruit in the garden, thinking that perhaps somehow things might turn out differently'.[16] But it was not possible to shut out the ominous signs. Ellen Wilkinson had written to Naomi that there was no way the war could be stopped. In her view, what needed to be addressed was how political activity could be sustained to ensure that, whatever else happened, out of war would come socialism.[17] It was the one grain of hope, that if a war had to be fought, at the end of it everything would be different.

2

The Bull Calves, Naomi's first Scottish historical novel, was published in 1947. It was the only major writing she was occupied with during the war years. It is prefaced by a poem, 'Clemency Ealasaid', about the death of her one-day-old daughter in July 1940. The novel draws together much of Naomi's effort to engage emotionally, intellectually and politically with her Scottish inheritance. The poem provides an intense convergence of private and public pain that was very much in the present.

The baby 'was to have been a binding between me and Carradale',[18] a commitment to a place but also to the future, a gesture of faith in wartime.

How shall I stay here, how go on with the little things,
How not hate Carradale, the flowery betrayer,
Dagger in fist?
How be crushed into such humility as can continue
The daily work, alleviation of meals and sleep and slight laughter?[19]

Naomi began working on *The Bull Calves* the following year. The poem and the novel together sum up much of what was important to her over five years or so, and they were crucial years, in respect of the many strands of her career and of her emotional life. They provided the opportunities she wanted and needed to live life on her own terms. At the same time, they were acutely difficult, dominated by war and the demands of life in a small, circumscribed rural community.

Most of the time was spent in Carradale. The detailed diary Naomi kept for Mass-Observation charts her efforts to establish a worthwhile place in the community and the ebb and flow of her ambivalent feelings for Carradale's people. She was often frustrated and angry at local intransigence; there was also frustration at being so far from London, however pained she felt about the London literary highbrows and their negative attitude to her work. And as well as coming to terms with the loss of her daughter, she had to deal with the first symptoms of menopause and the realization that there would be no more children. The war, bringing its inevitable news of the deaths of friends and reminders of the terrible losses of the First War, intensified an anxiety about the children, which runs through most of the diary.

There was also a basis for optimism. The defeat of Hitler might bring not only a socialist future, but a measure of independence for Scotland. This became increasingly important to Naomi. It was inseparable from the need to understand the past, to draw out of history the materials for commitment. 'Clemency Ealasaid' moves from dark depression,

> *as I am now*
> *Unable to imagine the new times, because of the blackness*
> *Steadily ahead of me, the still curtain*
> *Over my dancing daughter...*[20]

to a willed and unromantic statement of hope for the future.

> *The roughest day is to come. We shall perhaps*
> *Live through it, or others will. In a hundred years*

Things may seem in order, making sense, drawing a new map:
Human endeavour going round about, unselfishly...[21]

The poem captures a moment in Naomi's personal history. *The Bull Calves* explores a moment in Scotland's history, the year following the defeat of Prince Charles Edward at Culloden in 1746, but it also draws heavily on the present. It reflects both Naomi's growing political involvement with Scotland and personal involvements with individual Scots, so much so that when the present failed to co-operate, progress on the novel was seriously impeded.

Naomi's Mass-Observation diary is an invaluable source for these years. Mass-Observation was founded in 1937 by her friend Tom Harrisson, Charles Madge whom she also knew, and Humphrey Jennings. Its object was to document the lives of ordinary people all over Britain, in an attempt to piece together a social anthropological picture of the way Britain lived and thought. It was easy for Harrisson to recruit Naomi. He was with the Mitchisons in Vallay in 1937 and must have discussed the new project with her then. Her contribution ran to 1600 pages of typescript.[22] She wrote it almost every day (with one significant gap from November 1939 to March 1940), often producing entries of several type-written pages. It chronicles all aspects of her life: the activities of running a house and farm, the stresses of the war, her involvement with local and national politics, and her personal relationships. It gave her a splendid opportunity to write the script of her life as she was living it, and to do so with a purpose.

The diary begins on 1 September 1939, the day German troops invaded Poland. Two days later, war was declared. Naomi and her friend Tony Pirie, who was staying at Carradale with her son, had washed their hair – "'I'll start this war clean,'" Tony had announced – and sat with family and others listening to Chamberlain on the radio, 'sounding like a very old man'.[23] All the children were at home. Denny was on vacation from Cambridge University, where he was studying medicine. Murdoch, Lois and Avrion were all on holiday from their boarding schools, and Val, only nine, was about to start at the local primary school. Hanging over the family, and all the Carradale families, was the possibility of call-up. For Naomi it was an agonising time, as inevitably she was 'thinking of the second war in terms of the first one, thinking how can I keep these boys out of the army'.[24] She wrote a very depressed letter to Aldous Huxley, in which she said she felt paralyzed by a feeling of moral failure. 'If one were a brick-layer, it would be possible, I suppose, to go on laying bricks, but it's hell trying to write.' How was it possible to reconcile a profound anti-war conviction and a feeling that if necessary there should be violent resistance to war-mongering? She suggested a 'new kind of patriotism', but could not find a way of articulating it.[25]

Dick arrived from London two weeks after the outbreak of war. He disagreed with Naomi, supporting Britain's entry, while she felt that socialists should stay out of what she identified as a contest of capitalist states. Her view was that Nazi rule was bound to destroy itself sooner or later, and the world should sit it out. But her reaction was as much emotional as rational. 'I was very conscious of what [the First War] had been ... and there it was coming again, and I was very much against it.'[26] At the time she wrote:

> The alternative seems to be a very long and increasingly horrible war, effectively smashing all that we care for ... The ending of a civilization, and above all the killing of people, the extermination of a generation. I don't see how that is to be avoided if the war goes on.[27]

Naomi felt an acute 'sense of personal loss, as though years of work and hope and idealism had been wiped out'.[28] In October, the Carradale Labour Party passed an anti-war resolution, and Naomi was anxious to keep as many Carradale men as possible out of the fighting. Gradually this resistance to the war diminished and later she would find herself wishing that she could make more of a contribution to the war effort. But she never lost her protective urge on behalf of both her own family and members of the local community.

As Naomi went about her business through the Highland autumn, there was an air of unreality about the war. On 12 September she had driven to Oban for a meeting of the Argyllshire District Nursing Association (she was president of the Carradale section). North of Lochgilphead she passed Loch Graignish.

> The loch was still that paint blue, with the queer shaped islands sloping out of it like the backbones of megatheriums. Everywhere the rowans were orange to scarlet; harvests were being gathered. There was no sign of change. I, who am trained to use my imagination, could not at that time imagine or be moved by the war one knew for certain was happening.[29]

Dick's arrival from London, from the centre of war alertness, did not dispel this detachment. The departure of Murdoch and Lois for their schools was a wrench, but the lack of credibility continued. 'I hardly believe in this [war] yet,' she was writing on 4 October.[30] In some ways life went on very much as before, although there were some immediate problems and issues. Evacuees from Glasgow had already arrived in Carradale, and hundreds more were expected. It was clear that Glasgow and Clydeside, with their concentration of key industries, would be a principal target for German air attacks, and Kintyre was initially identified as a safe area. (Later, this designation was revised; the whole of the Clyde estuary was vulnerable.) Preparations were made to receive evacuees, both at Carradale House and throughout the community, though in the event nothing like the four hundred expected came, and many returned to Glasgow after a short stay. Naomi already had a Jewish refugee staying with her, Elgé Pibram from Austria, and later accepted the three Gibson children from Glasgow – Betty, Matthew and Ina.

There were, however, enough evacuees in the area to cause some friction, as Carradale families tried to adjust to stressed slum children and problems of lice infestations, bed-wetting and various kinds of aberrant behaviour. Naomi often found herself in the role of trouble-shooter, soothing indignation, sorting out clean sheets and assisting with feeding and educating the incomers. In a letter to the *Glasgow Herald*, she drew attention to the fact that when the evacuee children were weighed and measured six weeks after their arrival, they were found to have gained weight and to be generally healthier than when they arrived.[31] She wanted to be practical, to take a lead, whatever her reservations about the war. There was a call for various kinds of patriotic activities, for example to gather sphagnum moss, which was useful for bandages. Naomi went out on to the hillside to gather it, and tried to persuade others to help, but, to her disgust, there was little local response to this or other national efforts to stir the public to action.

Naomi felt she should set an example. There were the responsibilities of landlord and landowner, borne mostly by Naomi as Dick was never in residence for long, and the need to respond to the first of the wartime regulations and deal with the accompanying paperwork. And all the time there were the demands of the land, the harvest, potato lifting in October, later the threshing, in which Naomi participated. She took her place beside the farm workers, stooking corn, snedding (cutting the tops off) turnips. She learned to handle Jo the horse, ploughing and harrowing, and to drive a tractor:

> The tractor was ill to start, a great heaving and jerking,
> The gear lever jars through palm and bone[32]

She fished and shot - there was a heightened purpose to these activities now as fish and game were a valuable contribution to the larder - and was able not only to gut a salmon but to gralloch (disembowel) a deer.

These were years of very hard physical work. Naomi's children may have felt sometimes that her talent lay mainly in organizing others to do the work, but there is no doubt that she made enormous physical demands on herself. She was often exhausted and sometimes ill, and this was exacerbated by wartime stress and personal sensitivities. By 1943, she was increasingly beset with symptoms she identified as menopausal, and twinges of rheumatism would plague her from time to time. Her emotions, always near to the surface, were often rawly exposed - love and anger, enthusiasm and frustration, forbearance and impatience. A recurrent theme of the diary is her ambivalence towards the Carradale community. Her profound wish was to expand the horizons of the village, to use her position of privilege for the community's good. She liked being an employer, she liked to be liked by the men, 'to be teased and petted and advised – and on the whole respected as a worker'.[33] Yet she was aware of the fragility of her 'superior' role.

> I'm willing to give them a good deal, of time and energy and thought and love. Take, eat. But what good is it going to do? Mightn't they be better left alone? Is it possible to do anything from above? I have to sacrifice a good deal in order to live here: above all the privacy that a big town gives, the privacy of the crowd in the Underground, in which one can think one's own thoughts and let one's eyes cloud with any kind of imagining. Here I have to be good ... all around are men and women waiting to catch me out. Sometimes I could scream. How can a writer work in these conditions?[34]

There were times when Naomi wanted to share as an equal in Carradale life, and times when she wanted to draw all of Carradale to herself as its life-giving centre – a touch of the priestess role she had often invoked. She liked to bring Carradale within the walls of the house, under her influence, but also providing vital links with the environment in which she was trying to place herself. When, for example, she listened to Jemima MacLean's fine voice rendering traditional Gaelic songs, she experienced it as part of the blending and building process. Naomi often asked Jemima to sing for Carradale visitors.

But the blending was far from smooth, and sometimes, as this passage indicates, she felt she was being watched by a suspicious community, who were made uneasy by this unorthodox laird, a socialist and a feminist who told them what they needed. 'Living in a village is walking/ Among snare wire', as she put it in her poem 'Living in a village':

> *Watched on, edible, spied and lied to,*
> *From burrows, runways, witch-twisted bushes…*[35]

Surely London was her more natural habitat? Yet London denied her precisely the sense of community that she found simultaneously so valuable and so exasperating.

The more positive aspects of Carradale often centred on fishing, a collective activity which summed up much of what Naomi sought. She derived an emotional fulfilment from sharing in a practical and productive activity, which depended for its success on intimate co-operation and understanding of the task. One day at Tarbert she watched the *Alban*, subject of a long poem she was writing at the time, coming in.

> I watched her berthing. Everyone was busy on the other boats; one or two waved to me; the *Cluaran* was there. I liked watching those men whom I now know so well doing their work, coiling ropes and jumping and handling the boats skilfully. It was like watching someone in a lab, or a sculptor … [the fishermen] part of a community of which I believe I know something. And the wind blew cold and sharp and the sun shone and everything was lively and bustling with movements and shouting.[36]

The poem 'The *Alban* goes out: 1939' concentrates not only Naomi's experience of herring fishing, but much of Carradale.

> *We are working all the season, boat near to*
> *boat in the nights,*
> *And danger may come on us quick, no time to*
> *stand upon rights,*
> *When all our hands are as net-cut, and our eyes*
> *as sore from the spray,*
> *How can we think of our neighbours except*
> *in a neighbourly way?*[37]

The poem is a lyrical and precise account of the Carradale fleet on a night's ring-net fishing, and catches the sights and sounds with a vivid immediacy.

> *Men and engines grunting and haaling,*
> *The nets dripping, the folds falling;*
> *The spring-ropes jerking to the winches' creaking*
> *Wind in by fathoms from their sea-deep seeking,*
> *Steady and long like a preacher speaking.*
> *But the flow of the net we must all lay hold on,*
> *The cork-strung back-rope our hands are cold on,*
> *As we thrash at the net the dead fish falling*
> *Gleam and break from the tight mesh mauling,*
> *Show what we'll get from the bag of the net!*
> *And fierce and straining and shoulders paining*
> *We drag it out from the sea's wild sprawling,*
> *From the lit wet hummocks' twist and spin;*
> *And the leaded sole-rope comes slumping in.*[38]

The poem is a celebration, and also a statement of Naomi's place in it all. She is part of the 'we'; there is no distinction made between herself – woman, laird and incomer – and the fishermen, in particular Denis Mackintosh, though he is not named.

> *You kneel on the rocking deck*
> *And the two boats kiss,*
> *As the two brother skippers,*
> *Fine and handy at this,*
> *Bring them alongside gently…*
> *And the waves tumble and shove*
> *At the Alban and Cluaran,*
> *And sometimes your face is below me,*
> *And sometimes above.*[39]

This intimate comradeship was what Naomi wanted from Carradale, indeed what she had always wanted wherever she had been, and what she would continue to seek. Sometimes she found it. Often the men and women who were a vital part of this alliance could not forget her difference, and she was acutely aware of this. The lines 'And the hand on the gunwale by mine/ Is a grimed and working hand' contain both intimacy and separation.

3

'The *Alban* goes out' was written before war overtook life at Carradale and made her much more a part of the community than seemed likely at the time. By the end of 1939, Naomi was pregnant. She was forty-two years old; it was her seventh pregnancy. It did not stand in the way of her vigorous involvement in an Argyll bye-election in March, in which a Scottish Nationalist candidate, William Power, stood against a Unionist: it had been a Unionist seat. The wartime electoral truce kept the Liberals and the Labour Party out of the contest. Although Naomi was still a member of the Labour Party, her concern for local social and economic issues attracted her to the Scottish Nationalists, and she supported Power, though she had greater regard for his agent John MacCormick. MacCormick had been a leading nationalist since 1928, when the National Party of Scotland was founded, and was already developing ideas for an all-party Scottish Convention, in which Naomi would play a part. In Argyll in 1939, the Nationalists attracted quite substantial support, but not enough to dislodge the Unionist.

The war continued to seem remote, although everyday practicalities were affected. First petrol and then food was rationed. Naomi was growing fruit and vegetables, and there were hens, but efforts to adapt to wartime shortages were often ineffectual. Fruit bottled with less than the usual amount of sugar, in an attempt to stretch the ration, resulted in the fruit going off. There were periods when the hens did not lay or the potatoes rotted. Supplies of meat and fish were sporadic. And there were often large numbers of extra people in the house, all needing to be fed whether or not they had remembered to bring their ration cards with them.

June 1940 saw the evacuation of the British Expeditionary Force from Dunkirk, the fall of Paris and the entry of Italy into the war. The future looked bleak. 'Are we completely beaten?' Naomi was asking herself on 17 June.[40] For the first time, people were talking as if defeat were possible. Depressed, and with her pregnancy now well advanced, Naomi was longing for the company of women friends. 'I feel they're more likely to be sane than a man, less certain of themselves, less arrogant, more able to see two sides to any question. Perhaps if they had men's power they'd become as destructive, though: the best argument for the subjection of women!'[41] But she was also finding separation from Dick harder to deal with than she had in the past. 'We have grown together too much.'[42]

With the baby's birth only weeks away, Naomi was out on midnight fishing expeditions with her fishermen comrades, relishing the calm beauty of the night and the quiet co-operation. She had decided that the baby was to be born at Carradale, although it meant making special arrangements, engaging a nurse and bringing an obstetrician, Dr Hunter, from Glasgow. Additional help was being provided by Rosemary Jones, an Australian whom Naomi had taken on to act initially as her secretary. Rosemary and the nurse began to get things ready for the birth. Naomi sorted out baby clothes. Denny had arrived from Cambridge with his girlfriend Ruth Gill, whom Naomi was meeting for the first time. From the start, they got on well – 'she is extraordinarily nice and level-headed,' Naomi commented[43] – and Ruth would prove a great support.

It was decided to induce the baby, although it was not quite full term. On 1 July, a hot bath, quinine, castor oil and pituitrin got things off to what turned out to be a false start. Naomi's diary entry is interspersed with war news and confirmation of the death of a young friend of Murdoch's who was in the navy. She writes a letter to *Time* suggesting that the USA accept more anti-Nazi refugees, and starts to read Agnes Mure Mackenzie's history of Scotland. Three days later she is worried that there could be something wrong. There have been a few contractions, but nothing significant. On 4 July a baby girl was born. Although there was some concern, as she seemed a little weak, Naomi asked for the red flag to be hoisted above the house. The following day the baby died of a heart defect and the flag was lowered.

Dick was on his way from London, but was able to stay only briefly as he had to get to Yorkshire on a Ministry of Labour job. Their daughter was buried at sea, taken by the *Cluaran* out into the bay. Over the next few days, Naomi longed for something purposeful to do, to be more fully involved in the war, to be with women friends for a few hours. It was natural that her thoughts should turn to another form of creativity, a new book, but there was little solace. 'If only I had my baby I wouldn't need to write a book that probably nobody wants to read.'[44] A feeling of emptiness and uselessness persisted.

> All springs of action gone, all confidence gone; I don't see that I'm likely ever to be any good at anything. I don't feel I can tackle any new situation, or even any old one ... I have been in the past ambitious, not, I think, for power, nor for money, to be creating perhaps. I've wanted a bit of fame, or at least encouragement; I've wanted that more because of being a woman than for myself – something to break the myth of feminine inferiority. Above all, I think, I have wanted my values to be accepted: I have lived in loyalty to them; the values of the *clerk* – truth above all, reason as opposed to passion ... Now I am left completely useless and valueless. That's defeatism, but I know my values are defeated, whatever happens.[45]

Such negativity was understandable, and from time to time over the next few years it would recur. Personal loss intensified the damage to her self-confidence as a writer, which was not the source of solace it might otherwise have been. She expressed her negativity not only as defeatism, but also as a complete absence of sympathy. 'I feel unkind now, the opposite of innocent: nocent, hurting, because of having been hurt,' she was writing on 16 July.[46]

As always, all the varying strands of Naomi's life were woven together. Pain or disappointment in one area deeply affected everything else. The shock of losing the baby spread through all her concerns and activities. This was something she accepted, and made little attempt to counteract. Nevertheless, she did continue with her reading of Scottish history and began to plan her next book. She was writing book reviews. She was soon turning her attention again to local problems and the concerns of the children, who by the end of the month were home for the holidays. Lois was bored and awkward, not getting on with Eglè, who was also difficult. But Denny announced his and Ruth's intention to marry, and Naomi approved; it was an affirmation of life which she needed.

In the middle of August, Dick returned, with Douglas and Margaret Cole, with whom he was now living in Hendon. In some ways this added to Naomi's problems. It meant 'extra complications about food'[47] and about drink: Dick and the Coles were used to drinks before and during dinner, a habit Naomi not only did not bother with when she was running the household for herself but about which she also had equivocal views, especially as Margaret consumed a fair amount. She was abstemious herself and had little time for the overindulgence of others, whether her intellectual friends from London or local fishermen. Although Margaret and Douglas were close friends, she found their presence a strain. She felt excluded from the talk of London life and politics. An undated comment in a notebook mentions 'the sense of inferiority that one tends to feel when confronted with hard-working left wingers' and this may also have been a factor in her unease.[48] She wanted them to take an interest in her concerns, the practicalities of farming, Scottish history and Scottish issues, but they did not share her enthusiasm, although Douglas responded to the extent of producing his piece on Carradale for the *New Statesman*. Dick was now working closely with Douglas on the Manpower Survey initiated by Sir William Beveridge. He remained personally close to Margaret, who worked with the Fabian Society. Naomi was distanced from this involvement with large issues and direct contact with the war effort, and she never took kindly to being left out.

Margaret Cole's accounts of visits to Carradale do not refer to any specific time, but suggest a rather different picture. She pays tribute to Naomi's warmth and sympathy, but also recalls her 'verbal truculence' and her delight in scandalizing her listeners.[49] There were times when Naomi's originality was simply odd. She wore peculiar clothes 'which were sometimes beautiful, sometimes reminiscent of an old peasant woman subsisting on cast-offs from gentry'.[50] The clothes may have been sometimes a genuine unconcern, but there were certainly occasions when they were part of the theatricality, the pleasure of dressing up. Much of her writing shows her interest in clothes, in the ways the body could be adorned, and she was highly aware of their symbolic function. If Naomi was feeling left out, she probably used clothes as well as words to make her statements. It is quite clear that she wanted people to know that she – unlike some others – was truly involved with real people, and getting her hands dirty.

4

Naomi was still struggling with her grief and wondered whether she should try to have another child. Dick found it difficult to respond sympathetically. As always, he kept his own feelings battened down, and Naomi felt correspondingly inhibited. She records an August walk with Dick to nearby Dippen: 'oh I did so want to talk and I couldn't get any of the things I wanted to say to the surface'.[51] Preparations for the wedding, planned for September, were a welcome distraction, although it meant learning to detach herself from her eldest son who would be only just twenty-one.

The wedding itself, almost exactly a year after the declaration of war, went off well. Naomi rose to the challenge of getting together food and drink for some sixty people. Another problem was what to wear: she settled for 'my old blue linen and embroidered coat, newly ironed' and changed into a green organdie dress for the evening.[52] Ruth wore blue. It was a high-spirited occasion, culminating in a splendid ceilidh at which Carradale let down its hair. Denny, at that time a member of the Communist Party, was scathing about Carradale's traditionalism, but for his mother the wedding ceilidh at Carradale House, whatever undertones of feudalism were present, was not only an important and symbolic collective celebration, but immensely enjoyable. Her own words capture the occasion:

> Peter got more and more drunk and affectionate ... Eddie's lovely red-haired baby crawled about at first, and then slept through it all, and Eddie got very gay, but stayed on his feet. Lachie was dead sober and smiling and danced exquisitely, in exact time; Denny M. was sober too, and a grand M.C. Willie doesn't need even a drink to behave like an imp at a party, with his superb head, and curly, greying hair. Strip the Willow got wilder and wilder with Duncan Munro wanting to dance with everyone, and Jock just not tripping over his feet and Eddie dancing well but recklessly, and Lachie giving a little high cry in his throat ... I danced with [Duncan Semple] ... and he danced marvellously, throwing his head back and laughing ... I had an eightsome with Peter and Jock in it, and Peter was singing a peurt a beull [mouth music] at the top of his voice, and suddenly he gave one leap too many and he and I were on the floor.[53]

The fiddler passed out. Duncan Munro had a whisky bottle hidden up a tree. The party eventually ended at 2 a.m. In addition to the unofficial supplies the company had consumed two dozen bottles of champagne, six of whisky, tea, lemonade, passion fruit drink, sandwiches and biscuits, 15 pounds of cake, half a wedding cake and ten dozen small cakes.

Naomi reflected on how different this was from the last war, when 'I never danced once; everything like that went.'[54] (It seems that although Naomi clearly enjoyed dancing greatly, she was not in fact very good at it.) The feeling that life went on pretty much as usual underlined the distance of the war. With the wedding over, Naomi was much occupied with the harvest. Work on the new village hall, a project initiated and nursed by herself and Dick, was nearly complete, and she was working on a play, *A Matter Between Macdonalds*, which would be performed in the new hall at Christmas. On 19 October, the hall was opened. Dick came up for the occasion and made a speech. There was a concert followed by tea for two hundred. Naomi had gone to Glasgow in search of crockery, glasses, kettles, trays, dusters and all the other items needed to equip a community centre – a daunting task in the face of wartime shortages.

With the hall open, Naomi's efforts focused on rehearsing the play, with Duncan Munro, Denny Macintosh and other Carradale folk. She had written the play for them, deliberately setting out to produce something that Carradale would enjoy, and also in a sense writing herself into Carradale's life. There were parts for herself and for Val. The play became not only a symbol of what Naomi saw as the creative responsibilities of the Big House, but a focus of complicated emotional entanglements which were an important part of Naomi's life during these years.

Her relationship with Denny Macintosh developed and strengthened. Naomi's need for a quasi-maternal role, which had emerged at a very early stage in her life, remained as strong as it had ever been. Although she expressed doubt at taking on the role of leader she responded enthusiastically to opportunities of taking control. It is manifestly clear that she enjoyed being laird of Carradale, however deeply and genuinely she rejected the traditional aspects of that role. She wanted a relationship of mutual respect and affection with the people of Carradale – not only with the men and not only with Denny. Denny became a key figure in her emotional life, but her particular feelings for him were tied into a more general need to give as much as to receive.

> ... this awful feeling of love; these people I had not known at all three years ago, and now I love them so much I can't begin to get it into words and I a poet: the feeling one must protect them but one *can't*. One wants to be their sacrifice but one doesn't see any way at all to do it.[55]

The echoes reverberate of earlier books and lives. At the same time she was aware of the maternal nature of her feelings, perhaps intensified by the loss of the baby and her heightened protectiveness. All her children were now absent most of the time.

Her respect for the practical skills of Carradale's fishermen was expressed in 'The *Alban* goes out' and later in *Spindrift*, a play produced in Glasgow after the war (there was a second play about west-coast fishing, *Guilty Together*, never published or performed) and *Men and Herring*, all collaborations with Denny Macintosh. She described Denny as 'true, generous and gay, silent when need be, with the beautiful manners that come from natural kindness'.[56] He spoke English, Scots and Gaelic, and Naomi seemed to find the Gaelic language particularly agreeable and seductive. There was a strong physical attraction too, which she had no wish to deny, but equally no wish to allow to get out of hand. Both Denny and Dougie Campbell, of whom she was also very fond, were married and Naomi got on well with Lilla, Denny's wife, and with Chrissie Campbell. However, neither man was averse to taking an opportunity if he found one and neither seemed to need much encouragement. Naomi was not the only woman to whom Denny was attentive.[57]

She was conscious of the responsibilities, and the exposure, of her position, did not want to take advantage of it or hurt her friends or disrupt their marriages. She knew that the code of conduct accepted by London friends and associates, and which she had good cause to understand did not guard against the raw emotions of jealousy and rejection, would not transplant to Kintyre. Apart from other considerations, there were conventions of class involved as well as of morality. But the need for physical contact, for warmth and kindness, the word she uses often as a synonym for sexual contact, was powerful. Her nature was spontaneously tactile, which could be disconcerting for those who were less relaxed about touching.

On several occasions, Naomi and Denny M. exchanged hugs and kisses and endearments. Her diary descriptions of these episodes show her unerring instinct for drama and the symbolic gesture as well as the personal value she placed on physical contact. One summer night in 1941, Naomi and Denny were out hunting. Denny shot a stag, and the two of them, triumphant, lay down in the heather.

> Hard, hard to say no for the sake of a thing you can scarcely put into words he would understand, into words valid enough to stand against the thing in the blood, the great kindness. Hard to say no to someone who has no reproaches, nothing but kindness and laughter and agreement that this is best; but the wavy bright hair among the heather, and the gentle fox-eyes behind the long black lashes, and the strong, thin body that might have had its way with me as with the deer: and all the time biting at me, the knowledge of the things the Big House had done. Yet it was sweet enough to lie side by side on the heather, with the gun and the stag beside us...[58]

Sometimes, Naomi commented, the people in her life were like the characters in her books – and vice versa of course. And sometimes she wrote about her own experiences as if she were writing fiction. She knew, of course, that this particular diary would be read by others.

The fact that it was not only Denny to whom she was attracted, and that Denny himself was susceptible to others, perhaps made it easier to keep 'the thing in the blood' at bay. She enjoyed physicality for its own sake – the labour of ploughing or hauling nets, the casual contact of working alongside someone, the touch of a dancing partner, the affectionate embrace of a friend or a child. She placed a high value on mutual and sympathetic expression through physical contact. And where earlier in her life sexual activity contained a political as well as a personal message, perhaps now there was less urgency in pushing back the frontiers of feminism. It seemed more important to be emphasizing what was shared, between men and women, Big House and croft.

Naomi clearly needed admiration; Dick's affectionate support was not enough. She relished spontaneous gestures and if the men had reservations about kissing the lady of the Big House, she found ways of reassuring them. Dougie Campbell was a partner, sometimes Dougie, Denny and Naomi together, indulging in friendly and sometimes prolonged embraces. Duncan Munro, one of the foresters, was another, although at the same time as entangling herself with him, Naomi was encouraging his involvement with the girl whom he would eventually marry. Duncan and Naomi shared a memorable journey, necking in the back of a bus from Tarbert in the company of a large Carradale contingent who, although it was in the dark, were probably aware of what was going on. There were times when Naomi enjoyed knowing she was shocking the community. Being careful went against the grain. Fifty years later she was still saying, 'I don't like being careful.'[59]

Whoever else was in receipt of her attentions, Denny M. was never displaced from his position at the centre of Naomi's experience of Carradale. He played a leading role in *The Bull Calves*, both as the model for William Mackintosh of Borlum, and as a more general inspiration and sounding-board. He himself clearly found it difficult to understand his multi-stranded value to Naomi and frequently, often inadvertently, let her down. He would promise to visit and fail to turn up. He would appear to be unresponsive to what she was trying to achieve. Naomi was deeply hurt by what she felt as acts of betrayal, even though she realized these were the result of awkwardness and misunderstanding rather than a deliberate intention to cause pain. She had a similar problem with Duncan, whom she also identified as a key if unconscious collaborator in *The Bull Calves*. She inveighed against Highlanders who made facile promises which they knew they would not keep, who said what they thought she wanted to hear even if it bore little relation to truth or intention.

Whatever value she placed on physical contact, words were pre-eminent. This was another complication, for most of those around her in Carradale did not share this sense of the worth of words, and sometimes she felt acutely this lack of understanding of a crucial part of what she was. She would write letters to Denny M.

and to Duncan, trying to explain her needs and how they could help her. 'Probably I was wrong to put so much weight onto your friendship,' she wrote to Duncan, 'but I was lonely and wanted to talk to you about my book.'[60] Her facility with the written word almost certainly did as much as her residency of the Big House to emphasize the gulf she hated to acknowledge.

There were other ways, perhaps, of bridging the gulf. Duncan's fondness for whisky was a problem, and disrupted rehearsals of the play, in which his role as Prince Charles Edward was important. His unreliability made Naomi angry and exasperated, and increasingly anxious about whether he would be sober on the day. When he let her down just ten days before the performance, she was provoked to extreme action. She made him promise to give up drinking, sealing the promise with a gesture straight out of one of her own novels. She cut her hand and his. They clasped hands, mingling their blood, and Duncan kissed her bleeding hand and then her lips. When the day came, he was drunk again, but scraped through his part without disaster. Even in her anger she sought and found an explanation. 'I am angry thinking of these gentle and delicate minded Highlanders who have been oppressed and hurt until they have to drink.'[61]

With Christmas approaching, the family gathered at Carradale. Murdoch, who had followed Denny to Cambridge, also to study medicine, was depressed and unhappy, thinking about leaving university and joining the navy. He was anxious about the future and the family, clearly concerned that no two members were in the same place. Even Val, whose status as the youngest was intensified by the loss of the baby, was now away. She had been unhappy at Carradale school, where an encounter with the tawse (for not being able to say the Lord's Prayer) had been a shock. After a term being taught at home, Naomi had sent her to a tiny progressive school near Castle Douglas in Dumfriesshire, where she was enjoying herself. She was aware of the contradictions of her life as a daughter of an unorthodox Big House, where conflicting messages echoed the contradictions implicit in her mother's role. Murdoch worried about whether Dick and Naomi would be in the same place when the war was over. Naomi's diary suggests that Murdoch's perception of strain was accurate. 'What I feel, but don't say, is that Dick and I are much happier if we don't see one another all the time, though it would be nicer to see a bit more than at present.'[62] Jack and the Coles also arrived for Christmas.

Naomi's relish for celebratory events meant that she put considerable effort into making Christmas pleasurable, but the war cast a pall over the choosing of presents and planning of food for large numbers. She felt depressed:

> An awful lot of coming and going and swapping round of Christmas presents and the young rushing down to the shops for last minute things ... but who are we bombing this Christmas Eve, Christmas Eve, who are we bombing on Christmas night, when the snow lies thick on the ground? This bloody silly war.[63]

She was relieved to find that in fact there had been no bombing over Christmas. But there was a certain amount of combat at home. Jack and Douglas Cole engaged in political arguments, which made Naomi feel very uncomfortable. When Rosemary pointed out that they were playing boys' games, scoring points off each other, she felt better. 'Felt that I may be a coward and inaccurate but at least I'm not a man.'[64]

Shortly after Christmas came *A Matter Between Macdonalds*, two performances on the same day. Naomi put a huge effort into making it all work, in the face of Duncan's inebriation, general nervousness, an overloaded generator and a variety of technical hitches. The performances accomplished, more or less successfully, Naomi was presented with a sgian dhu, a small, black-hilted Highland knife in which she at once invested talismanic importance. The play was followed by a party at the House, but Naomi was exhausted and deeply hurt by Duncan's disaffection. He was morose and self-pitying, but she was determined to jolt him into an awareness of how he was letting himself down as well as her. The dancing continued, but the atmosphere was fraught; a drama was being played out as tense as anything that had been performed earlier. It concerned not just the relationship between Naomi and Duncan, but the place of both of them in the eyes of others.

Naomi slept with the sgian dhu under her pillow. Later she began to write 'The cleansing of the knife', a long poem addressed to 'Donnachadh Bàn' – Duncan the fair-haired and also the name of an eighteenth-century Gaelic poet, Duncan Ban Macintyre, who wrote powerfully and poignantly of the defeated Jacobites. In the poem she weaves together the personal and the political.

> *Friend, is this how you are,*
> *Is this the man I know:*
> *A Highlander and lonely,*
> *Oppressed by historical causes,*
> *Aware how things should be,*
> *Not how to make them so?*[65]

The year came to a quiet end. Naomi was planning to go south. 'I wonder whether I shall be as frightened of raids as I think I shall.'[66] But on the first day of 1941 it was Carradale that dominated her thoughts, with no hint of anger or disappointment. 'I kept on thinking how much I would like to stay here and have another child and write enormous poems and never go back to London.'[67] But the knife and all it represented went with her.

> *Now I go south to the war:*
> *The sgian goes with me*
> *I am not forgetting Scotland.*
> *Here at my heart's core*
> *Lie all of you my friends.*
> *Across wild land and sea*
> *Love goes quicker than bombers*
> *To its own mixing of ends.*
> *Your wish for death and passion—*
> *Deirdre, Mary Stuart*
> *And the girls in the old songs—*

Flares with my sense of life,
Of direction steadily kept
And a steady righting of wrongs
And a cleansing of the knife.
See yourself, Donnachadh Bàn,
And I will stand beside you;
In the cold morning mirror
I will let no phantoms ride you.[68]

'Now what I feel for Carradale is mostly love,' she wrote a few days before going to London.[69]

5

Throughout the war, Naomi made visits south, spending time in London, seeing her mother in Oxford, Denny and Ruth in Cardiff, Murdoch in Cambridge, Lois and later Val at Badminton School evacuated to Devon and Av at Leighton Park. She tried to maintain contact with a number of friends. Travelling south meant getting to Campbeltown or Tarbert by bus or car, then on to Glasgow by air from Campbeltown or on the steamer to Gourock or Wemyss, and then on by train. The steamer no longer called at Carradale pier. From Glasgow she went by train to London. The children made the same journey at the start of each school term, travelling overnight on the train, pausing in London, perhaps fitting in a visit to the cinema before catching their connections to their schools. London and the south were not as accessible as they seemed in 1937.

Wartime travel meant queues, long, slow journeys, crowded trains, and the blackout. Naomi had always been accustomed to writing in unlikely places, and often found she could make better progress with work in trains and waiting rooms, away from the incessant demands of Carradale. 'I can write standing in the Underground in rush hours.'[70] Early in 1941 Naomi had other things on her mind. The war was going badly, though the German bombers shifted their attentions from the London to the west-coast ports.

This meant a quieter time for Naomi in London, but the Clydeside blitz in March brought the war very close to Carradale. The British were in retreat in North Africa; merchant shipping losses were heavy. In the midst of this, ideas for the new novel was growing. It was to be 'about the two kinds of life', Highland and Lowland.

> The Highlanders with the death wish and the passion and the foundation of things on the Celtic civilization ... and also the feeling for some kind of communism ... I suppose essentially predatory, unsettled, fishing and raiding: and the Lowlanders with their reasonable Protestantism which was also hierarchical, which insisted on the individual and life and redemption through God, not any fusion with God.[71]

She planned to set the novel's action in the early eighteenth century (in fact, she shifted the action to the mid-century but included an element of flashback) and to people it with her own forebears.

For the rest of the war *The Bull Calves* was a major preoccupation. It was slow going at first, and Naomi took some time to make up her mind whether it should be fiction or social history. And throughout she continued to be affected by the circumstances around her, and above all the people.

> I know I mustn't ask too much. But by god I am fed up with Denny and Duncan; it wouldn't be so bad if I wasn't just beginning a book. If I was in the middle of writing I wouldn't care two hoots in hell who was or wasn't nice to me. But when one's beginning the whole thing is so bloody depressing, one feels this intolerable weight one can't lift, one feels weak, one demands an accession of strength from everyone. A book is conceived in misery of the spirit. It was begotten in dire woe. I suppose the answer is that just now books don't matter, everything like that can go to hell, all I am good for is agriculture and looking after people from the war area who are convalescing.[72]

The struggle to write was not confined to the early stages. There were periods when she was unable to work on the book, because people or farming or the house demanded her attention. Often, as this passage suggests, the lack of progress left her in doubt of her own abilities. But at other times both the research and the writing went well. On occasional visits to Edinburgh she would slip into the Signet Library for a few hours of research and feel exhilarated. 'Historical research is one of the greatest pleasures of life,' she commented,[73] and she soaked herself in eighteenth-century texts, both in Edinburgh and at home where she gathered source material. Edinburgh was relatively peaceful, a haven from Carradale and less affected by the war than Glasgow. She stayed with her cousin Archie Haldane in the New Town and walked around the city which was so powerfully imbued with the past about which she was writing. She visited Jenners, the Princes Street department store, and was amazed at the quality and quantity of goods still available.

These visits were a respite, but her more arduous, and sometimes dangerous, journeys also seemed to be good for her work. Most of the obstructions rested in Carradale. The farm labour was constant. When there was no work to be done with crops or animals, there was paperwork, accounts to be wrestled with, forms to be filled in, applications to be made, wages to be calculated. Wartime regulations and controls vastly increased bureaucracy and Naomi was impatient with the detailed and time-consuming attention they required. People also got in the way of writing. There always seemed to be some kind of worry or problem with one or other of the children. Her maternal concern extended to the workers on the farm and in the house, to neighbours who sought advice or help on everything from dental treatment to education, to the many friends who came to stay, to the Free French refugees convalescing in the house from experiences in prison camps and the front line. Yet visitors were also a stimulus. She liked having the Frenchmen Pierre Marienne and Gilbert Morisson at Carradale. She liked to mother them and to flirt with them, though they were not necessarily popular with other members of the family.[74] It was not only that demands were made on her, emotional as much as anything else, but that she herself had a profound need to give, to help, sometimes to interfere, but never to hold herself aloof from the hurly burly of human exchange.

There were the daily demands of the domestic front, particularly exhausting when there were visitors. It was sometimes difficult to get help, as every able-bodied man and woman was either in the forces or in some form of directed labour. Farming, fishing and forestry were all reserved occupations, and although there was a tradition of mutual help it could not always be available when required. When, at different times, Sarah, who worked in the house, and Bella the cook left, there were major problems. Naomi herself sometimes did the cooking, though it was never her strong point, and Val when she was home from school was adept at producing meals for a throng of people, but every meal meant stretching limited resources. The addition of their own produce, game shot by the family or fish caught locally was always welcome, but often Naomi sent this off either to another Carradale household or to friends and family in the south.

There were other less tangible inhibitions that interfered with writing. Was there any point in writing novels any more? Would anyone read them? Was she trying to do too much? Self-doubt was interwoven with passionate commitment. She desperately wanted to write this book, for Carradale, for Scotland, yet was sometimes unsure of her ability. She still felt bruised by the London highbrows. *The Bull Calves* was 'for people here ... to make them confident and happy. But I don't want to write for the New Statesman boys, for the international culture of cities.'[75]

> I feel nervous about it; there is something deep down, I feel defensive and passionate, as I do about being a woman. Not quite reasonable. I feel I don't care about being in the same tradition as Shakespeare and Beethoven if only I can do something for my own people in Scotland. I would like of course, just for once to be a best seller.[76]

Naomi had always poured herself into her novels, and this was perhaps more true of *The Bull Calves* than of previous novels. She was consciously reflecting ideas, emotions and circumstances of the present, as she had done before, and weaving herself into a tapestry of her Haldane heritage, which had never seemed so important as it did now that she was living in Scotland. In a sense, *The Bull Calves* was also a statement of her commitment to Scotland. However inconsistent her attitude to Carradale, however clearly she saw the limitations of life in a remote village that was a long way from London which remained a magnet to her, the hold of Scotland and Scotland's future was strengthening all the time. This commitment was knotted into her relationship with Carradale. 'I would never have written it if I hadn't come here, or if, having come here, I hadn't wanted to live differently from the old order.'[77]

Through the character of *The Bull Calves*' Kirstie, Naomi was able to give herself a Scottish voice. There are frequent passages in which Naomi's own understanding, of farming for example, is readily transported back two hundred years and directly communicated by her central character.

> …one is thinking about the men that are working, and one's own man most, and the weather and the wee looks of growth or of shrivelling, and the great plans we have, and a time coming, maybe, when we will keep our kye on neeps in the winter, even in the Highlands, and have our eating beef between October and July, and early-calving cows, and all the bairnies throughout the length of Scotland the better of good milk. Of the value of such things, in pounds sterling that mean prosperity, that mean an easing of the hard yoke on the backs of countless men and women. Or better ways of feeding and droving.[78]

She was concerned about getting both the history and the language right. Denny M.'s role was not only as Black William, Kirstie's Jacobite husband, but as a sounding board for the language, vocabulary as well as tone and rhythm. One of the characteristics of her earlier historical fiction was the fact that she deliberately employed contemporary colloquial language, making no attempt to create an illusion of the archaic. What she aimed for in *The Bull Calves* was a consistent and convincing Scottish voice, and she achieved it, with marked success, by combining 1940s Carradale with an eighteenth-century context.

She also wrote into the book her sceptical view of Highlanders. Black William, Denny M.'s *alter ego*, is a complex and shifting figure. It is a portrait of a man morally as well as physically damaged by war and politics, but the characterization was almost certainly affected by Naomi's responses to Denny's unreliability and readiness with 'Highland promises' – promises meant to please rather than to be kept. William is redeemed by his unfailing and genuine love for Kirstie. This suggests a belief on Naomi's part that Denny's insouciance was redeemed by his affection for her. The fact that Naomi specifically asked Louise Annand, the book's illustrator, to model her depictions of Kirstie and William on Naomi and Denny supports this.[79]

When the writing went well Naomi was full of confidence. 'When the immediate strain of Carradale is taken off, I always feel very creative,' she commented in October 1941.[80] There were days when interruption was particularly frustrating.

> I dug in and wrote my book through all the interruptions in the morning, the difficulty being that I still want desperately to go on writing! And it takes a time to work up. But I couldn't go on because there were a lot of chores, and Mr Thomson from the Agricultural College turned up...[81]

But there were other times when, the adrenalin flowing, she would write into the night, even though she knew she would pay for it with nightmares and 'feeling rotten' the next day. But always the relationship with Denny M. weighed in the balance of the book's progress. 'I tried to get on with my book, but it jammed. I wish either of my Highlanders would come, and un-jam it. But neither Denny nor Duncan came.'[82]

It took over four years for Naomi to reach the end. She was writing the penultimate chapter and planning the last in February

1945, the war in its last phase, on the train to Cardiff to visit Denny and Ruth. But there remained much revision and rewriting to do, and it was another two years before the book was published. In Naomi's view, it received little publicity and did not sell well, although there were respectful reviews (not in the *New Statesman*, however) and it established in Scotland her reputation as an historical novelist. Naomi reflected later that the problem may have been that the book did not fit into any convenient category. She felt, nevertheless, that it was a valuable work, and emphasized the importance of the historical notes included at the end of the novel. These amplify the context of the action, and also explain the liberties she took with 'the facts', but although a genuine aid to the reader, they almost certainly contributed to the reticence of reviewers.[83]

The tradition of Scottish historical fiction is a long one: indeed, it was in this genre that a distinctively Scottish fiction was first put on the European map, through the novels of Walter Scott. *The Bull Calves* inevitably invites comparison with the work of Naomi's contemporary and friend Neil Gunn, whose novels have received much more attention, at least in Scotland. In some respects Naomi's has a greater clarity of purpose and expression, uncluttered by the highly-charged imagination which is such a feature of Gunn's dense style. Gunn is more concerned with place and character than with ideas. His intention is not to capture an historical watershed as *The Bull Calves* attempts, but to evoke a many-layered way of life. Nevertheless, his clotted prose is often less accessible than Naomi's straighter, less colourful and detailed approach. Naomi herself felt that she had caught an authentic Highland speech more successfully than Gunn: it was something that concerned them both. But they were mutually sympathetic, and corresponded for some time before they actually met, after the war. The contact helped Naomi to feel more a part of the Scottish cultural scene. The sympathy expanded to include an element of spirited and good-natured flirtation.

6

The Bull Calves was Naomi's first novel since *The Blood of the Martyrs*, and a re-confirmation of her creativity as well as a statement of faith in the future, just as another child would be. 'If I could start a baby now, during the worst time, and write a book as well, then it would be something won against the enemy. Also of course it would be a bit of a risk, but the kind of risk I should feel would be worth running. I want to be in danger, but not uselessly, not as a sight-see-er.'[84] Publishing a book was also a risk, an exposure of herself to critical comment. In the event, there was no pregnancy and a long gestation period for the book.

Her faith wavered, as did her sense of self-worth, but neither lapsed for long. The war may have diverted her energies in a number of exasperating ways, but it also offered the possibility of radical reconstruction without revolution – assuming, of course, that Hitler was defeated. Naomi never lost her horror of war, sharply intensified when Stephen Spring Rice, Margy's son, was lost when his submarine was torpedoed, and Jim MacKinven, the young son of neighbours, was killed in the Clydeside blitz of March 1941. News that Jim was missing sent her and other Carradale folk to Glasgow, where Jim's body was eventually dug out of the rubble by Denny Macintosh and Sandy Galbraith, also a Carradale fisherman. Later she took a tram out along Dumbarton Road – 'houses down, pouring over the road, and still smoking', people in the street looking 'incredibly strained and tired, grey-faced'.[85]

> A lot of buildings were burnt out, others badly cracked and unsafe, some completely smashed. Off the main road it was worse; here and there houses were being demolished, blasting going on sometimes, traffic being cleared, here a bridge being propped up, there a loudspeaker van telling people where to go for money or food. All windows gone everywhere … everywhere was the smell of plaster and burning, everywhere this incredible mess, everywhere people trailing about with a mattress or a bundle or a few pots and pans.[86]

A month earlier, Campbeltown had been bombed and the local procurator fiscal, Mr Stewart, killed. Carradale was unscathed, but not untouched by this direct contact with the blitz, which made a powerful impact not just on Naomi but on the community. (It is likely that it influenced Naomi's description of the mining accident in *The Bull Calves*.)

Jim MacKinven had visited Naomi at Carradale and she had encouraged his first attempts at writing poetry: 'You came on summer evenings/ With your head away in a cloud.'[87] He had played the piano at Ruth and Denny's wedding. He was one of several youngsters Naomi helped: Dick Galbraith, Denny Macintosh's nephew, was another, as was Christine, Dougie Campbell's daughter. Jemima MacLean she especially encouraged, and helped to persuade her parents to let her go to Glasgow to train as a nurse. The poem she wrote about Jim's death is elegiac rather than bitter, reflecting perhaps her own efforts to console his parents. Jim, like other Scot's boys who had died through violence or poverty or drowning at sea, was part of the river of Scotland's past. The last lines, 'However cruel the present,/ Nothing can hurt the past,' expressed something she must often have had occasion to say to herself and others.[88]

An erosion of the spirit was inevitable, the drabness, the nagging worries and the endless effort with meagre results were taking their toll as much as the loss and destruction. A visit to Jack in Harpenden, living in what Naomi perceived as communal squalor, provoked this comment: 'Will after-the-war mean this amount of grubby, mild but very discouraging, discomfort for everyone, and especially the women?'[89] From time to time she wondered with a certain wryness whether, when the revolution came, she would always have to wash her own dishes. But if she was sometimes disturbed at the possibility that socialism might bring a colourless levelling, her political resolve did not falter. She was critical of the Labour Party, initially because she felt it had too readily fallen in with capitalist militarism, later because of its lack of real concern for Scotland. This, Scotland's future and in particular the future of the Highlands, became the focus of her political interest.

She had supported the Nationalist candidate in the 1940 Argyll by-election. Subsequently, John MacCormick, William Power's agent, visited Carradale and Naomi often saw him and other Scottish Nationalists when she went to Glasgow. She had a high regard for MacCormick, and supported him in his initiation of the all-party Scottish Convention, launched in 1943. He was a clever man, sometimes too nimble to be easily followed, and this may have contributed to the Convention's eventual demise. Naomi's attendance at Scottish Convention meetings and participation on the Convention's education committee gave her opportunities to develop ideas about reconstruction. It had never been enough to write; she had already demonstrated her need to act and she also wanted a wider sphere than that offered by Carradale. The war concentrated that need. Plans to rebuild and to redirect political energies in Scotland were important for morale. The Scottish Convention was also good for Naomi's morale, as she felt confident of what she could contribute, and also that she was respected by those involved. If London did not take her seriously, here was an arena where she could operate quite independently and forge a role for herself.

Denny Macintosh shared her views, or appeared to, accompanying her to meetings in Glasgow. Dick, on the other hand, seemed distant from Scottish concerns, although he did play a part in a key local issue, the campaign for a new pier at Carradale which was gathering pace through 1942. He was much involved in research for the Beveridge Report, which was published in December of that year. Naomi was encouraged by the report, which provided a framework for what would become the welfare state, affirming the need for state provision of health and social security services.

Through 1942, Naomi's mood swung, affected by progress on the book, personal relationships, whether Carradale seemed kind or obstructive. Her own waywardness was partly a factor. At times she was determined to run the farm effectively and to be actively involved, taking her cattle into the ring at the market at Tarbert, haymaking, lifting potatoes in the rain and mud, carting dung: 'I rather like it, I feel completely like a farmer about it, think of it as fine and luscious: just as well as one gets all over dung...'[90] The need to put as much land as possible under crops strained resources. There were subsidies for ploughing up marginal land and to encourage increased production, but these brought a cascade of paperwork as well as the need for able-bodied workers. To help her, Naomi had three successive landgirls as well as the men she employed. She also tried to press offspring and visitors into service, not always with success.

The year 1942 began and ended badly. Its start saw Singapore falling to the Japanese. Germany again seemed poised for invasion. It was not until June, with the German invasion of Russia, which drew the immediate threat away from Britain, that there seemed some cause for optimism. But it also provoked guilt amongst Naomi and her associates as Russia bore the full brunt of the war. The losses as the Germans approached and then laid siege to Stalingrad were huge.

Naomi's periodic depressions intensified the relationship with Denny M., which continued to be close yet erratic. A diary entry in October frankly addresses part of the problem.

> There is something missing in our relationship. Possibly that comes of the intervention of the social conscience; when one is very tired and lonely one wants the short cut of love-making and if that is ruled out, and obviously we are socially right to rule it out, then things jam a bit.[91]

Interestingly, it is the *social* conscience that Naomi identifies as the controlling factor, not the moral conscience, which she, in any case, could not divorce from social relationships. Yet her concern to avoid hurting people, and her awareness of how easy it was to get hurt – for someone who took so many emotional risks she was herself extremely easily bruised – might be more readily associated with moral than with social scruples.

Carradale seemed also to have changed her relationship with Dick. Their spheres of existence were more distanced, and not only geographically, than ever before. He lived his life in London, at the political and cultural centre, and however genuine his interest in Carradale itself, the opportunity to shoot game on the estate remained a high priority. Although at times he helped with the accounts, for which Naomi had little patience, he remained remote from everyday activities. His involvement in the harbour campaign aggravated Naomi. It was important, as the fishermen respected him and he had political clout, but he was encroaching on territory that she had made her own.

> ... it's no good Dick and I trying to work together on this; we don't do things the same way and anyhow I'm so tired of always being the woman, the one who types things out and makes suggestions which may be accepted but aren't the main thing - I think this is all very wrong of me; one oughtn't to want recognition and all that.[92]

Wrong it may have been, but it was real, and characteristically Naomi did not attempt to disguise her resentment.

When Naomi was in the company of Dick and his political friends, she felt out of touch, and often distressed by political argument and gamesmanship. The couple wrote constantly to one another, as they had always done, and sometimes seemed to communicate better by letter. 'Dick and I discussing by letter and with great helpfulness all the things we never manage to say,' she recorded on 16 October.[93]

There were times when Naomi felt diminished and confined by Dick's rather patronizing view of Carradale activities and her own part in them. His role was a national one, hers local. But her vision was much more than local, and it was precisely the discussion of major issues and principles that she missed. Dick would insist on talking about 'herrings and horses' when Naomi wanted to 'get down to principles a bit': '... feeling passionately that I didn't care what happened in the way of tuppence extra on herring, all I wanted was revolution and the chance of killing people myself ... I feel like an eagle in a small cage.'[94] There were times when Naomi's need for violent expression echoed a current in Jack's personality.

Christmas 1942 was not altogether happy. Neither Murdoch nor Denny had been able to come home. Ruth and Denny had just had their first child, Su, and Naomi's feelings were ambivalent, pleasure at becoming a grandmother conflicting with reminders of the loss of her own baby and the diminishing possibilities of her conceiving again. In her usual open fashion she records her jealousy.

> I feel so shaken up about the baby. Odd to feel jealous of one's own daughter-in-law for having a daughter! One can always face and ultimately deal with, a straight emotional situation, but this isn't. And I can't let it show.[95]

Later, when Ruth was again pregnant, she and Su stayed for some time at Carradale and Naomi clearly enjoyed getting to know her granddaughter and looking after her. Su provided another outlet for her maternal interests and protectiveness.

On Christmas Day, she and Duncan kissed under the mistletoe. This prompted the following reflection in her diary:

> I wonder if I am normal for my age, or over polygamous. Difficult to get data. Most of my friends admit to romantic feelings, to deep affection, to love and distress, to deep emotions of various kinds, but not to this light and savage enjoyment ... I don't believe in promiscuity through the year; one hasn't time and it takes the mind off the things that matter, one's job and one's duty to one's neighbours. But at the life-giving seasons?[96]

This passage is full of clues to understanding Naomi. Her scientific curiosity is genuine, and works in partnership with her emotional recklessness. But that recklessness, she felt, had a place and a season. It couldn't be let loose all the time. For her the celebratory rituals of *The Corn King and the Spring Queen* were not confined to a distant past and an alien culture but were an integral part, or should be, of every human community. We can read this as a kind of justification for behaviour which of course Naomi knew was unorthodox and offensive to some people. It also reads as an honest, if perhaps self-conscious, assessment of her own particular needs, in the context of her understanding of the social and psychological functions of community patterns and rituals.

The urge to help, to champion victims and support worthwhile struggles, manifested itself in many ways. With so many people either staying at Carradale House or seeing it as a centre of their lives, it was impossible for Naomi to avoid getting drawn into personal worries and crises. When Dorothy Melville, an evacuee teacher who had arrived early in 1941, incurred the wrath of Mr Mackenzie, one of the local ministers, through her attempt to start a bible study class, Naomi leapt to her defence. A fierce quarrel with the Mackenzies, especially Mrs Mackenzie and Mr Mackenzie's sister, ensued, in which Naomi called the two women 'cowards and bullies' and they responded with a string of accusations levelled at both Dorothy and Naomi. Although Dorothy was extremely upset at this episode, Naomi clearly enjoyed the battle.

Love affairs, too, tended to attract her like a magnet, although she sometimes grumbled at the consequences. She was generous with advice – to Murdoch, for example, and his girlfriend Eleanor whom he brought to Carradale – though one can guess that it was not always welcome. Duncan Munro's complicated love life often received her attention. When her secretary Rosemary got involved with a married naval officer, Naomi was alternately supportive and irritated, but always concerned. War intensified all aspects of human relations, including Naomi's own responses to other peoples' problems.

Love was one answer to war. Naomi's maternalism can be detected in her adolescence, when she shepherded Jack and his friends in the performance of her plays, so the impulse was there before the First World War. But the experience of both wars increased and extended it. Her large family, her talent for friendship, her urge to encourage and help those less privileged than herself, can be understood as part of a deep-seated urge to counteract destruction with warmth and creativity. Although she often found the residents, permanent and temporary, at Carradale House difficult and emotionally wearing, her instinct was always to offer the security and care that she felt she and the house could provide. Among the recipients were many friends from the south, members of the forces based at Campbeltown who came for meals and dances, Young Communist League campers who borrowed books and sometimes helped in various household and garden tasks, and the Free French refugees. It was after the departure of Pierre and Gilbert, who had arrived thin and tense and left fatter and happier, that Naomi recorded:

> I feel the same passionate tenderness towards them that I feel towards Murdoch and Val and sometimes the fishermen, this longing to protect. No doubt it is partly sexual, why not? I wouldn't feel this way if I wasn't a woman ... It's also that one has to throw a hell of a lot of love into the balance as against what has been done to them. And unfortunately one can't, being human and limited in time, do it for more than a tiny minority of hurt people. I suppose if one thought one could do it for everybody, by being crucified or whatnot, one would. I suppose the pain I feel now, which is bloody real, is what I am trying to buy them with.[97]

She took the pain of others upon herself. Tied in with this was a sense of *noblesse oblige*, of creating relationships (which figure in her novels) where the bond depends on the ability of one to give and the other to receive. When Dougie Campbell helped with the potato harvest and refused payment, she wished that he was in her employment. 'I would like him to be my man, I would like to defend him and help him and show him beautiful things.'[98] In such a relationship, the receiver's acceptance is a response to the giver's need to give. At the same time, many of Naomi's relationships are flavoured with what one can only describe as benevolent paternalism.

The one-to-one rapport was only part of the story, part of the structure of 'living in good relationship'. Individual relations were the bricks out of which a more communal intimacy and sharing could be built. This is a theme that runs through almost everything that Naomi wrote. The search for harmony is reflected in most aspects of her life. 'I like any of the kinds of basic sharing,' she wrote in April 1941, 'work or food or bed (no doubt).'[99] It was both a personal and a political search, and she was most likely to find what she was seeking if she could weave the two together. She had clearly tried to do this in her relationship with John Pilley, but the balance seemed skewed by his left-wing orthodoxy. At Carradale, the distorting factor was, inevitably, class and the hangover of feudalism. Nevertheless, there were occasions when, if only momentarily, Naomi found what she sought. Having tea with Denny and Lilla Macintosh in January 1942 she sat on the floor making toast, 'and thought there was a feeling of agape, of eating-together, of atonement'.[100] Agape is a key word in Naomi's vocabulary, and she uses it in both its meanings, as a sharing, generous, unerotic love, and specifically as a communal meal taken in a spirit of love, mutuality and commemoration, like those of the early Christian church which she describes in *The Blood of the Martyrs*.

A few months later, at an impromptu ceilidh following a planning session on the new harbour, she experienced an affectionate bonding with her three Carradale men, 'the three men I like best in the world to dance with, Denny, Duncan and Dougie, all at once and all sober'. She added, 'what pleasure can be greater than that, when one has been working a day's darg [work] before?'[101] In September, she was in Glasgow for a Scottish Convention meeting, with Denny and Dougie. Away from Carradale there was a certain liberation. The three of them celebrated their 'very odd friendship', lying on a hotel bed together exchanging confidences, Naomi feeling they were 'closer than if they'd had my body, and that this wasn't really what they wanted from me'. Although at times Naomi could be almost childlike in her determination to match circumstances to her requirements, on this occasion she was aware of the fine line she was treading:

...none of us had taken anything from the others that should not have been taken or might have hurt anyone else; but we had been in such a state of love and trust, and both of them had got away from themselves as they might never have done otherwise. Yet I knew I must be careful, for I wasn't sure where the border lay between agape and eros, and one might get addicted to this; for surely there is nothing one cannot do too much or too often except pure contemplation of ultimate reality.[102]

On this occasion, Naomi succeeded in weaving together the political and personal. At other times, she experienced deep satisfaction at the physical harmony which shared work could bring, especially when a class or wage relationship did not intrude.

7

Gradually the tide of war turned. The Soviet Union held its own at Stalingrad and then drove the Germans back. In Britain, there were mounting calls for a second front. At last, on 6 June 1944, Allied troops landed in France. That day, Naomi 'went about ... in three layers of consciousness, partly fidgeting about this, and being so remote and out of it'. Germany retaliated with flying bombs, V1s ('doodlebugs') and then V2s, subjecting London to another blitz. Naomi worried about Dick, Denny and Ruth, now living in River Court, and her London friends. She recalls an occasion when she was at River Court and Denny, discovering an unexploded bomb lodged upstairs, threw it out of the window.[103] The Coles' home was damaged by a doodlebug, bringing the ceiling down on their son Humphrey. In spite of this, there was a growing feeling that the war would soon be over. Naomi and Val, home for the school holidays, began to use up some of the hoarded tins of food. When Naomi was in London in November, doing her usual round of visits to children and friends, the bombs were still falling: 'I was more or less frightened almost all the time, except perhaps immediately after a bang when one felt at least that one hadn't been hit.'[104]

Increasingly, reconstruction and the possibilities for Scotland after the war took up Naomi's attention. In particular, she concerned herself with fishing, forestry and education. She edited and contributed to a Scottish Convention publication on *Re-educating Scotland* (1944). It expresses the view that education in Scotland was too narrow in approach. It called for more nursery schools, more and better school buildings, smaller classes and a wider curriculum. Naomi believed that many people she knew in Carradale would have benefited greatly from better and more appropriate educational opportunities and did her best for those she thought she could help, lending books, giving Dougie's daughter Christine French lessons, campaigning for more adequate transport to Campbeltown to get children to the only secondary school, or, as she did for Jemima MacLean, persuading reluctant parents to allow their children to pursue education and training away from Carradale.

Fishing and forestry were the dominant local concerns. For much of the war the herring fishery was more profitable than it had ever been, with government subsidies dramatically increasing the price fishermen received. The Carradale men operated with fairly well-equipped boats, ring-net fishing mainly in Kilbrannan Sound but sometimes venturing further afield. But they were heavily dependent on the middle-men who bought the fish at the quayside. The government encouraged the herring fishery but sometimes there was little demand for the catch, and it was dumped. Naomi felt that it should be possible to organize a co-operative which could sell direct. The scheme for a new harbour at Carradale was, she believed, crucial to the community's future. Throughout the war, the Carradale fleet had to put in at Tarbert, Campbeltown or Ayr to sell their catch. She also dreamt of having a share in a boat, with Denny Macintosh and others. On forestry, too, she had strong views. This she saw as vital to Carradale's and Kintyre's future, but it needed to be run with some concern for the needs of the forestry workers and their families and an understanding of the nurture of trees.

On the broader political front, there was Dick's future to think of. He still had parliamentary ambitions, and was selected as Labour candidate for Kettering. Then Naomi herself was asked if she would be interested in standing for one of the two Dundee constituencies. It was a difficult decision to make, but she said no, because she felt she should support Dick in his campaign. She also realized the problems that would arise if she got in and Dick did not: both the Dundee constituencies were safe seats, Kettering was not. However strongly she wished to be taken more seriously in the political arena, and however unappreciated she sometimes felt, she had in fact achieved more distinction in her own fields than Dick in his. Dick badly needed a role. The war had given him one, but he was depressed at the prospect of this role coming to an end. Naomi recognized that his need to make a useful contribution to public life crucially affected both his well-being and their relationship. She reluctantly closed the door on the possibility of a national political identity for herself.

The war had also led Dick's personal life to diverge from Naomi's. Although the Coles came often to Carradale, and Margaret was as close a friend to Naomi as to Dick, his relationship with Tish Rokeling was more separate. Tish, her daughter and then her granddaughter were all involved with the family, but there is no suggestion that Naomi was a personal friend to Tish, or that she influenced Dick's relationship with her, as she clearly had done with both Margy Spring Rice and Margaret Cole. This may have made it harder for Naomi to accept that Dick's life in London had, in one respect at least, areas that she hardly entered. Lois and Val certainly felt that their father's involvement with Tish caused difficulties for them. They remember occasions when the door was closed to them because Tish was with Dick, and they walked around London until the coast was clear.[105]

Naomi continued to participate in the work of the Scottish Convention, and wrote articles for *Forward*, a socialist paper edited during the war by Emrys Hughes, who became Labour MP for South Ayrshire in 1946. It was clear that, whatever else happened, political activity would remain an important strand in her life. *The*

Bull Calves was all but finished, but there was plenty of material stored in her mind for more books. When the war and all its accompanying demands were over and the general election that followed it out of the way, she was released to write, and there followed a prolific period. The children were growing up and moving away. Val was fifteen, Lois had won a scholarship to Oxford, and Avrion was working temporarily in his uncle's laboratory. A grandmother again – Ruth and Denny's second child Graeme had been born in Glasgow – Naomi would have no more children of her own.

Victory in Europe was declared on 8 May 1945. Naomi had travelled overnight to London. Her diary description of VE day is rather subdued, as if she were deeply tired. She and Dick, with Av and Val, spent much of the day wandering around London. Jack, his colleague and future second wife Helen Spurway (he and Charlotte were divorced in 1945), and Denny joined them for dinner at the White Tower, a Greek restaurant in Soho. Later, back in Hammersmith, Naomi danced a reel with a drunken Glaswegian sergeant. The night ended on the roof at River Court, with 'the searchlights whirling round and reflected beautifully in the river'.[106]

On 25 July 1945 Naomi flew from Campbeltown to Renfrew on the flimsy 'silver paper' plane that was now so familiar to herself and Dick and many of the wartime visitors to Carradale House.[107] She looked down at extraordinary cloud effects.

> It was so beautiful that I can never quite forget it; I kept on thinking about it all the time. It was an immense glittering alpine landscape with solid cliffs and hills that were so obviously snow that the slightest movement in them was snow shifting. We went smoothly, not on wings; I kept on wishing it would stop and let me walk; I kept on thinking there must be edelweiss or some such things, scrub brick perhaps, below the top level of snow. At the edges of the immense plain there was a rift and an ice-blue river or glacier. I thought that beyond that again I could see spires and battlements, or at least that

they were beyond the next ridge. It was astonishing and shocking when it suddenly opened below our feet and there was a small green and brown world, not noble and empty and glittering but full of things, crawling, an underworld. And a patch of sunlight on it.[108]

Unwittingly, in recording this experience, Naomi was creating a picture that could stand as a metaphor for her own life and its mixture of vivid idealism and practicality. For the next fifteen years or so she devoted most of her energies to this 'small green and brown world', moving beyond Carradale itself to the county of Argyll, working in it, trying to improve it, writing about it.

CHAPTER SIX

Highlands and Islands

Aware how things should be,
Not how to make them so.

The Cleansing of the Knife

1

W ITH THE war not yet over, and the buzz bombs falling on
London, Naomi attended a Labour conference at the Caxton
Hall in Westminster. 'I was sitting in the balcony and kept thinking
that if one landed in the middle of the hall it would take out all the
Labour Party leadership; it was in some ways an exhilarating idea.'[1]
This remark is a typical piece of Mitchison mischief, but it also
contains a clue as to the way her mind was working. What would it
be like to start completely afresh in politics? What would be the
effect of a line-up of entirely new faces, new ideas, new talent? But
for all her impatience with the Labour Party, her socialism was not
eroded. She had written to Tom Harrisson towards the end of 1944
that she was 'a keener socialist than ever I was. In fact, I doubt if
anything short of revolution is going to give the country folk the
kick in the pants which they definitely want, or rather need.'[2]

A general election came in July 1945. Naomi's political
ambivalence was the result not of doubt, but of impatience with

practicalities and people. However, she recognized the importance to Dick of parliamentary politics, and having made her choice, to forego national politics herself and support Dick's fight for Kettering, Naomi threw herself into the campaign with her customary vigour. Kettering needed her: 'surely I had to throw my not inconsiderable weight – I was a good public speaker by this time – into a Labour victory for Kettering'.[3]

Kettering was a pleasant market town with some light industry, including shoe-making and the Co-op corset factory. The constituency also included Corby, where Stewarts and Lloyds steelworks had moved from the Clyde, taking their Scottish work-force with them. It was a marginal seat, which was perhaps why the BBC decided to film the campaign, the film unit causing some disruption as they pursued candidates and their workers. Naomi stayed in Kettering for the duration. Her own beliefs were straightforward.

> I believed strongly in the simple case for a reasonable society in which liberty, equality and above all fraternity were genuine ideals, towards which we could all work and which seemed almost attainable...[4]

But she had problems adjusting to the narrow conformity of small-town socialism. She conceded a wedding ring, but refused to wear a hat. Years later, a Communist supporter told her that 'he had watched the Labour candidate going by in a city suit with an umbrella and briefcase but after him a "gipsy" with a scarf over her head and a bright striped shirt... who was eating chips out of a bag'.[5] She may have frightened off the more conventional but it seems she mitigated Dick's rather establishment image with the more radical sections of the electorate.

She was an old hand at electioneering, having served her apprenticeship at King's Norton: 'canvassing, envelope addressing and general amiability were no bother for me, nor yet writing bits of printed matter which blew in the wind and collected in gutters.[6] She did some speaking herself, and drove others round the countryside to address meetings with audiences varying from a few dozen to several hundred: 'occasionally we would stop at some rural crossroads and address a few cows'.[7] She clearly relished the campaign, the contact with people, the current of action.

> Remember, there was no telly nor yet even local radio. People had to bestir themselves to take an interest, but once tea was over and washed up the meetings were a good way to pass the time, so people told me. The last day was a tremendous build up to the eve of poll meetings which were where nearby candidates swapped appearances with one another and broke the speed limit between halls. There were usually enjoyable rows going on, often leading to fisticuffs but nobody was ever really hurt.[8]

After the long wait to gather in and count the Forces' votes, which took three weeks, Naomi and Dick learned that the country had voted in a Labour government and that Kettering had returned Dick as their MP. Naomi's ambivalence about orthodox Labour politics inevitably affected her role as an MP's wife. Although supportive of Dick and committed to his political career, she was herself both a deeply political animal and resistant to conventional expectations. It was clear that she needed a political role of her own, and that she could do nothing for Dick that involved wearing a hat. Dick's career as a Labour MP did not progress as he and Naomi hoped. His alliance with the left wing of the Party was a barrier to office, and having a wife who did not hesitate to speak her mind and lobby for her own adopted causes was hardly an asset. Although she had been able to forego the opportunity to stand for parliament, preserving a strategic silence, particularly on Scottish and later African issues, was contrary to her nature.

Naomi spent more time in London, though Carradale remained her base and by this time she was firmly identifying herself as a Scot. River Court was sold, and much of its contents taken north, as clear a sign as any of where Naomi saw her future. She had never really lived in River Court since she had written her poem 'The house on the Mall' in 1940, when windows broken by bombs suggested that something had come to an end.

> *... it's odd how memories accumulate*
> *Round a bath-tub or a gas fire, let alone*
> *A nursery fire.*
> *That piece of life is ended.*[9]

The piece of life that had ended was more than a change of environment. She was nearly fifty. Everything that River Court represented was over. There was no need for a nursery fire. The ancient world no longer commanded her imagination, although she would return to it again on occasion. Life with Dick had metamorphosed. The centre held, but Naomi's commitments were increasingly distant from his, and her nomadism took her all over the world while now Dick was pinned to Westminster.

He moved into a flat in the Temple, but it was never home for Naomi in the same way as River Court or Carradale, although she did her duty as an MP's wife and entertained Dick's colleagues and fellow politicians. 'We had very simple food and red or white wine but lots of talk and a mixture of ages.'[10] Later, she was inviting her own contacts, students from India and Africa. Dick, as always, was kind and welcoming, but not always clear who his guests were.

Back in Carradale there were visitors too, not only the old friends and regulars, but new faces, who were equally likely to be pressed into service, haymaking or weeding. Westminster colleagues of Dick's were often invited. Louise Annand, who made her first visit to Carradale at about this time, recalled, 'I think Naomi invited some of them quite deliberately without too much in the way of correct instructions about how to get there, so they realized the difficulties of living in the west of Scotland, the hard way.'[11] Louise Annand was there to work on the illustrations for *The Bull Calves*. She found a house full of people to whom she was not introduced, and was at first disconcerted by the informality and the problem of identifying members of the family and distinguished guests. Mitchison hospitality was heartfelt but haphazard.

In August it was likely that both Dick and Naomi would be at Carradale. During the day, when not out on the hill (Dick) or on farm business (Naomi), the two might be found at their desks in different windows of the drawing-room. Offspring and visitors wandered in and out, read, talked: Naomi never lost her preference for working in the thick of things. In the evening, Dick dispensed his favourite single malt whisky, not always easy to come by in the years after the war. Guests assembled for dinner at the long table in the dining-room, Dick at one end, Naomi at the other. The conversation flowed, *badinage* mixed with political argument. After dinner, the aroma of cigars drifted through the house.

Even as Naomi was declining to stand for Dundee, she was formulating a plan to participate in local politics. It was a natural step for her to take: she had steeped herself so thoroughly in local issues and knew she had the courage of her convictions. She needed a forum, a sphere of influence that was more than the ambivalent territory of her relationship with Carradale. She needed an activity to balance Dick's Westminster preoccupations, and to provide an outlet for her raised consciousness of Scotland. Through the war she had continued her involvement with the Scottish Convention, in spite of some reservations. She wrote to Compton Mackenzie that it was dull, but worthwhile: 'it doesn't matter what it is so long as it wakes people up. And it is doing that.'[12] But she wanted a more active role, and so decided to stand for Kintyre East in the County Council elections, in which she was successful. At this time, local elections in the country constituencies were non-party political (only the burgh candidates stood for a political party) which almost certainly helped Naomi, whose particular blend of socialism and nationalism was likely to make the orthodox in each camp uncomfortable.

She relished the challenge of 'getting things done'. Her great ally was John MacNaughton, an engine driver based in Oban and convenor of the Council's Education Committee. 'He and I and Jack Reid [an aluminium worker from Kinlochleven] would go off together for tea, planning how we were going to work together on some County Council ploy.'[13] A strong friendship developed between John and Naomi. Just as she liked to demonstrate that she had practical skills and did not shrink from getting her hands dirty, she was drawn to practical men. Part of the attraction of the men of Carradale was their work as fishermen, foresters and farmers. Part of the attraction of John MacNaughton was the fact that he drove a huge steam locomotive: 'he would look down at me from the cab of his engine like a giant'.[14]

Over and over again Naomi records the satisfaction she got from hard, physical work. She was not an arms-length farmer. She prided herself in her ability to drive a tractor or shape a haystack – this comes through vividly in the pieces she wrote regularly for the *New Statesman* throughout the 1950s. Equally, she was not an arms-length politician. Council work took up a great deal of time and was often frustrating. Her feeling that what could be achieved by elected representatives was minimal did not deter her from trying, especially in the areas of education and transport. Gradually she got to grips with issues and problems, and sat through interminable council meetings, dominated, of course, by men.

> ...a great many of the meetings were deadly boring except perhaps for the few who had special axes to grind. There was always a lunch break; most councillors went to the nearest hotel for a drink at the bar and then soup, meat and two veg, pudding and tea. Naturally they had to sleep it off in the afternoon session.[15]

As a woman, Naomi was an uncomfortable presence at clubby gatherings in the bar, and tended to avoid them. Her natural allies were those who felt excluded for different reasons such as class.

Her political activities were instinctive and emotional. At their base lay her own vision of community, but she was not necessarily prepared to play the political games that were sometimes necessary. When she did, she played them her own way. But often she felt, as she confessed in a letter to her friend Bettie Baxter, 'our local politics are horrid'.[16] Although she knew she was not sufficiently hard-headed, or hard-hearted, there is no suggestion of regret when she wrote to Tom Harrisson, 'I am afraid I am completely feminine, Tom, I do nothing from the head, everything from the heart.'[17] The horridness of local politics was particularly brought home to her when she failed to be re-elected in 1948. Bad weather prevented the fishermen, her main supporters, from getting back in time to vote. She found it hard to forgive them, or a system that allowed this kind of disenfranchisement. But three years later she was back on the Council.

She counted three significant achievements from her nearly twenty years as a councillor. One was preventing the use of herbicides on grass verges; another was championing a Mull family who had taken their children out of school. But the most notable and lasting was her initiation in Argyll of a school picture scheme. Naomi was concerned that visual education was being neglected, and proposed that the Council should buy contemporary paintings, thus supporting Scottish artists, and loan them to schools. She was given £100 to get the scheme going, and raised additional money by writing round to 'such Argyll lairds as I knew or knew about and got £5 here and £10 there'.[18] She also went to the Gulbenkian Fund, which agreed to support the project. She then set out to acquire pictures, going to shows, visiting artists. Amongst the early pictures she bought for the scheme were two by Joan Eardley, who had set up her studio in Glasgow in 1949, for £50. Other artists included Robin Phillipson, Ann Redpath and William McTaggart. Jim Tyre was recruited to go round the schools with the pictures, not just to put them on walls but to encourage a response and stimulate artwork. It was a demanding task, as many of the schools were remote. Pictures went to primary schools for a month, and to secondaries for a term. For many, children and adults, this was their only opportunity to see original paintings and sculpture. Although this was not an entirely innovatory scheme – Naomi herself had been impressed by a similar project in Yorkshire, and Dr Honeyman in Glasgow had been operating a neighbourhood scheme, taking small exhibitions to schools and other centres – it was a significant acknowledgement of the needs of remote communities.

The picture scheme was an important venture, both for the schools and for Naomi. It was another way that she could make a contribution, have a role in her adopted community, and strengthen her Scottish credentials. She kept in contact with the scheme long after she ceased to be directly involved. But generally the County Council was limited in the opportunities it offered for political or educational effectiveness. More rewarding, though in many ways just as frustrating, was Naomi's work on the Advisory Panel on the Highlands and Islands.

2

Naomi and John MacNaughton were nominated to represent Argyll, one of the crofting counties, on the newly constituted Advisory Panel on the Highlands and Islands, which soon became known as the Highland Panel. It had grown out of the Hillary Report, an attempt to set the agenda for post-war Highland development. The Panel included each of the Highland MPs, seven of them, and representatives from the councils of all the crofting counties. The political flavour was traditional Tory, with a sprinkling of more radical voices. The secretariat was provided by Scottish Office.

> Looking back on the Highland Panel days I find myself wondering whether the Panel itself was designed by the politicians of the time - the Labour Government - ably assisted by their civil servants, as something which would look as though it was a big step towards helping the Highlands. However as it had no power and no money it would be totally unable to achieve anything and so would not in the end bother anybody. It would be simply advisory and would be designed only to give a push to plans already being formulated by the Scottish Office.[19]

No power and no money: certainly, the Highland Panel had no

executive role, but it was a wonderful opportunity for Naomi to pursue some of her ideas on Highland development and to feel she was actively engaged in post-war regeneration. It also allowed her to add to her experience, and to her knowledge of the Highlands and the north of Scotland, from the Mull of Kintyre to Shetland. And the panel was not altogether emasculated. She goes on, 'It did in fact manage to get a few things done which might not have been done otherwise and drag quite a lot into the light.' She herself, she adds, was one of those who 'dragged things into the light and nagged people'. On several occasions she was knocking on doors at St Andrews House and would even resort to tears: 'but I never went into tears twice on the same floor of the Scottish Office'.[20]

In the early years of the Highland Panel, which began life in 1947, hopes were high. Its primary concern was with economic regeneration, and the industrial development and the infrastructure, especially transport, essential for it. Naomi frequently articulated her views, in reports and memos, drawing on her decade of Highland experience, building on ideas that she had been pondering over recent years. On the question of forestry, for example, she had been agitating in a private capacity for some time. In a letter to the *New Statesman* of December 1944, she had voiced her criticism of the Forestry Commission, too hierarchical in structure and not sufficiently integrated in its approach.

> State-owned forests democratically run might be a splendid thing; afforestation employs more men than sheep-runs do – far more of course than the same area of deer forest. If forest industries were to be encouraged, still more could be employed, including women. But that would mean a different outlook in the Forestry Commission.[21]

She saw able Carradale men denied promotion, without the educational opportunities that might open doors, and the area without the infrastructure needed to sustain communities – which would, in their turn, benefit the Highland economy. Fourteen years later she was expanding on the same theme at a Highland Panel meeting. Her view was that 'regard would have to be paid to moral considerations as well as economic factors. They would have to ask themselves what was the good life and if its attainment was possible in viable agricultural holdings which would make for a happy and creative population.'[22] And later, in a memo of 1960: 'What is our object in any Highland policy? Presumably to get the maximum satisfaction out of the land: both in production and in human happiness.'[23]

It was clear that Naomi's main concern was with people, and there were times when this kind of sentiment was out of tune with the tenor of debate. John Gibson, who was secretary to the Panel from 1955, remembers an occasion on North Uist when members were 'deep in discussion about the possibilities for vehicle ferries'. Naomi came in late, having been walking on Vallay strand. 'It was a June night, absolutely heavenly. And she came in, in a complete state of poetry about it, and was unable to get to grips with the hard, flinty discussion.' Yet Naomi's susceptibility to poetry and concern with people was her main asset. She reminded the Panel 'that they were dealing with people's lives, not just the economy'.[24] More practically, her particular talent was as a mediator, reconciling local perceptions with broader needs, helping communities to see how their requirements fitted, or in some cases did not fit, with strategies for development.

Something of her style is illustrated in her comments on the *West Highland Survey* put together by Fraser Darling in 1950. She was impatient for action.

> The Highland Panel has done enough observing. We have all been on various groups and seen a good deal. Many of our preconceived ideas have been knocked sideways by real life.[25]

And she goes on to suggest that the Panel should tackle some of the most difficult areas: 'If we can do anything with them the rest will not be so hard.'[26] She proposes a strategy that was clearly impractical, but just as clearly full of sense. A group of men and women should examine closely one particular place – she suggests an area of 100 square miles – seeing everyone living there, and making recommendations 'in relation to the whole community'. 'The people who do this must be devoted,' she went on. 'They must have a vocation. They must not be hankering for the desk and the tea-cups all the time.'[27] Her idealism was sometimes expressed in rather more blunt terms. J.A. Ford, Scottish Office assessor, remembers a meeting in Stornoway in which Naomi was getting carried away with ideas for expanding agriculture and forestry. He pointed out there was a limited amount of money in the till. 'Fuck the till,' was Naomi's rejoinder.[28]

The Panel seems to have tolerated (and quietly ignored) Naomi's more idiosyncratic notions. But there was a measure of general consensus. Whether driven by human or economic motives, Panel members were united in their view that the overriding need of the Highlands was population. In the past, efforts had been made to repopulate destitute areas, through land settlement programmes intended to provide crofts and give crofters a stake in agricultural development. Naomi had strong views on the repopulation issue, and on the provisions and responsibilities that it involved. Typically, she championed the unsuccessful Knoydart land raid, an attempt to replicate the land raids of 1920 on Skye and along the west coast, which had led to estates being divided amongst crofters. But the mood and the economic realities were different.

She argued consistently, in memos and reports as well as at meetings, that Highland survival depended on there being not only jobs but amenities, not only economic investment but social and cultural investment. If youngsters were to be encouraged to see their future in farming and forestry, it should be possible for them to receive their training locally. If a rural community was not to see the younger generation irresistibly drawn by the temptations of towns, it must itself provide some of the town's attractions. She had campaigned successfully for a village hall in Carradale, and seen it put on plays and ceilidhs and show films. She now launched herself into a campaign for village halls throughout the Highlands, with a missionary zeal equal to anything that resistant ministers could supply. It was uphill work.

In her novel *Lobsters on the Agenda* (1952), Naomi captures the conjunction of the Highland Panel's endeavours and a small west coast fishing community. The novel is a striking vignette of a Highland village, aware of its losses – "'In the old days Highland people would come together for work, to build a house it might be, or to cut peats, and they would come together at nights for a ceilidh. But now it's all past'" – and uncertain about the future – "'we've somehow got to find some way of holding together, or – or we're clean done'".[29] The community's concerns, about transport, about employment and leisure, are focused by a visit from the Highland Panel, amongst whom is Mrs Mitchison herself, 'a woman with a dark handkerchief over her head and her hands deep in the pockets of a huge old leather coat ... short and solid ... [with] knitted stockings and heavy shoes'.[30] The Panel, it is explained, is there 'to get the feeling of everything that needed done in the Highlands'[31] though the main object of the visit is to look at the harbour and assess the needs of the fishermen.

The central consciousness is that of Kate Snow, a doctor, war widow and county councillor, through whose eyes Naomi reveals a divided community. A village meeting votes in favour of a village hall, but a powerful church faction is against it, seeing it as an invitation to licentious behaviour. The fictional Mrs Mitchison encounters the opposition, which prompts her comment to Kate: "'I'm allergic to Ministers.'"[32] This 'allergy' had led Naomi into a number of confrontational situations, not least in Stornoway on the island of Lewis, where John Gibson remembers she was more incensed at the Presbyterian attitude to village halls than at any difficulties encountered over harbours, transport and the fishing industry – issues that were all dear to her heart.

The portrait of a Highland community, its people and its divisions, its often obstructive traditionalism yet concern that opportunities may pass it by, is both sharply observed and affectionate. When Kate wonders, 'Was there ever going to be ordinary, peacetime expenditure in the Highlands? Bridges and harbours and all that. Or would there always be some excuse?'[33] the voice of Naomi's own experience is clear, though it is gentler than its expression elsewhere. The novel ends on a note of quiet optimism, and an assertion of the value of collective will. This certainly reflected Naomi's aspirations, but veils the frustrations of local politics.

The Highland Panel had no teeth, yet, though she cursed at times and wept at times, she stuck with it. And not only that: she brought a sense of fun as well as commitment. John Gibson remembered the occasion on which he first met Naomi, joining the Panel on a trip to the Western Isles. With them on the boat from Oban was a group of Free Presbyterian ministers from Lewis who had come to meet a colleague who had been a missionary in Peru. In his long absence he had grown unaccustomed to the Minch weather, which proved too much for him and he had to make a sudden exit from the lounge, accompanied by a companion. Shortly afterwards the companion returned, saying, 'Wasn't it a terrible thing, he comes all the way from Peru to lose his teeth in the Minch!' John Gibson added, 'This was the kind of thing Naomi adored.'[34]

Naomi found various ways of enlivening proceedings. At one meeting she passed the time writing additional verses to Louis MacNeice's poem 'Bagpipe Music' and passed them surreptitiously to John Gibson, probably the only member of the panel who would appreciate her efforts. Yet, in spite of boredom and frustration, Naomi's commitment did not flag. She rarely missed the bi-monthly meetings, usually in Inverness, and continued to reiterate her views, however apparent it was that expediency and what she considered to be narrow-minded bureaucracy obstructed them. She stayed with the panel until its demise in 1965, when it gave way before the Highlands and Islands Development Board. In the early days, she had written to Bettie Baxter in the same vein as she had complained about Argyll County Council. 'The Highland Panel is rather hell as we are never allowed to do anything.'[35] Over her eighteen years with the Panel, things did not change a great deal. But she had learned useful lessons, and by 1965 she had identified another arena for her commitment, which would provide her with a more satisfying outlet for 'getting things done'. She transferred her energies to the urgent needs of an often overlooked southern African country about to embark on independence.

3

The Panel was not, of course, Naomi's only area of energetic activity. In 1949, she fulfilled her dream to own a fishing boat when she and Denny Macintosh together bought the *Maid of Morvern*, a fifty-one foot, Eyemouth-built boat equipped with 120 horse-power engine, echo sounder and radio. Naomi and Denny brought the boat from east to west coast through the Forth and Clyde Canal, so little used that they had to struggle to open the jammed sluices in the locks. They did not know it, but the herring fishing industry was entering hard times. After the boom years of the war, when price controls had ensured a decent return for the fishermen's labour, there was a deterioration. In 1939, there had been 120 men of the parish of Saddell, which included Carradale, occupied in fishing, running twenty-four boats. By 1955, there were only fourteen boats, and less than a hundred men. (Naomi records that at this time there were sixty Carradale men working on the boats.[36]) There was a host of difficulties, among which the inadequacy of the pier at Carradale and marketing arrangements which left the fishermen at the mercy of middle-men loomed large. After the war, the speed of change accelerated, sometimes leaving behind men who had spent decades, their entire lives, at fishing. Naomi felt that Denny himself was 'not modern enough, and not I think good enough on machinery'.[37]

The days of plenty had not lasted long, and often the boat's catch was sold off cheap for fishmeal. The return was hardly worth the effort.

> The boat's receipts are divided up, week by week, one share for each fisherman, four for the boat. As part-owner of a boat I get my divide, one and a third of a working-share, in grimy, purplish Clyde Bank notes, shillings and pennies. It may be

nothing; it may be £10 or more. But what's the good? Back it has
to go into insurance, engine repair, replacement of nets, hire
of radio equipment, paper for echo sounders.[38]

At the Highland Panel meeting of December 1958, Naomi reported
'genuine hardship among the Campbeltown and Carradale
fishermen' and said that they were 'apprehensive' of the Herring
Industry Board.[39] The Board was based in Edinburgh, at a distance
from the fishing communities whose work – and, inevitably, lives –
it attempted to regulate. It was the Herring Board which provided
the loan for Naomi and Denny to buy their boat, and the Herring
Board that foreclosed eight years later, leaving Denny 'pennyless'
and Naomi angry. 'We had to go to Edinburgh and sign things. I was
very, very upset and sat on the cold stones and wept like a pig.'[40] And
in a letter to Bettie Baxter she wrote:

> The Herring Industry Board forclosed [sic] on the boat and it
> is gone. I felt it was very unfair, as the secretary would not
> listen to anything we said and obviously disbelieved us. In fact
> I suppose it was quite good for me to be treated as an
> under-dog, but I can't bear the idea that he is getting away with
> doing this to the fishermen.[41]

The problem of the pier was more happily resolved, although at
first the proposal was turned down and it took many years of
relentless persuasion to get it built. When the Mitchisons came to
Carradale, the pier was both in a state of disintegration and not
capable of taking the larger vessels on which the fishing industry
was increasingly dependent. A proper harbour was needed. Naomi
and Dick both embraced this cause early in their Carradale
residence. 'The harbour may go through, but if the fishermen can
contribute so that we need only ask for 90% grant, then it's more
likely to happen,' Naomi wrote in her diary entry for 27 June 1942.[42]
It was a genuinely collective effort, with the community
contributing to a harbour fund – the estimated cost was £30,000 –
and Naomi representing their interests, on both the County Council
and the Highland Panel. At last, plans were approved and public

funds were granted, but it was September 1959 before the new harbour was opened by Tom Johnstone, who had been Secretary of State for Scotland during the war. Although the herring fishing has all but gone, the harbour is still in active use, by boats fishing now for prawns and scallops. Naomi's contribution to the survival of a fishing community is quietly acknowledged in the buckets of fish that are left at the back door of Carradale House.

For Naomi, the fishing was serious. Although she was certainly regarded with some scepticism by the fishermen, at least initially, she proved herself, not only sharing their work but determined to get a real understanding of what was going on. Her impressive poem 'The *Alban* goes out' demonstrates this. In 1950, *Men and Herring* was published, described as a 'documentary' and written jointly with Denis Macintosh. In it, ring-net fishing is described in some detail – the net a hundred fathoms long and twenty deep, towed between two boats, whose symbiotic relationship is so vividly portrayed in 'The *Alban* goes out'. *Men and Herring* is rich in descriptive detail, anecdotal, capturing the same rhythms as the poem, and laced with the fishermen's backchat and banter. It deals not only with the fishing itself, but the selling of the fish at the quayside at Tarbert – some fresh, some to be kippered, some to be tinned, dependent on the buyer who samples and assesses the quality. And at the end of it all, the reckoning up and the division of the slender return after the deduction of expenses.

Much of this is distilled into the play *Spindrift* Naomi and Denny also jointly wrote, which presented the same world and featured a boat for which the *Maid of Morvern* was clearly the model. The play was produced at Glasgow's Citizen's Theatre in 1951, to some acclaim. It chronicles the fortunes of a boat and its crew and a small fishing community from 1938, when prospects were gloomy, to the years of success immediately after the war. On the page, the language and speech rhythms give the play a rich authenticity. The poetic, almost ritualistic, cadences are captured in this exchange between the fishermen.

ROB You get terrible fond of a boat. They are alive some way.

JUCK They are like folk. They are better than folk.

HAMISH A house is kinna cold, standing still and alone. But a boat is aye moving. A boat is so lively and nice.

ROB A woman may be working against a man, but his boat is working wi' him.

JUCK Well, well, here's the day coming.

ROB The breeze is down.

HAMISH Aye, there's a smell o' morning in it. (*He looks out to sea.*) Ah see, there come the rest of the fleet now.

ROB (rising) The bonny, bonny boats. Many's the time I've miscalled the fishing, but to see them coming home ... Yonder the *Righin Og*.

JUCK Yonder the *Silver Birch* - yonder the *Dorchus*.

HAMISH Yonder the *Maid of Morvern* and the gulls crying round her.

JUCK Morning herring...

ROB Yonder the *Honest Lassie* - yonder *Kitty Mor* - yonder the *Sireadh*. A decent crowd, all of them. Aye, a decent crowd.[43]

The values affirmed by the play, of community, collective action and mutual support, take up a familiar theme in Naomi's writing. The word 'decent' is a loaded one, in its sense of 'fitting' and 'adequate': Naomi had little time for respectability. The life of a West Highland fishing community was, or could be, 'decent' if government worked with it rather than, as she felt was often the case, against it.

Naomi credited Denny with the lion's share of authorship. A lifetime of his experience went into the play, and his contribution to the language must have been considerable. But Naomi by this time had more than ten years of direct involvement in Carradale fishing, and had already demonstrated her sensitive ear for idiom and rhythm. Without both, it is very unlikely that the writing partnership would have worked. It did not survive, however, possibly because Denny had little natural inclination towards writing, perhaps because their personal relationship was beginning to dissipate, with both recognizing that they were pulled in different directions. Denny's life was deeply rooted in Carradale. Naomi's world had always been larger, but now her specifically Highland arena took her beyond Kintyre. A second play, *Guilty Together*, also drew on west-coast fishing for its subject, but it was never published or performed and there is no reference to Denny participating in the authorship. She also wrote a crofting play, *The Reel of Payment*.[44]

Her Highland knowledge and identity expanded and deepened during this period. With the Highland Panel she came to know well the west coast, the Inner and Outer Hebrides, Orkney and Shetland. In a book she published in 1958, *Other People's Worlds*, stimulated by her visits to West Africa, her Highland identity is communicated with firmness and conviction. It provides the territory of comparison with everything else. Africa, she felt, was both a problem area of the world, and a 'growing point'.

> I come from another problem area, the West Highlands; but it is not a growing point. I wish it was. I grope uncertainly at the kind of conditions which make it so, but see little chance of getting them.[45]

Often dispirited, she nevertheless sustained her efforts to make the West Highlands grow, not only in the public and political spheres. Her writing was a part of it, with Scottish themes predominating at this time. She was sure of her identity, and sure of the audience she was trying to reach, however unreceptive it proved. 'I myself try to write for my own race, to write intelligibly for the ordinary man and woman in Scotland, to shake them a little out of their bad dream of respectability. I get little encouragement either from them or from the neighbours.'[46] And, more literally, farming at Carradale was also a way of making Scotland grow.

In 1951 Naomi began writing regularly for the *New Statesman*, and continued throughout the fifties. Many of the articles chronicled the farming year at Carradale, providing vivid snapshots of farming life and a rich source of sociological and ethnographical information in a period of transition between traditional agricultural methods and increasing mechanization. Naomi's own pleasure in physical work, and in being literally close to the earth, is evident, as when she describes raking – 'easy if one does it the right way, sliding the smooth handle effortlessly through the supporting hand, moving in rhythm'[47] – or cutting bracken:

> The smell of the cut bracken is as strong and exciting as Bond Street; the sun blazes on one's arms and neck. I watch to see that the snicking blades don't jam on whin stalks or hummocks of earth. If they do I must stop and clear them.[48]

Part of the attraction of farming, as of fishing, was the sense of co-operative effort. It was not just wartime emergency that had brought people together to help each other out. For generations, survival had depended on it. Ploughing, harvesting, threshing, sheep shearing: all the focal points of agricultural effort relied on co-operation. Naomi was quick to spot the nature of the satisfaction involved:

> ... none of us will see the rest stuck if it is a matter of lending a hand. It seems lighter, some way, to do a thing for someone else. One can take one's time and yet, for all that, one is showing off. Work is no longer just the thing which is paid by the hour, but something on its own: a social value.[49]

In a sense, Naomi is also showing off to her *New Statesman* readers. She was perfectly aware of the fact that, in this case, she was not writing for a Scottish audience, but for a predominantly English left-wing intelligentsia, readers who had probably never lifted a scythe and certainly had not extracted maggots from cattle or made dinner for a dozen workers at the threshing.

> We put on potatoes, cabbage and stewing apples and I made a rather complex milk pudding, doubling everything in the recipe, putting on my spectacles to read it and taking them off

to stir, because they are the kind that keep on dropping into things.[50]

The columns of the *New Statesman* gave Naomi a public outlet for moans as well as celebration: 'my main depression, the thing that brings me nearest to just sitting down and screaming, is the farm accounts'.[51] Eighteen years of hard work and gradual modernization had transformed the farm, but not its profitability or the headache of debts:

> At least it looks like a farm now; and every year whatever profit I may have goes for some essential farm implement ... After the valuation (and my poor bull's leg is still swollen so I have to depreciate him quite a lot) and the cash paid out and cash received and the allowances, it remains to consider debts owing and debts owed. On the one side there are a few dozen eggs; on the other solider things like the tractor fuel and Dunkie's lambs. But should I really count Dunkie's lambs as something owed, seeing he wouldn't dream, dear Dunkie, of sending me a bill for them? Better to shut one's eyes and think of a number – possibly doubling it. If only Dick won't ask me if I'm sure it's the right one![52]

Maintaining the house was also a headache, although the opening of the Lussa Hydro-Electric Scheme in 1953 at last brought an electricity supply, which did away with the need for the rather unreliable generator, which for many years had frequently plunged the house in darkness. The Hydro-Electric Board was a child of the war, set up in 1943 as one of the foundations of post-war Highland regeneration. It not only brought electricity to private homes, it provided employment and opened the door to industrial development. Naomi was aware of all its implications (though ultimately she found it no less disappointing than other projects), just as she was aware that most of her *New Statesman* readers had no conception of what life without electricity was like, nor of the economic potential that its arrival released.

Even with electricity, running the house could be wearisome,

although she was a bit perturbed at the direction Val was taking. Her comment in a letter to Bettie Baxter – 'Val taking the church part so seriously is a bit disconcerting'[54] – was a sign of Val's divergence from her mother's views which, in spite of her historical interest, were not tolerant of Christian orthodoxy. Naomi had to accept that in some respects she and Val were out of tune with one another, but she became very fond of her son-in-law. In the war years, Val, of all the children, was caught not only in the often frenetic activity at Carradale, which must inevitably have overlooked at times her adolescent needs, but also in the emotional backlash of the death of the baby. Val soaked up some of the overspill of love, filling in for the lost child.[55] Clues in Naomi's wartime diary suggest that at times Val received too much attention, at other times not enough. The others were either old enough to escape this dilemma or, in Avrion's case, more detached.

Murdoch and Rowy, Av and Lorna, Val and Mark were soon adding to the grandchildren. A new generation was growing up, and it was perhaps this that encouraged Naomi to concentrate more on writing for children. Some of her best books about and for Scotland were for younger readers, and they are an important part of her investigation of Highland life. *The Big House* (1950), *Little Boxes* (1956) and *The Far Harbour* (1957) all draw in some way on Carradale, *The Big House* perhaps most directly. In it, the heroine Su (the name of Naomi's first grandchild, daughter of Denny and Ruth), living in Tigh Mor, the big house, befriends Winkie, a crofter's son. Su feels out of place in the village school (as Val did at the school at Carradale) and Winkie is at first resentful of her 'superiority'. Traditional lore and Naomi's relish for magic combine with everyday detail to produce a time-travelling tale that reverses roles and upturns convention. It is also imbued with the historical ambiance of Argyll and its ancient communities, and in particular Dunadd near Lochgilphead, site of the crowning of kings.

The response to *The Big House* was mixed. While the *Times Literary Supplement* commended its originality[56] and the *New Statesman* found it 'magnificent',[57] *Scotland's Magazine* took her to task for her realism and treatment of class consciousness. 'These things are learned with sadness and all too soon when history is studied seriously and there is surely no place for them in the golden land of fairy-tale.'[58] Naomi employed myth and magic freely, and not only in stories for children, but for her these were means of illuminating reality. There was no boundary between history and 'fairy-tale': that was precisely the point. A later story for children, *The Fairy Who Couldn't Tell a Lie* (1963), explores the awkwardness that ensues when it is impossible not to tell the truth. It questions certain assumptions about morality through fairy characters, often malevolent, whose environment is not at all 'golden'.

The Far Harbour touches on themes handled in *Lobsters on the Agenda*: the problems of a fishing community, the impact of tourism, the erosion of tradition. The fact that it focuses on children, dealing with a classic theme in children's fiction, of the young forced by circumstances into adult responsibilities, does not in any way dull its relevance to Naomi's critique of Highland society. Most of her children's stories have a didactic intention, if only an aim to educate her readers about life in marginal areas. Often she is tackling issues – class, the difficulties of remote communities – which were not the customary territory of tales for the young. Sometimes a serendipitous quality bubbles through, or occasionally completely dominates, as in *Graeme and the Dragon*, written for Ruth and Denny's children, which reads like a story spun by their grandmother to entertain them at bedtime. Dick was also a story-spinner, and had a hand in *The Two Magicians* (1978), tales of Upsidonia which were initially told to his own children.

For *The Rib of the Green Umbrella* (1960), Naomi moved outside Scotland. It was directly inspired by a visit to San Gimignano after the war, and is set in a German-occupied town in wartime Italy. Its theme is the partisans' resistance to Fascism and the violence is not disguised – a small child has her feet blown off by a land mine, two youngsters come upon an Italian collaborator who has had his throat cut. Naomi believed that stories for children should not pull their punches, that they should deal the real world. As the Germans retreat, their commander, whose wife has been killed, goes to the town museum where he had become friendly with the curator. He takes the curator's favourite Etruscan treasures. "'It is right," he said, "that all should suffer as I am suffering now. Your town will suffer too!"[59]

In a *New Statesman* piece of 1955, she discusses writing for children. 'We have no right to simplify moral issues. Normally we leave out certain aspects of sex ... But we must not leave out love; and we should not leave out hate.' Violence, also, should not be left out, but should be presented in such a way as to explain 'what is really happening to people: that is, to show the historical consequences of actions'. She felt that there was a distinction to be made between violence and cruelty. Children 'appreciate violence ... they want a bang. What they don't need and should not want is a *cruel* bang.'[60] It is a useful and valid distinction, if a very difficult one to apply. To omit violence from the picture of human action is a distortion, but so is to dwell on cruelty.

Naomi's books for children brought her into prominence as a writer for the young. They reveal a sure touch and essentially the same approach and style as in her adult fiction. She knew what she wanted to say to children. She was also incapable of condescension: indeed, in some respects there were fewer inhibitions. She could play with ideas of magic and the supernatural and present elemental confrontation and misunderstanding, uncluttered by adult assumptions, conventions and rules. In this respect, her own unregulated attitudes, her directness and her impatience with synthetic morals and mores is childlike.

This perhaps explains why some of her books are hard to categorize. *The Land the Ravens Found* (1955), for example, is a simple but compelling story based on a chronicled Viking journey from Caithness to Iceland. Reviews of the book reflected the impact of its vivid reconstruction, as appealing to adults as to older children. It is closely linked to *The Swan's Road*, published the previous year, in which Naomi traced Viking journeys not only to England, Scotland and Ireland but to the Mediterranean, Byzantium and eastern Europe, and across the Atlantic. Her fascination with Scandinavian culture was fostered by her continuing visits to Denmark. In many ways, *The Swan's Road* is a fine example of what Naomi was best at, blending history, myth and the imagination, dwelling with fascinated care on details of costume, ornament and artefacts, celebrating courage and vision. The book was in effect a tribute to Norwegian and Danish heroism under Nazi occupation and to these societies which she believed to be in advance of Britain.

Other hard-to-categorize books are *To the Chapel Perilous* and *Travel Light* (1952). The former is a clever, entertaining but curiously convoluted interpretation of the grail quest story. The central idea, assembling journalists from rival newspapers at Camelot to investigate a story that Sir Galahad has found the grail, is promising, but here Naomi's attempt to fuse together different genres does not quite come off, although there are some splendidly comic vignettes, including the moment when the press is faced with several knights and several grails. Naomi wrote into it Val and Mark. Not surprisingly, although the book was very widely and on the whole positively reviewed, some critics were puzzled.

The family also enters *Travel Light*, a book obliquely for and about her daughters, particularly Lois, whom Naomi was with in Pakistan while working on it. A quest novel of a rather different kind, it returns to the Black Sea territory of *The Corn King and the Spring Queen*, and can be read as a kind of sequel to the latter, as Elizabeth Longford pointed out in her forward to the 1984 edition.[61] In *The Swan's Road*, Naomi had written, 'if people thought that [dragons] were real, ought not we, if we are trying to see what those people were really like, to assume a kind of reality for dragons or anything else of the same kind? That may lead us into some rather curious places.'[62] In *Travel Light*, she explores some of those curious places. Halla, the heroine, has been brought up by dragons to value the acquisition and hoarding of beautiful things, but learns how to 'travel light', unburdened by possessions. It is Naomi writing at her most lucid and resonant, blending fairy-tale and historical realism, this time with striking success.

Halla's dragons lived and protected their treasures in caves. '"Those who live in caves, die in caves,"' says the Wanderer, the mysterious figure who sets Halla off on her travels.[63] We can read

Travel Light as a statement about where Naomi felt herself to be in the early 1950s, poised to become a citizen of the world at the same time as she vigorously pursued citizenship of Scotland. Travel would continue to be very much on the agenda for the next thirty years.

5

The end of the war meant that it was possible to cross frontiers again. A post-war holiday in the South of France was particularly relished because it had been out of bounds for so long. 'How lovely to get south and see vines and olives and oleanders, and walk up small paths through the scented maquis and sit in cafés again,' she wrote in *Mucking Around* (1981).[64] The Mediterranean continued to draw her, and the French Riviera was often a holiday destination over the next two decades. She travelled in Italy also, walking in the Apennines, spending time in Tuscany, Rome, Ravenna, and as responsive as ever to the spirit of place.

> I expect to let go to places, encouraging them to sink in and start a fertilization process which might end in a story or poem. Sometimes I felt that I had been seized hold of by something with a kind of personality. As in the train leaving Rome I felt entered into by the ghost of a girl, some kind of martyr, for suddenly I smelled burning wood and felt oddly sickened.[65]

Wherever she went, Naomi was looking for stories, not in the journalistic sense but rather as a way of understanding where she was. Finding a story established a link, gave her an identity, validated her citizenship, and gave her presence a purpose. She was drinking coffee in the piazza of San Gimignano when the story for *The Rib of the Green Umbrella* came to her, 'clear in my mind, plot and main characters all in a town like this. It was like a complex crystal but I held it in my hands; all I had to do now was to name the people and write it.'[66] The episode is almost like a consummation.

She resumed her regular visits to Denmark, usually staying with Sonia Meyer. Denmark not only stimulated the Viking interest but also gave rise to *Karensgaard, The Story of a Danish Farm* (1961), a fictionalized history of several generations on the same farm. She takes the story from the late eighteenth century to the Second World War. Denmark had always spoken to her particularly strongly, not only with an historical voice, but through social and educational attitudes which Naomi found highly relevant to Scotland. Scotland, she felt, could learn a lot from the way the Danes approached community education, transport, the support of agriculture. While in Denmark, she visited Karen Blixen, and the title of Naomi's *Karensgaard* is a clear echo of Blixen's *The Story of an African Farm*, about Blixen's farming experiences in Kenya.

Naomi had become a member of PEN in 1938, an international organization of poets, playwrights, editors, essayists and novelists, founded in 1921 to promote freedom of expression and co-operation between writers. She was active for some years in Scottish PEN, attending meetings in Glasgow, and was at PEN conferences in Zurich and Amsterdam and the 1950 conference in Edinburgh. It was a similar concern that drew her into the group of writers who in the fifties set up the Authors' World Peace Appeal, an attempt to bring writers' influence to bear on Cold War intractability. The Appeal was founded on a belief that communication and negotiation might break down ideological barriers between the Communist world and the West; and it assumed that writers had influence, which Naomi felt was truer then than when radio and television began to have a more immediate effect on opinion.[67] The exercise was fraught with tension from the start, as any attempt to suggest that communication with the Soviet Union might penetrate the obduracy was regarded with huge political suspicion. The AWPA was seen as a Communist front, and was proscribed by the Labour Party.

In July 1952, a group of AWPA members set off to visit the Soviet Union. Naomi, who was vice-chair of the organization, was one of them. In June, she was writing to Robert Graves that she was busy organizing a delegation of writers, 'rather like organizing a flock of sheep'.[68] The group was led, however, by the poet and short story writer A.E. Coppard, and included Richard Mason, Doris Lessing, Douglas Young and Arnold Kettle, the last a Communist Party member whose role was to make sure the group did not make any political gaffes while in Russia. But their visit was constrained by formality and over-management, and although they were well looked after and entertained, there was little opportunity for real conversation. They talked to Russian writers, who politely declined to stray from the official line. The group 'disagreed and even quarrelled so much among ourselves that we had little energy left for disagreement with our Russian opposite numbers'.[69] There was a sense of disappointment.

> It may well be that we expected too much. Truth is perhaps not a commodity for such easy exchange. It may be that what happened was not entirely deliberate, but the result of a cybernetic lesion, a lack of real communication, masked by flowers and friendliness and a certain sympathy that British and Russians easily find for one another. But the result was that even without swallowing everything, we were considerably misled.[70]

Naomi found the experience much less interesting and rewarding than her first visit twenty years earlier. Its biggest gain was probably the start of a friendship with Doris Lessing, with whom she shared a room.

A return visit by two of the Russian writers was arranged. Naomi and Doris Lessing went to meet them at the airport and immediately ran into difficulties with Soviet embassy officials who were reluctant to release their charges into the women's care. Naomi employed characteristic tactics:

> I took one of them by the shoulders and shook him. I burst into tears, always I found effective with males. Heads were turned in our direction. There were quick consultations. Then the

man said yes, it could be arranged ... I took him by the ears and kissed him.[71]

Naomi was able to carry out the original plan, and took the Russians to Scotland, where they visited Compton Mackenzie on Barra and the Iona Community, before being entertained at Carradale. Later, Naomi reflected that very little had been achieved. She felt that it was probably more worthwhile for writers to write rather than try to influence politics by addressing people directly. 'Is anybody going to listen to the writers? I am afraid this is most improbable.'[72] At no point, however, did Naomi herself follow this advice. There was always a cause to be taken up, a campaign to be fought. Wherever she went she had an eye for issues, and was ready to take action as well as write them into her response.

There were several reasons to go to the Indian sub-continent. Lois had stayed on in Pakistan and was teaching in Karachi. Denny went to Madras to set up a laboratory for the treatment of tuberculosis. And in 1957, Jack's toleration for professional and political life in Britain finally ran out and he too went to India, taking up the offer of a research professorship at the Indian Statistical Institute at Calcutta. His wife, Helen Spurway, was also offered a research post. He was only three years from retiring from his University College London professorship. His official explanation was that he was leaving in protest against British and French intervention in Suez in 1956, but it is likely that he had been preparing for the move for some time.

Naomi's first visit to the sub-continent was in 1951, to see Lois. But of course she did not stay in the same place for long, and in *Mucking Around* describes a trip on the back of a student's motor bike, which took them 'up from dry, rocky, barren land, and over a mountain pass by hair pin-bend roads, and up, up and then all at once down into the valley of Swat, a green paradise foamed over with palest pink almond and apricot blossom'.[73] During this visit, she was working on *Travel Light*. In 1958, she was in Madras visiting Denny and then went on to Calcutta to see Jack. There the two of them swam at night in a tank where kitchen refuse floated and Naomi was grateful for the darkness which kept it from her sight. Some of the old closeness was restored, partly due to the mediation of Helen. Jack, who had declared that sixty years of wearing socks was quite enough, padded round in bare feet and comfortable Indian cotton clothes. He embraced the Indian way of life, became a vegetarian, and engendered a vast amount of professional and personal respect.

Naomi found India difficult to grasp. 'You go east to India, say, eagerly, all your sensibilities open for whatever the east will do to you. But nothing means what you think. There is always an underlying opposite.'[74] This did not inhibit her from writing about India with her customary confidence, but there is a note of discomfort. She may have found it difficult to accept the apparent ease with which Jack 'became' Indian, especially as she herself found no Indian community with which to identify in the way that Jack had. Her brother and her children had roles which she could not replicate. She took an interest in the position and education of women, commenting on the fact that there was no feminist movement and that although Indian men wanted educated wives they did not want them to move out of the home. There were few professional opportunities for women.[75]

While in Madras she wrote the children's story *Judy and Lakshmi* (1959) which centres on a visiting English girl's encounter with India and is an effective vehicle for some gentle didacticism. Reviewers in Britain liked the book's straightforward handling of ethnic and cultural differences, while in India the *Hindu*, a Madras paper, approved it as 'a bridge of understanding.'[76] Apart from its appeal as a story, it is an excellent example of Naomi's ability to capture the ambiance of place and culture without fuss or pretention.

Naomi visited Nehru, whom she had known and liked since pre-war River Court days. He introduced her to the pandas he kept at the bottom of his garden. After Jack's death from cancer in 1964 she returned to India to see Helen, who continued working there, and to inspect the Haldane Institute which was set up in Kerala. But the sense of unease remains detectable, and no major writing came out of these visits. India was one country which she could not seem to adopt. But by the mid-fifties the spell of another continent, Africa, was beginning to weave itself into her life.

CHAPTER SEVEN

African Journeys

I go in the dark through a strange country.

Tribal Country

1

AFRICA BEGAN with Egypt in the spring of 1956. The trip took in Israel, about which Naomi's views were ambivalent, and Jordan. About Israel she commented, 'Somehow I never cared that much for being in Israel. Indeed I never felt very happy in any community with a strong religious base which is founded on a father-god.'[1] This coloured her responses to Islamic countries also, but there is less reserve in her accounts of Jordan and Egypt. Jordan was ablaze with tulips, iris and anemones. But, whatever the delights of the flora, it is the personal nature of her response to a struggling peasant culture that comes through. There were scenes and activities that tuned in with her experience of Carradale and, as always, she identified with the underdogs, not with the driving success of the Israelis.

At the same time, her political senses were alert. She stayed with friends in Israel, refugees from Austria, and understood their longing for a secure and permanent home. A Jewish home created displacement in its turn, manifest in the Palestinian refugees in

Jordan. Naomi saw inflexibility on both sides, the suffering of individuals manipulated by politics, attempts to alleviate the situation condemned as compromise.

The near east was close kin to the Mediterranean cultures she knew, and she had anyway been in the Lebanon and Saudi Arabia before: this was not new territory. West Africa, however, was another story, and when, the following year, she was in first Nigeria and then Ghana, she threw herself into the living and telling of a new tale. The grip of Africa never relaxed. In Nigeria, staying in such places as the district officer's house at Uyo and the official residence at Calabar, she experienced what she described as 'the old world of District Officers and colonialism, perhaps at its best'.[2] But she was also taught to dance the High Life by students at Ibadan University, which stood her in good stead when she moved on to cover the Ghana independence celebrations for the *Manchester Guardian.* At midnight, Kwame Nkrumah spoke:

> ... after the last words he burst into a dance of achievement and joy which was taken up all round. But not by the journalists, who piled back into their buses, most of their minds on drinks and typewriters, a few slightly shocked at the carry-on. However, the buses became firmly embedded in joyous crowds and it seemed a waste of opportunity not to join in. I slipped into the High Life, a constant bath of happiness.[3]

The liveliness and colour of West Africa captivated Naomi. The vivid expression of identity also stirred her. At the opening of the Ghana parliament she wore a tartan scarf, 'the nearest a poor news-girl could get to national costume'.[4] The gesture was important to her.

Part of the attraction of West Africa was that it was 'one of the world's growing points'.[5] so that whatever the problems, it was full of promise, and, inevitably, underlined disenchantment elsewhere. The frustrations of Scotland were never far from her mind. In the thirteen years since the end of the war, she had worked hard to push the Highlands in the direction she was convinced was right, and had experienced profound disappointment. She may not have been consciously seeking new ground, but her responsiveness to Africa suggests she needed it. Nor, perhaps, was she consciously looking for a parallel to Jack's India, but she could see how easily he had slipped into another culture and that it seemed to suit him. Possibly there could be similar gains for her.

It was three years before Africa reasserted its spell, in the shape of a young man who found himself in the garden of Carradale House in the summer of 1960. Linchwe, paramount chief designate of the Bakgatla, a people spread from northern South Africa to the southern part of the British Protectorate of Bechuanaland, had joined a trip to Scotland organized by the British Council. Linchwe had been sent by his tribe to school in Gloucestershire; this was his summer holiday. The British Council tour took the group to Campbeltown, and Naomi invited them to Carradale and entertained them in the garden. Linchwe was the only African amongst them. Naomi remembers 'a young-looking darkish brown boy who had no particular friends with him' whom she approached.[6] She asked him if he had ever seen the sea, and when he said no, took him through the garden and across a field to the shore where he took off his shoes and waded in. She adopted him from the start, not just because he was African and rather apart from the others but also because her interest was fired when she learnt he came from southern Africa: 'At that time I didn't know where Botswana was.'[7] They were soon discussing South African politics. By the end of the day, Linchwe remembers, 'we were friends'.

> I remember very well that at that time I was not used to mixing freely with white people, and she struck me straight away, she did not strike me as a white woman, she struck me as a mother, just a human being … the way she was approaching me, she was relaxed, I felt very comfortable with her, I felt at home.[8]

Naomi was drawn by the predicament of an intelligent young chief designate, with ambitions for his tribe, constrained and frustrated by political and social attitudes. Bechuanaland, though a British Protectorate, was governed from Mafeking, inside South Africa. If apartheid did not formally function in Bechuanaland, its effects and those of British colonialism, perhaps driven more by class than by race, were profoundly felt. Linchwe's tribe was divided by a political boundary, with a large part still in South Africa, and as apartheid bit deeper and resistance grew, refugees made their way across the border. Bechuanaland, Botswana from 1966, could not detach itself from events and developments in South Africa.

Although a schoolboy, Linchwe was twenty-five when he met Naomi, with a strong sense of the responsibilities of a tribal chief. The plan was that he should study law, and so equip himself for his future role. Naomi was not impressed by what he told her of Woodchester Park School and suggested that he come to Carradale in the holidays and read under her guidance. He accepted the invitation, and visited several times, meeting Dick and the children: 'I became part and parcel of the family.'[9] He moved on to the Southern Municipal College in Southend-on-Sea to take his A-level exams, but his plans to study law were curtailed. He was summoned back to Mochudi, tribal centre of the Bakgatla. His uncle, acting as regent in his absence, had a drink problem and it was felt that it was time Linchwe returned to take up his responsibilities. Before he left the UK, he invited Naomi to come to stay in his own country.

The attraction and sense of trust between the two were mutual, though inevitably different in kind. On his part, he appreciated her warmth and concern, which impressed themselves on him on that first occasion. He recognized that she could help him without patronizing him. On her part, she responded to his graceful good looks as well as to a situation in which she felt she could help to shape an individual for leadership. The nature of his responsibilities was not so different from the way she saw her own. Both depended on a complex network of relationships between land and people.

At Carradale, Linchwe occupied one of the upstairs rooms, read the books recommended by Naomi, and talked with her about his hopes for the Bakgatla. He discussed his people, his position, and the importance of the chief standing up to the British in Bechuanaland as well as to South African attempts to push the border northwards. It was the beginning of a more than thirty-year relationship. He seems not to have doubted that she would come, and come she did, arriving in the middle of the night at a dark empty railway station in the autumn of 1962. With her extraordinary gift for adopting people and places, she was soon one of them, a Mokgatla (a member of the Bakgatla), and the 'we' of all her writing about Botswana confidently asserts her African identity.

That first time, she got off at the wrong station, at Gaborone, which was then little more than a railway station and a hotel, rather than Pilane, much nearer to Mochudi, Linchwe's village. It was in the hotel at Gaborone that Linchwe eventually found her, greeted her as 'mother', and embraced her. 'And then it all began,'[10] a new phase of Naomi's life which would command her attention and dominate her writing for the next quarter of a century.

2

Mochudi was, and still is, a large, sprawling village of scattered huts, courtyards and cattle kraals, connected by dirt tracks and paths. Traditional rondavels, often decorated with coloured clay, still predominated, although now rectangles, breeze blocks and corrugated iron are taking over. The centre of the village is the *kgotla*, meeting place and court, presided over by the chief, roofed against the heat of the sun and shaded by trees, but without walls. It is there that tribal issues are resolved, judgements given and punishments handed out. Naomi spent many hours there, observing, taking notes, recognizing what was valuable but not holding back from criticism, for example of the beatings which were a traditional punishment. Her criticism was all the more pertinent for her empathy with the whole idea of tribalism.

The keys to survival for the Bakgatla were water and cattle. Wealth and status were measured in cattle, and without water, there would be no cattle, and no crops. *Pula*, rain, is the watchword of Botswana and the name given to the country's currency. Water is the theme around which all activities turn, a dry and landlocked country's lifeblood. 'First there must be rain,' as she wrote in *Ketse and the Chief* (1963).[11]

Naomi, primed by her talks with Linchwe, lost no time coming to grips with the life of Mochudi. One of the first projects was the setting up of a library. Naomi and Linchwe had talked about it at Carradale. A joint letter to the *New Statesman* appealed for books, and packages were soon arriving. Schools drew her attention: education was the key to the future of the Bakgatla and of Botswana. Mochudi needed a new secondary school; children and parents both needed encouragement. Health, nutrition and birth control were issues she could hardly avoid. And of course water, how to control it, how to conserve it, how to make it accessible.

Within a few months of her first brief visit, Naomi was back in Mochudi. Linchwe was to be installed as chief in April 1963. Now acknowledged as not only Linchwe's 'mother' but as 'mother of the tribe', she felt she had to be there. Linchwe's own mother was mentally unstable and institutionalized. His stepmother seemed not to resent the taking on of the maternal role by a white stranger. And Naomi herself was in her element. Her love of ritual and ceremony, which she had written about so vividly in her fiction, and which was always being thwarted and undermined in Scotland, was given free rein. She did all that was expected of her, and more, helping to prepare – and improve on – Linchwe's ceremonial outfit, taking very seriously her guardianship of the leopardskin which marked Linchwe as chief, making the most of the inherent drama of the situation.

A piece she wrote for the *Scotsman* describing Linchwe's installation reveals her exaggerated hopes for him: 'he may be the nearest thing that exists today to Plato's dream of a philosopher king'.[12] We can read this now as a warning signal – how could he possibly live up to such expectations? – but at the same time recognize the heightened sense of future possibilities which the ceremony itself, and Africa, encouraged. Naomi talked of the 'extraordinary classless society of the tribe' but political realities were not far away.[13] Those Bakgatla who crossed the border from South Africa to attend the ceremony were stopped and searched.

In a sense, the installation may have been almost as much of Naomi as of Linchwe, for, however incidentally, her place among the Bakgatla was confirmed. She had by this time made friends and talked with many members of the tribe and was confident about what she could contribute. She felt valued. She was living a life that was perhaps closer to that celebrated in her books set in ancient tribal worlds than anything she had encountered before, or would encounter later. Yet Botswana, however much it dominated her thoughts, could only ever be an interlude. Although from now until the journey became too much for her, in the early 1990s, she would visit the country almost every year, it could never be more than a visit. She had found a home of sorts, but it could replace neither Carradale, nor her London-centred life, and indeed, if anything, accentuated the contrary pulls and pressures that had always been so much a feature of her life.

Before she had met Linchwe, Naomi had written, about West Africa, 'As a writer, an intellectual, one is *engagé*. One must be part of the change one writes about. There is no external, unbiased attitude possible. I am not unbiased about West Africa. I liked it too much.'[14] In Botswana, it was not just a case of liking, but a total involvement. Yet her reflections on West Africa were a useful preparation. They helped her recognize the responsibilities of the outsider.

> You have to learn the political myths and the class myths, all with their special words. You have to realize what happens to people when these myths collapse as social and political myths have a habit of doing, leaving them to face the jungle unarmed with the magic word, the pathfinder.[15]

This of course, applied to Scotland as much as to Africa.

Sandy Grant arrived in Mochudi towards the end of 1963. A twenty-six-year old who had done his apprenticeship in West Africa, he had met Naomi, recently returned from Bechuanaland, before he left London. His task was to help set up a community centre. With the Bakgatla divided between Bechuanaland and South Africa, refugees from across the border gravitated to Mochudi, and part of the community centre's purpose was to assist them. Instrumental in setting up the project was Martin Ennals, secretary of the National Council for Civil Liberties, backed by a committee in England. Naomi was a member of that committee.

In Mochudi, Sandy Grant found unopened parcels of books stored in the village granaries – the response to the *New Statesman* letter. There were books, but as yet no building, certainly no librarian, and no materials for setting up a cataloguing and borrowing system. Sandy opened up the packets and started to catalogue the books, but the shortage of basic materials continued to be a problem for some time. The Mochudi library would eventually be a success story, but its early days epitomize the nature of the task required for development. It was not so difficult to initiate projects: finding the means to sustain them was another kind of challenge which was not always met.

By the time Naomi was back the following year both the library and the community centre projects were making progress. But Naomi had reservations about projects which were dependent on foreign volunteers. To Eric Linklater she grumbled:

> ... a lot of well intentioned young people come and do community development. Of course, of course, they are doing lots and lots of good ... building lovely classrooms and clinics and organizing women's clubs and boy scouts and all that. But wouldn't it have been possible to think in terms of the culture that was here, that could live and grow? If one suggests that, one is told not to be tribal. Tribal, Jesus bloody Christ. And I think of what the Highland Panel might have done if we'd still had the clan lands.[16]

This was a theme she would return to often. She was convinced that traditional social structures provided the best foundation and the best resource for development. Her voicing of such opinions was not popular in some quarters.

The library and the community centre were real gains for Mochudi, but they were not enough for Naomi. Education was also high on the agenda of her concerns. She particularly championed Segale Primary School and its principle Mrs Maribe, and recognized the need to expand provision at a higher level. Mochudi's only school to offer secondary education, on the top of Phuthatikobo Hill with its stunning views, was dilapidated and inadequate. A new school and more secondary provision were badly needed, and equipment and materials. Naomi launched herself into another campaign, assisting and supporting David Maine who became headmaster of a new junior secondary school, writing letters to her wide range of contacts as well as British officialdom in an effort to win money, books and equipment for Mochudi schools. It took time. A letter from David Maine to Naomi written in July 1964 is gloomy about prospects for the new school.[17] But Naomi was digging into her own pocket to help, and the same letter thanks her for donations of books and science apparatus. There are other thank you letters, and many requests for advice – on education, on training, on opportunities abroad – and sometimes scarcely veiled approaches for money. A white woman, almost by definition, had cash resources beyond the dreams of most Bakgatla.

She did what she could, which was a great deal. She gave advice, enlisted the help of others, wrote endless letters to individuals and organisations, and was often instrumental in enabling young men and women to study abroad. She set up a revolving fund to pay school fees, the idea being that the fund would be perpetuated by the repayment of loans from successful pupils. It foundered, as did other projects, but although Naomi was sometimes frustrated and depressed, she persisted.

It was never a one-way relationship, as Norman Molomo, who got to know her well, commented. She spent a great deal of time with members of the older generation, those in positions of responsibility. One of these was Francis Phirie who, as tribal education secretary, was a key figure in efforts to develop schools, and for Naomi a source of valuable guidance. Norman Molomo himself was a member of the legislative council, and later became an MP. 'We were the only people who could provide traditional information – she wanted to know about Botswana cultural values and traditions.'[18] That reciprocity was vital to Naomi, both personally and in terms of her effectiveness. It was the same mutual trust that Linchwe had recognised in Carradale. Without it, almost certainly, Naomi Mitchison would have been treated courteously in Botswana but would never have been able to get out of her white skin.

Talk was important; participation equally so. Naomi was now in her sixties. That did not prevent her undertaking long and difficult journeys, sleeping rough, eating minimally – there was severe drought in the mid-sixties and food supplies were limited. In one of the diary notebooks she kept during her stays in Botswana she records travelling on the train from Francistown and feeling overcome by compassion when she saw drought-bound landscape.[19] A piece in the *Scotsman* records 'Bechuanaland today looks for hundreds of miles like nothing but a desert scattered with dead leaves, with here and there the brown, nasty smoke of a dust whirlwind.'[20] Wherever she went, she relished involvement in physically demanding escapades. In February 1965, she wrote to Dick about going on an ostrich hunt, with obvious pleasure.

> … there I was in the front seat between Rampa and Maribe and nursing the guns and there was a time when I wouldn't have been able to read, under the external differences of skin colour and different muscle structure, Maribe's kindness and deucency and Rampa's skill and political intelligence. I wouldn't have felt completely at ease.[21]

But now she did. In the same letter she wrote, 'With me, everything goes easily and lovingly; we are on the same job. It is this intense feeling about [Linchwe's] people that goes on: I wonder if one could have that without being born to it.' And goes on:

> I am being taken completely and warmly for granted, which is nice, and makes one think one isn't just a milk cow. Linchwe is being more charming than I can say. I sleep like a log, with not so much as an aspirin. Masses of things coming up to be done but all so to speak, about one main thing, so that I am not dispersed, and still all is gathered up into the tribe.[22]

Other escapades were more provocative. On a pre-independence visit to Mafeking with Linchwe and a refugee from South Africa, they were denied entry to Crewe's Hotel where they went to have lunch. Naomi was welcome; the others would have to go round the back. The same thing happened at the Grand Café. Naomi was irate. In a mood of defiance, they bought food and went to sit in a 'white park', thus attracting the attention of the police. Naomi revelled in having provoked a racial 'incident', and Linchwe needed little encouragement to make rebellious gestures. The following year, 1964, he took a gun into a whites-only bar in Mahalapye after he had been refused service, and in 1969, on his way to Washington to take up his post as Ambassador to the United States, he was involved in an incident in Jan Smuts Airport, Johannesburg, when he attempted to walk through a door labelled 'whites only'. Linchwe and Naomi were in many ways kindred spirits. She needed someone to adventure with. Once it had been Jack. Wade Gery and John Pilley had in very different ways been fellow adventurers, in ideas more than in actions. Denny Macintosh had been an adventuring companion; Dick perhaps less so. Now it was Linchwe and some of the other men, such as Greek Ruele and Skara Aphiri. They walked and hunted in the bush. With Linchwe, who was and still is a keen horseman, Naomi sometimes went riding, which was a good way of seeing the country, especially as wheeled vehicles were in short supply. Eventually she bought a second-hand car, and helped the community to acquire its first tractor.

With her determinedly positive attitude to tribal values, Naomi supported an important development in the sixties which echoed the traditional, though eroded, generational regiments which had been a foundation of tribal structure. The village of Serowe, north of Mochudi, had devised a system of brigades to provide a work-force which could be directed to a range of collective tasks. The key player in this initiative was Patrick von Rensburg, who with his wife ran Swaneng Hill School at Serowe, which Naomi visited often. At Swaneng, Patrick and Liz von Rensburg were committed participants in the community, and Naomi admired their achievement. She and Linchwe were convinced that Mochudi also should introduce the brigade idea.

The von Rensburgs lived in a one-room rondavel with an open fire for cooking. When Naomi was invited to dinner, she dressed for the occasion, 'sweeping into our rondavel in her long dress'.[23] There were certain establishment standards that the anti-establishment gadfly maintained, less, perhaps, because she set store by such things than because she enjoyed challenging expectations. In Africa, as elsewhere, Naomi's compulsion to be provocative and theatrical remained keen. She believed in comfort, and would travel in old clothes and comfortable, well-exercised shoes and with a battered corduroy suitcase. But there were occasions which cried out for dressing up, and they were not necessarily those one might expect.

At Serowe, Naomi met Bessie Head, a young aspiring novelist of South African mixed-race origin, who had recently come to Botswana to teach. Although Naomi found her a difficult personality, she encouraged her work and advised her on her first novel, *When Rain Clouds Gather* (1969), which deals with issues of political exile. Bessie Head went on to write several works of fiction and *Serowe: Village of the Rain Wind* (1981) about Serowe itself. There was little literary activity in Botswana, and Bessie's insecure position probably contributed to the severe depressions that afflicted her. Although her relationship with Naomi seemed uneasy, Naomi corresponded with her and tried to help her with advice on seeking treatment in England as well as on her books.[24]

The community centre in Mochudi came as a response to

Linchwe's open-door policy towards refugees from South Africa, enabled by the encouragement and active help of the London committee and its recruits. When the brigades were set up, it became their operational centre. There were workshops and tools, and volunteers were brought in to help with the training. The brigades worked on agricultural and building projects, and made a very significant contribution to developments in Mochudi. Naomi was a strong advocate of collective purpose and effort. Her keenness to mobilize tribal cohesion in constructive ways echoes her commitment in the Highlands, just as her exasperation with what she saw as Batswana fecklessness echoed her Highland experience. She was always ready to encourage by example. At Swaneng, she was mixing concrete for a new school building. At Mochudi, she was scrubbing down walls for painting: 'I hope the sight of me doing that will encourage some Batswana – though I did have a headmaster helping me last week-end.'[25]

3

Naomi was game for anything, but a particular source of satisfaction came from her contribution to education. Getting the schools built and maintained was the first challenge. Swaneng had pioneered a self-help system which involved the pupils in constructing and looking after their own school, but, unlike the brigades, this did not transplant to Mochudi. Getting buildings up was a slow and agonizing process, continually held back by lack of cash. Then the schools were in need of the most basic equipment, and Naomi was constantly appealing and agitating on Mochudi's behalf. She also taught. During each visit to Mochudi, the priority was to get into the schools, to talk to the children and take classes. She felt strongly that children should 'feel that they are not shut out of the exciting new world of the adult'[26] and encouraged them to ask questions about whatever provoked their curiosity. She rapidly became aware that, in its imitation of a British system, much of what was being taught was irrelevant to African experience. There was a dearth of African teaching resources. Naomi adopted a multi-cultural approach, focusing on African topics as well as Shakespeare or the origins of democracy. A constant theme was the vital need for science education, and included in this was access to knowledge about birth control.

This was familiar territory to Naomi, but it was tricky. The idea that women could control their own fertility gave them a power that went contrary to tradition. If there had been a problem in North Kensington for middle-class proselytizers to win the confidence of working-class women, the barriers in Botswana were both more considerable and more subtle. Naomi realized she needed not only Linchwe's backing in what became a crusade, but tribal support. There was a meeting of the *kgotla* at which the issue of birth control was discussed. The occasion is described by Linchwe's wife, Kathy:

> I remember when we went to *kgotla*, there was a terrible row there, but she was adamant that women, especially women ... must know something about contraception ... We really got some fireworks from the men. But she just wouldn't care ... she wanted people to know about this. Because society was sort of shy about this kind of thing, and yet we had children we couldn't look after. Big families were created, with no income sometimes, and then you end up with children not even going to school ... It was hard for women to talk about it freely at *kgotla*, because you were afraid that ... society is going to be looking at you differently ... men would say, it means there is going to be promiscuity.[27]

Naomi was not content simply to discuss the issue; she pursued it in a number of ways. She smuggled in supplies of contraceptive foam tablets and enlisted the help of trained nurses. One of these was Eva Moagi, whom Naomi helped to study at Edinburgh and who later became matron of the hospital at Serowe. Another was Angelina Rampa, 'Nou's number one lady',[28] who became one of the first woman councillors in Botswana. Nevertheless, and in spite of Linchwe's support, there were bastions of resistance to overcome.

Afraid of their husbands' reactions, women took the pill in secret. In an effort to bring down the level of teenage pregnancies, nurses were trained to ask no questions when young girls turned up for contraceptive advice, although this went against the grain.

The issue of birth control was integral to wider issues of the position of women, which also, inevitably, concerned Naomi. Always she had to tread with care the thin line between alienating those with traditional views, women as well as men, young as well as old, and providing encouragement and support. Sometimes she lost her temper.

> We were seated one time in the house and we were talking, and somebody said, 'No, women can't do this,' and she just stood up and banged her fist and said, 'Fuck the women! What are you saying about women? Why don't women stand up and do things for themselves?'[29]

Botswana was a society in transition, which threw many of these clashes into sharp relief. There were tantalizing possibilities of progress, a sometimes painful letting go of old ways, and simultaneous suspicion and interest in new ones. Naomi recognized the potential for the role of mediator, but it meant she had to accept brickbats as well as bouquets.

Drought was the hardest enemy to tackle. Most families depended on being able to produce at least a proportion of their own food. When crops failed and cattle died, parents were unable to feed their children, sometimes unable to care for them. Many of the men looked for work in South Africa and were away for months on end. Women were left to look after the home and the 'lands', the cultivated areas which were often at some distance from the village, and young boys to look after the cattle at the cattle posts, again at a considerable distance from home. Small children could be left in the charge of only slightly older siblings.

Kathy, Linchwe's wife, became a key partner in many of Naomi's activities. Naomi had taken a keen interest in the marriage, going to visit Kathy in Johannesburg, where she was training as a nurse.

When they first met, in a public area of the hospital, Naomi embraced her. Kathy was taken aback; in South Africa, white women and black did not publicly embrace. It was no surprise when, not long afterwards, Naomi became a proscribed immigrant, in both South Africa and Southern Rhodesia.

Kathy had been told about Naomi, and realized she was being 'checked out'. Nevertheless, they soon established a close relationship, which enabled Kathy to endure with reasonably good humour Naomi's strong views and criticism of the way in which Kathy and Linchwe were setting up house. It was a new house, specially built for the couple. Naomi's involvement was not appreciated by the builder, who on at least one occasion threatened to abandon the project if she were allowed to continue to interfere. Years later, Naomi was still complaining about the house's defects, particularly the lack of ventilation, and blaming the builder.

Kathy was often Naomi's companion as she visited schools and addressed groups of women. She was a signal that Naomi had the backing of the chief (in the early days, Linchwe's stepmother had performed a similar function) and could also act as interpreter, for many of the Bakgatla did not speak English and Naomi never learned more than a few words of Setswana. But Kathy had her own difficulties, as she herself was not a Mochudi girl and to some extent an outsider. However, it would have been uncharacteristic for Naomi to have allowed herself to be dependent and she often struck out on her own. Kathy herself described an occasion when she accompanied Naomi on a visit to an elderly woman with whom she had no common language. Naomi told her to leave them together. When Kathy returned, she found the two women comfortably lying on the floor side by side, not understanding each other's language but nevertheless clearly able to communicate.[30]

Naomi's currency with the Bakgatla women was strengthened when she elected to join her age regiment. (In the event, she joined the regiment of a younger age group as she had more in common with the younger women and they were more likely to speak some English, thus exercising a choice which no Mokgatla had.) She was known, she had an identity as a Mokgatla which was more than self-imposed. She participated in ceremonies and celebrations, wearing the uniform blue skirt and red scarf. It was important to Naomi to have this identity, to share in tribal solidarity and to be recognized wherever she went. At the same time, she did not want deference or fuss. On one occasion, when a school she was visiting made elaborate arrangements to greet her, with a guard of honour and the school drum majorettes parading, she insisted on Kathy taking her round to the back entrance.

She did not want fuss, but she did want a forum and she wanted to be listened to. Her efforts to stir women out of submissiveness often brought little reward. She would call meetings of women to which only a handful would turn up, and sometimes those who did were only there because they received instruction from their chief to attend. Often those who did come were late. Frequently, Naomi lost all patience. She also felt let down, and it was perhaps harder to accept when it was women, in whose interests she worked so vigorously. She saw herself as their champion, but it was a championing that must have seemed irrelevant to many women's lives and perhaps came too soon to do more than prepare the ground for later development. Women had found ways of coping with things as they were, however unjust or painful their situation. And the actions of even the best-intentioned whites had often brought complications with which they were not equipped to deal.

Naomi may sometimes have fumed at Mochudi intransigence, just as she fumed at Carradale, but she did not curtail her efforts. When feeding schemes were set up to mitigate the worst of the effects of drought, and a 'child to child' programme was organized to help the childcare problem, Naomi was vigorously active in both. The latter was organized by Modiegi Manyatso, a local teacher, whom Naomi helped to send abroad for further training. A shelter was built beside the school where young children with no parents at home could wait for their older siblings who were pupils. While at the school, they received some informal teaching and were also fed. But there were many discouraging experiences. Kathy and Naomi worked desperately hard to maintain a feeding scheme for young children, mixing and serving huge quantities of donated meal powder. Mothers were happy to send their children to be fed, but when they were asked to help run the scheme they refused to do it without payment. Naomi had to return to Britain and Kathy was pregnant: the scheme collapsed and the donated meal went to another village.

There were some successes, to counter the disappointments. Many individual women owed much to Naomi's support – education, opportunities abroad, careers. Some came to visit her in London, or made their way to Carradale. Although sometimes she grumbled at being taken for granted, the maintaining of contact between her visits to Botswana was important. And her missionary zeal on behalf of women did not distract her from issues that tended to concern mainly men. Her privileged status – she was white, she was elderly, *and* had her acknowledged position as a member of the Bagkatla and 'mother' of the tribe - meant she could associate freely with the men and share in traditionally male activities. She could, and did, talk to them as an equal and demand their attention and respect. Men such as Norman Molomo, Amos Pilane and Greek Ruele regarded her also with affection and a fatherly concern. In a letter from Greek Ruele to Naomi after she had broken her leg, he gently chided her for dancing when the leg was still weak and then contradicts his caution: '... a Mokgatla never gives in. So you are not wrong to dance at this stage. Let us go on.'[31]

One notable success was the introduction of a printing press to Mochudi. Naomi acquired a cast-off press in London and arranged for it to be shipped out by the Crown Agents, which was not easy and required considerable help from Tish Rokeling's daughter. A volunteer, Johnny Gumb, came to operate it and teach others. Another press was acquired later and for a while there was a flourishing jobbing-printer business in Mochudi, producing letterheads, leaflets and a magazine. Naomi herself learned how to set type.

She experienced drought and she experienced floods. When the rains came, usually around November, the Ngotwane River often burst its banks. The ecstatic splashings of small boys could not make up for the fact that the water dispersed and disappeared very quickly. Rain signalled the time for ploughing and planting, and, with luck, there would be enough to sustain the year's crops. But often water was not there when it was needed. The answer was to build dams to contain and conserve water, and sink boreholes to enable access to water to feed stock and for domestic purposes. Many people, usually women and children, had to walk great distances to fetch water. More boreholes and a system of piping water at least to standpipes if not to individual homes would make a huge difference to domestic survival and to health and hygiene.

With Hugo Going, a civil engineer, Naomi tramped the country inspecting sites and assessing the practicalities of dam construction. Men were needed for the labour of digging and building. They turned up 'in rags and tatters of western clothing, some with sandals, some barefoot. There was no question of payment, but there would be porridge.'[32] There was some initial success. In a letter of August 1973, Amos Pilane includes the Borejane Dam and the Morwa Irrigation Scheme among Naomi's key achievements. But work was left incomplete, and in the longer term the dam projects, at least, did not live up to expectations. Even with limited success, part of what Naomi accomplished was the proof that action was possible, that, to some extent at least, people could take their future into their own hands. Often she used her own hands in an attempt to demonstrate this.

4

With all this activity, Naomi was also writing – letters to individuals and organizations, articles (she published several in the government-funded Botswana magazine *Kutlwano*, although her critical tone needled officialdom), pieces for the British press, and, before long, stories and books. She had her notebooks and her portable typewriter, and was rarely deterred by a lack of amenities. Long practice of writing in unlikely circumstances enabled her to work by the light of a paraffin lamp with her typewriter on her knees, though when reduced to a candle and a torch she gave up the attempt to write at night. The heat was often intense and the rain could turn Mochudi into a quagmire. Sometimes there was little to eat, and she lived off maize porridge and bread and sardines. An omelette cooked by Sandy Grant at the community centre was a treat. Sleep sometimes evaded her, and on occasion she took librium to overcome this.

In 1967, she reached the age of seventy. She still came to Mochudi, for two weeks, sometimes a month at a time, greeted with warmth and pleasure when she arrived, even if Linchwe failed to turn up at the station or airport. Age slowed her down a little, and as the years increased she found it more difficult to stay in Linchwe's house on the hill, and more often slept at the community centre. She could be seen, 'a little figure plodding up the hill', heading for the *kgotla* with her notebook.[33] There were times when it was a welcome relief to go to Gaborone, thirty miles away, and take advantage of city amenities. She eagerly accepted offers of baths and Howard and Fiona Moffat's invitations to swim in their small pool. (Howard Moffat is a descendant of the nineteenth-century missionary Robert Moffat, mentor of David Livingstone in Bechuanaland, and maintains the tradition of the missionary doctor.) In one of her diary notebooks, possibly 1966, Naomi records how much she enjoyed being entertained by Didon and Michael Faber at their 'very civilized house' in Lusaka.[34] She often saw them when she paused in Zimbabwe, *en route* to or from Botswana.

Botswana was changing, and Mochudi inevitably also. The discovery of diamonds put the economy on a firm footing. Gaborone was transformed, with new government buildings, a mall with shops and hotels, new housing, and an infant tourist industry. Foodstuffs and goods of all kinds came across the border from South Africa. Naomi was scathing about some of these developments. 'Botswana has the image of modernity but not the actuality,' she wrote in 1978.[35] She warned against undue reliance on 'foreign experts' and the dangers of adopting an alien culture along with the aid. The close relationship with South Africa disturbed her.

After only a few visits to Mochudi, Naomi began to write her novel *When We Become Men* (1965) which drew directly on her experience there. Mochudi becomes the village of Ditlabeng, which she used in other fictional contexts, and Linchwe appears, barely disguised, as Lelotse. The writing of this novel became almost obsessional, and forcefully underlined the divisions that pulled Naomi in different directions.

> I had become completely, alarmingly and joyfully committed; and I knew this was all wrong. I knew quite well that I felt myself at one time committed to Scotland, to the dream of Alba. The reality of working for Scotland had got rid of most of that, though occasionally I still got a breath of it. Possibly the same thing would happen here. Reality of Africans might kill the dream of Africa. Yet it was always being revived by people or letters. But I became more and more afraid that it was blotting out other necessary sympathies; I began to judge people by their attitude to my touchstone and that was all wrong.[36]

With all the contradictions involved, and all Naomi's awareness of them, Africa remained her touchstone for a quarter of a century and still, forty years after she sported a tartan scarf at Ghana's independence celebrations, tugs tenaciously at her. And embedded in that touchstone, and an important part of the writing of *When We Become Men*, was Linchwe.

Linchwe was often charming, but he could also be infuriating. He - and others - could fail to turn up at meetings, ignore agreed arrangements, arrive late or not at all to take Naomi to catch a train, or later a plane. And sometimes there were open quarrels. Naomi's ideas of the appropriate education for a chief did not always coincide with Linchwe's inclinations. She wanted to read Shakespeare aloud to him, while he wanted to be drinking in one of the Mochudi bottle stores. Her emotions were no further from the surface in Africa than in Britain, and in the course of one heated quarrel, much to his astonishment, she hit him. African men were not accustomed to unsubmissive women. Though she was normally his guest, on more than one occasion she packed up her bags and marched out in a fury, going down the hill to seek refuge at the community centre. A letter of September 1967, written to Linchwe from Scotland, reveals the intensity of emotion in their disagreements.

> I have wept so much, remembering the time when we were truly mother and son ... Perhaps it never really happened, it was only something which I imagined, a story. Yet I thought then that I could help you to keep the best values of being African – for you, of being the leader of a tribe – and at the same time to come to terms with the world of scientific knowledge and use it. But if you don't need me, that's all right.[37]

Of course, it was not 'all right'. Naomi had staked too much, emotionally and intellectually, on her involvement with Linchwe and Mochudi to accept rejection. 'I'm really deep in over Africa; I feel as if I'd got something like Spain, something to die for,' she wrote to her friend Bettie Baxter, after two visits.[38] Yet she could never be entirely confident that she was wanted, and her early uncertainty – 'I hope you really want me to come ... I must go back to you first, to make sure everything is all right: that we are secure together,' she had written in December 1962 – never disappeared.[39]

She was also aware that to tie her Mochudi life too closely to Linchwe himself was a mistake. She continued to visit Botswana when he was in Washington. Indeed, she made a point of drawing his attention to her participation in her regiment, in his absence, to demonstrate that 'I'm still part of everything even when you're not there'.[40] That in itself was a form of reassurance, that she had her accepted role, independent of his sponsorship. She also regarded it as signalling her support of tribalism, which may have had more force in his absence, both for the Bakgatla and for European sceptics.

Sometimes Naomi found the reassurance she sought, from Linchwe and from others among the Bakgatla, but she could never take it for granted. Linchwe, in true filial fashion, could be both devoted and delinquent. 'I always have you in my contemplation consciously and in my dreams. If you were my wife and decided to walk out on me I would shoot myself dead,' he wrote in an early letter.[41] The emotional ripples running through their letters express the closeness of their relationship, and its complexity. White and black, mother and son, colonialist (however benign) and colonized, elder and novice, teacher and pupil: all these feature, with an undercurrent of sexual awareness which from time to time breaks to the surface. The relationship had all the emotional charge of a love affair, at least on Naomi's side. 'I suppose I am making my usual mistake in love affairs of wanting to have things said,' she wrote.[42] In an undated diary, Naomi recorded an episode which illustrates her vulnerability. Linchwe announces that he is going off somewhere. 'I say this is rather hell, am I never to see you? I am really a bit upset. L. puts his arms round me, says Oh you are easily hurt.'[43] The physicality of the relationship is very apparent, indeed inseparable from any other aspect. The hugs and kisses were an important ingredient in the reassurance Naomi sought, but clearly signified more than that.

> I know so exactly the shape of his face against my skin, the feel of his arms; I find him very beautiful. I had thought that, what would have happened during the time I was away, would have been that the relationship would have grown on my side but not on his: I was prepared for him to love me less than I loved him. However it seems to be mutual; this is an unlooked for bonus or state of grace.[44]

At other times, she was full of doubt and bafflement. When she invited him to supper and he failed to turn up, she wondered if he was no more than a playboy. 'Does he do it on purpose or accidentally, casually?'[45]

These contradictions and strains were experienced on both sides. In January 1965, Linchwe wrote to Naomi, expressing his hurt that she should question her acceptance by the Bakgatla and reiterating a suggestion he had made before, that she should stay permanently in

Botswana.[46] Linchwe clearly saw the ways in which Naomi could be useful to him and his people and was not beyond attempting to manipulate her. But his influence was far from being control, and Naomi could be as unpredictable as he was himself. There was mutual exasperation. At the same time, his affection appears genuine. The relationship could not have survived a quarter of a century without both contributing to the emotional binding.

The tensions were not only centred on Linchwe. The frustrations in Naomi's attempts to make things happen, move things on, were huge. However enthusiastic and appreciative the people of Mochudi were, their carelessness and unreliability never ceased to be a source of upset. She would arrange to give extra coaching to a group of schoolgirls – only one would turn up. The community centre was, she felt, 'a muddle'.[47] The Mochudi men liked their beer, a reminder of Carradale which Naomi did not enjoy. She describes with some ambivalence a supper with Sandy Grant at the community centre, with an alcohol-inspired Linchwe holding her hand, echoing moments with Denny Macintosh.[48]

When things went wrong, when she felt, as she did on occasion, that it was all a waste of time and she might as well return to Scotland, she would make her way to the top of Puthadikobo Hill to find comfort and remind herself of why she was there. She describes one occasion when she was feeling particularly hurt at Mochudi fecklessness.

> I walked up and on to the great slabs of rock and saw down onto the river with the green trees, indeed everything looked astonishingly verdant, the river grey-green and a bit greasy, winding among the trees. More of the town than I thought was on the other side, a pattern of thatched houses, Square-shaped or round in their neat *lapas* [courtyards] here and there the glitter of a tin roof, shade trees dotted everywhere, no overcrowding.[49]

The strains were felt, too, at home, as Linchwe's letter implies. It was not just that Naomi visited Botswana, but that it remained a focus of her interest wherever she was. She spent a great deal of time lobbying on the country's behalf, using her own and Dick's contacts, pestering for support in cash or kind, as well as assisting individuals, some of whom came to visit, and, of course, writing about Africa. To friends and family it could seem obsessive. The family's coolness on the subject of Africa sometimes became exasperation. At one stage the grandchildren offered Naomi pennies for every hour she did not mention Africa. More seriously, her involvement with another continent was resented in Carradale and Argyll, and contributed to her losing her seat on the County Council in 1964. This only strengthened her commitment to Mochudi: she knew where she was wanted, though she also knew that the Batswana were no more consistent than the Highlanders.

5

Dick tried to be patient, but it was not always easy. In 1969, when Naomi was longing to get away, she was aware of his negativity. 'I'm afraid Dick would just not accept in practice my going to Africa ...'[50] Dick was having a difficult time. Naomi's growing passion for Africa coincided with a Labour Government which brought Dick a peerage and a short-lived post as Parliamentary Secretary at the Ministry of Land and Natural Resources. In less than two years he was displaced by Richard Crossman, at the insistence of Harold Wilson who felt Dick was too old to be effective. He was vulnerable and Naomi knew it. 'Poor Dick feeling like hell about losing his job,' she wrote in her diary, 'and no doubt I ought to be there. But equally I ought to be here.'[51] She was angry on his behalf, but there seemed more that she could usefully do in Botswana. But by this time Dick's health had begun to be a problem. He needed Naomi.

She recognized that need, although the African magnetism was powerful. Back in Britain, letters constantly reinforced the nature of her role there, from Norman Molomo, for example, and from Kenneth Koma, who also became a MP.

We are in a period of transition trying to move from the tribal society into the modern world and in this process we need somebody to hold us by the arm and encourage us to move forward not too fast and not too slowly.[52]

In a different vein, but equally difficult to ignore, were letters from Amos Kgamanyane Pilane, who was second only to Linchwe in importance to her. He, of all at Mochudi, articulated not only their need of her but her responsibility to them. 'I hope and trust you will agree with me that Almighty God elected you to become the real mother of our chief and above all to become the mother of the Bakgatla-Kgafela in Botswana, as your works among them speak for themselves.'[53] There is a hint of the missionary in this characterization of Naomi, and some have placed her in the tradition of the enlightened female missionary, of which Scotland produced several.[54]

Naomi's relationship with Amos was particularly close. He was philosopher and historian of the Bakgatla, roles which were valuable and attractive to her. They were possibly lovers, but it was a calmer relationship than that with Linchwe, indeed it may have helped to defuse the intensity and allay the uncertainty of that bond. Amos's knowledge and wisdom reinforced her view that tribalism provided a continuity and a collective ethos which the developing country needed.

Even if she had followed through her disillusion-prompted threats to abandon Botswana, after her first few visits it would have been almost impossible for her to do so. The ties were too strong and too extensive. Back in Scotland, letters arrived, not only from close friends such as Amos, but from others who kept her in touch with general news and her own pet projects. Mochudi was never far away. She was very much aware of the contradictory pressures, which were political and tribal as well as personal, as she suggests in *African Heroes* (1968).

I have obligations and loyalties to my little, struggling country of Botswana, and above all to my own tribe, which may sometimes, in some ways, conflict with my loyalties as a British citizen. But it also means, I think, that I have learnt to slip into an African skin, to think and feel as an African...[55]

But in 1967, possibly at about the time she was working on *African Heroes*, where she sounds so confident of her African persona, there had been a major upset, and she was writing to Linchwe as if mutual understanding were impossible:

You will be quite pleased that I shan't be there to bully you or perhaps make you feel guilty, for a long time. I won't write any more because it makes me feel too sad. I don't understand you; you don't understand me. Love is not enough. Perhaps that's the answer as between Europe and Africa.[56]

Moments of doubt were frequent but more of a reflection of a need for them to be denied than a lasting state of mind. In fact, she had begun the process of slipping 'into an African skin' when she danced the High Life in Accra. Whatever uncertainties Naomi had about her personal standing with individuals in Botswana, she never seemed to have thought that she could not 'become' African, just as she became Spartan, or Athenian, Or Marobian, or Scottish. It was a matter of culture and mind-set rather than national identity, and the result of her acute eye for the pivots of social and cultural intercourse. It was also the result of a generosity of emotion and her innate theatrical talents. To adopt individuals is one thing. To adopt causes is not excessively taxing. To adopt a way of life and a role within that life requires huge efforts of the imagination as well as an ability to portray 'the other', the essence of difference. And part of that role meant retaining her own otherness, for it was precisely the fact that she was white and well-connected that enhanced her value to Botswana.

Sometimes Naomi over-reacted and made others uncomfortable. Didon Faber remembers the embarrassment caused by her rubbing noses when she greeted Africans.[57] Others have commented on her exaggerated gestures in the symbolic juxtaposition of black and white skin, her hand on an African hand. Yet it was probably

Europeans who were made uncomfortable by these, in their eyes, misjudged actions. The Batswana accepted them, if sometimes with amusement, because fundamentally the British were odd and unpredictable by definition.

Nothing could have kept Naomi away from the independence ceremonies in September 1966. By this time Linchwe was married, and Kathy, his wife, recalls the moment when the Union Jack was being lowered to be replaced by the blue flag of Botswana. It was all too slow for Naomi, who seized the Union Jack and hurled it at the feet of the officials, declaiming, "'Stand not upon the order of your going, But go at once."[58] Another example of white unpredictability, to be remembered by Kathy with laughter, but typical of Naomi's talent for being theatrically provocative.

Naomi had many years of experience in provoking the British establishment. 'A career boat-rocker,' was how Sandy Grant described her, on the basis of her activities in Botswana, and she exasperated many members of The British ex-patriot community. 'Small wonder,' Sandy Grant continued, 'that the British Resident Commissioner, Sir Peter Fawcus, is reported as having once expressed his abhorrence of her Ladyship.'[59] Independence did not bring to an end the need for rocking establishment boats, for there was little immediate change. A period of 'phony independence' followed during which 'hidebound chiefs, missionaries and colonial officials continued to run the country and impose their values as if nothing had happened'.[60] Naomi, according to Brian Egner, who at that time edited the Botswana magazine *Kutlwano*, for which she wrote, 'helped to speed the departure of the colonial types in 1966-69'.[61] Norman Molomo remembered that she was unpopular with the government, and there were several European officials who saw her only as a trouble-maker. Dr Teichler, Superintendent of Mochudi Hospital, was described as referring to her as 'a tyrannical old lady' who interfered and stirred things up.[62]

Driving all her activities in Botswana were Naomi's ambitions for Linchwe. She saw him as a 'modern' African leader, with qualities that would enable him to draw together the best of traditional government and imported democracy. Her role was as his tutor and guide, to help him bridge the gap between traditional values and tribal cohesion and new ideas. Her seeking out of information that would extend her understanding was a crucial part of this, and her natural sympathies helped. Her affinity with, for example, traditional medicine was as valuable as her empathy with the idea of chieftainship. Her ability to utilize the rational without eliminating the irrational was an enormous asset to the process of acceptance by the Bakgatla, though it did not endear her to those for whom this was the handiest dividing line between white and black.

Naomi saw the tribal chief as a focus of community, drawing people together. She also saw traditional chieftainship as a counterweight to the increasing tendency of the new government to centralize power. Linchwe shared many of her ideas and was receptive to her notions of development. Indeed, part of what made the relationship work was that he, too, wanted to blend the best of old and new. That it required skilled tightrope-walking did not deter either of them from the attempt, but of course if there was a fall it would be Linchwe who had to live with the consequences. However deep her commitment, Naomi had another world to return to. If Linchwe offended his people or riled the government, escape was not so easy. A shared relish in rebellion was another part of their adhesion, but Linchwe's rebellion was sometimes directed against Naomi and that hurt her. He could not, he felt, always conform to her image of him, be always talking politics, 'intellectualizing'.[63] As late as 1979, there were still major rows between the two of them. In her diary of her visit in that year, she records an argument during which Linchwe burst out, "'Are you black or white? If you are black you agree with me, if you are white you are against me.'"[64]

In 1969, Linchwe was appointed Botswana's ambassador to the USA and his experience there seems to have hardened some of his attitudes. He clearly felt out of place, and was not prepared for the level of prejudice he encountered, nor for the deprivation of much of the American black community. Naomi felt that his appointment was partly a means of getting him off the Botswana political scene, where he was identified as a trouble-maker. It was when he returned from America, in 1972, that he re-introduced the traditional age regiment initiation ceremonies that had been banned since the time of Chief Linchwe I, who had become a Christian. The age regiments were adapted to modern needs, adjusted to the requirements of full-time employment and education, with circumcision carried out by doctors under hygienic conditions. They were a great success in spite of official opposition.

The government eventually supported the initiation ceremonies, but Naomi's view was that it was essentially hostile to traditional practices, as they fostered the influence of the tribe and were a hindrance to centralized power. 'The government are as quickly as possible taking away all that was good about tribalism and perhaps Africanism', she wrote in 1968.[65] A Land Act threatened the survival of traditional tribal lands, and opened up possibilities for private acquisition and development of large estates – an advantage only to those with access to resources.

Naomi was acutely aware of the inherent incongruities of developing Africa. In advising collaboration with tradition, rather than suppression, she was alert to the temptation of relying on foreign aid and advice, and its dangers. It led to the automatic rejection of traditional solutions, and left a damaging legacy, the belief that 'the white man always knew more, was the intellectual and moral superior'.[66] The element of assessment and choice, of responsibility, was in effect removed.

For Botswana, as with most ex-colonial African countries, independence meant struggling with an imported system of government. Naomi took pains to stress that democracy was not the invention of the 'mother of parliaments', but knowing that its roots were in Athens four hundred years before Christianity did not make its transplantation any easier. In Botswana, the system attempted to marry hereditary chieftainship with an elected assembly. The legislative house was partnered by a House of Chiefs, without legislative powers but nevertheless of at least symbolic importance. Having decided to retain the tribal chiefs, it was important to allow them a forum. Real political power nevertheless lay with the elected government, which did its best to ensure the chiefs could not challenge its authority. Linchwe's patrician instincts drew him to politics. Equally, they held him to the chieftainship. Naomi was aware of the potential for tension between national and tribal interests, but believed that there was a crucial political role for the chiefs.

Naomi was insistent that democracy required an effective opposition. She witnessed the emergence of a one party tendency with dismay. The fact that newly independent African states were 'kitted out with a "Westminster Constitution"' had not meant the automatic importation of an opposition that was not branded 'dissidence'.[67] At its best, tribal government was about consensus. What Naomi was asking for was perhaps more than democracy normally delivered. 'For genuine consensus to exist, discussion must be real and surely that means that so-called opposition opinion must be brought in and allowed to influence policy. This cannot happen so long as opposition is thought of and spoken of as "dissidence" or even "treason".'[68] She strengthened her point by allying herself with the opposition, in spite of which President Masire, successor to Botswana's first president, Sir Seretse Khama, attended her eightieth birthday party in 1977.

These tensions and contradictions provided fertile ground for conversations with Naomi. She had found herself another political arena at a time when it was clear that her previous political life was never going to deliver as much as she had hoped. In some respects, her role in Botswana was more effective than her role in the Highlands. Results were more evident, if often temporary and frustratingly makeshift. Her position was certainly a great deal more satisfactory than her vicarious role as a British MP's wife. She had more status (partly as a result of being an MP's wife, and later Lady Mitchison) and more clout. But whatever the rewards of her relationship with Linchwe, personal and political, inevitably her influence on the shaping of a modern African leader was curtailed. He was, as she acknowledged, a man of singular determination. 'You're a hard man, aren't you? ... You don't want to be deflected,' she wrote to him when he was in Washington.[69] She asked a great deal of him, and inevitably set the scene for disappointment. Again writing to him in Washington, she said:

> One thing comes out clearly; a leader in today's Africa must have some kind of moral principle. Kaunda is a kind of Christian. Clearly ordinary missionary Christianity is useless. Kaunda has gone beyond that. Can you? Or what else have you?'[70]

Although she was not alone in thinking highly of Linchwe it was never likely that he would lead his country. Perhaps she recognized that. It certainly emerges that although Linchwe brought her to Botswana and their relationship was profoundly important, once she had arrived there he became only one of many threads that bound her life to his country.

6

A recurring image for those who remember Naomi in Botswana is of her constant scribbling in notebooks or perched in some improbable place tapping at her little portable typewriter. She was writing letters, articles, book reviews, notes for what would become full-length works of fiction and non-fiction, all interspersed with odd lists and comments, messages and reminders. Words were her instinctive response to any new situation. The books began to appear a little over two years after her first visit, with *When We Become Men* leading the way. Both the novel and *Return to the Fairy Hill* (1966), which came the following year, were impulsive, immediate reactions to the newly-discovered territory of Bechuanaland. And they were also territorial markers. By writing these books she made real her identity as a Mokgatla. She wrote in *African Heroes* of African identity growing out of tribal identity. It was a notion that informed much of her writing inspired by

Botswana. She argued that the secure sense of identity provided by tribalism was the clue to an optimistic future for Africa:

> This awareness of identity survives and gives people something to be proud of, but, as different tribes and nations begin to know themselves not only as separate but, more importantly, as a whole, as Africans, they begin to think of a new time when they will no longer be taking orders from people of another colour and obeying blindly, just because they themselves were born brown or black. They are looking at a future when they will be counted everywhere as full human beings, to be respected as such, to be treated as fellow workers and colleagues.[71]

The erosion of tribal identity and of its historical wellsprings was a process which she felt needed to be countered, and *African Heroes* and her later book *The Africans* (1970) were attempts to do this, to make some restoration to 'people whose heroes had been taken from them'.[72] For this effort to be convincing, she had to establish her credentials; the books themselves were part of that, but nevertheless she acknowledged a need to spell them out. She was 'irrevocably a Mokgatla'.[73] Her Scottish background and Highland experience had been an excellent preparation for understanding tribal relationships and external pressures on them; and all her life she had been exploring the effects of physical and cultural invasion. Perhaps the strongest of her credentials was the simple fact that she was a writer. 'All writers are shape-changers,' she wrote in the introduction to *African Heroes*, 'or, if you like, so strong that they can play tunes in all modes.'[74] It was an ambitious claim, but is also a valuable clue to how Naomi saw herself. She was indeed a shape-changer, always looking for new scenes to release new shapes. Part of the inspiration of Africa was that it provided another stage.

The process of writing *When We Become Men* was of great importance to her. It was not only the thrill of engaging with a fictional world drawn so immediately from experience, but the particular excitement of being able to test her interpretation against the perceptions of those who provided her raw material. In January 1964, she was working on the book in Carradale and read some of it to visiting Batswana. 'It is like having got hold of a real Spartan or inhabitant of Marob to tell one if one was right,' she wrote to Henry Treece, a fellow historical novelist. 'So if I am right about the Batswana I am justified in my historical methods and perhaps the ancient world was as I have shown it. You will see how exciting this is.'[75] She felt she could tackle Botswana as a fictional entity in the same way she had approached the Sparta or the invented Marob of *The Corn King and the Spring Queen.* 'It will be the best thing I have done,' she wrote in another letter to Treece. 'I am using whatever tool it was that I used for getting inside the past but now I am getting inside Africans.'[76]

Those who listened to her chapters, in Carradale and in Mochudi - and they included Linchwe whose presence in the novel is so strong - seemed to approve. It is impossible to know to what extent this was African courtesy: after all, in the face of so much practical challenge, it was hard to recognize the relevance of Naomi's books about Africa, however intense her commitment to writing for an African audience. When asked thirty years later if he had read Naomi's books, Linchwe replied that he did not see the need to, since he had direct acquaintance with her ideas and views.[77] The value of Naomi's books may have been more symbolic than actual.

When We Become Men revolves around the character of Isaac, a South African resistance fighter on the run who learns the value of commitment, to a tribe and to a cause. (There are similarities here with Bessie Head's *When the Rain Clouds Gather,* although Head's novel is much less political.) By adopting an outsider's view as her main perspective, Naomi eliminates the problem of how to explain as well as present her portrait of the village of Ditlabeng. She tackles many of the tensions and anomalies of a society both in transition and under threat. She attempts to weave a whole fabric to demonstrate at least an idea of what she felt a modern African state could be, and it is full of clues to her own responsiveness to both old and new ways. Here, for example, she describes the chief's installation:

Everything done or imagined had value beyond itself. Everything was shared. Eyes spoke to eyes, hands to hands ... Songs and dances all had layer upon layer of hidden meanings, uncoiling and weaving in again among the close comradeship of bodies, the thudding of feet, the delight and laughter.[78]

Sharing, layers of interdependent meaning, comradeship: these are all at the heart of Naomi Mitchison's life and work. Africa allowed her – or perhaps impelled her – to set them free from the past.

The novel's fabric is not without its lumps and bumps and frayed patches. The characterization and the narrative are both strong, yet at times it founders as Naomi strives to pull together more arguments and illustrations than the plot can sustain. Observation and experience told her that the material she handles here is authentic; it is often vivid; but it is also sometimes close to moving out of the story, beyond the dynamic of fiction. Reviewers were cagey. John Fuller in the *New Statesman* suggested that her sympathies were too open, her hero idealized.[79] *When We Become Men* was Naomi's second attempt at a contemporary political novel, the first being *We Have Been Warned*. There is a curious echo in the titles, as if the link is partly conscious: the African novel is certainly the better of the two.

The personal nature of Naomi's African writing emerges clearly. She herself provides the evidence, in the books and in many letters. *When We Become Men* is much more than a novel, it is a statement of intent. The books that followed reinforced that statement, signalling a commitment that is, like so much of her life, both personal and political. Woven through everything she wrote was Linchwe.

Don't you know that I feel with you enough to have suffered insult and frustration and anger with you? You'll see it, I think, in my history book. I know that you yourself had schooled your own fierce and fiery spirit into courtesy and laughter. You know, I hope, that I would die for you, but not uselessly.[80]

Return to the Fairy Hill followed *When We Become Men*, and it too bears the hallmark of rapid and intense writing. It has a disarming frankness, expressing as much pain and resentment, about Mochudi and about the recalcitrant Highlands, as enthusiasm and engagement. It is a book about Naomi at a turning point in her life, rather than a book about Botswana. Africa, as she had written in that letter to Bettie Baxter, had become a cause, like the Spanish Civil War. From that first visit, she was hooked. 'I kept catching myself out in romantic plans; of doing something heroic, dangerous and painful; of proving my love for the tribe, for Africa: of undoing some of the harm which whites have done: of maximizing goodwill.'[81] Africa gave her something which Scotland had failed to provide, which Soviet Russia could not: what she called the 'open secret ... which binds all life together. The sense of continuity between past and present. The stream of life which makes the individual both more and less important, which takes away fear.'[82]

The zeal for Africa is backed by an aversion to Scotland. She felt that she could contribute less in Europe than she could in Africa, and questioned the value of her efforts in local politics and on the Highland Panel. The loss of her seat on Argyll County Council in May 1964 still rankled. And her adaptation to black skins was having a physical effect to which she gave an almost stagey symbolic expression. 'I wonder if they noticed me covering my eyes with my hands during the meeting at Tobermory so as not to see the craggy features, the extraordinary texture and colour of the skin, the alarming northern blue of the irises ...'[83] Yet, as she had made clear elsewhere, Scotland had prepared her for Africa, had made her receptive to clan society, to the impact of colonization, to both the crude and the subtle aspects of the operation of power.

Some of Naomi's best writing about Africa is found in her stories for children, and they seem to have had most impact in Botswana itself. *The Family at Ditlabeng* (1969) was on the school syllabus and has been read by a whole generation of Batswana. In telling a simple story about a girl who discovers a talent for making pots, family and village life are evoked and much detail of day to day activities is recorded. The family struggles through drought and failed crops. Mosaye's father goes to South Africa to work in the mines. Life is fragile. Through the agency of a Danish adviser, Mosaye is given the opportunity to study abroad. In case this is thought to suggest a betrayal of traditional values, it is made clear that Mosaye will return, 'to share the knowledge she had gained and the good things that came her way with her brothers and sisters, the men and women of Botswana'.[84] Other stories, *Ketse and the Chief* (1963), *Sunrise Tomorrow* (1973), the short stories in *Snake* (1976), convey the web of village life and values: 'so much of life was lived out there in the courtyard, with the hollow for the fire of sticks that never went out, and the earthenware pot, and the three-legged iron pot, and the kettle from the store'.[85]

In these stories, Naomi distils the best of traditional ways without playing down the negative aspects of life on the margins – problems of health and communications, the effects of poverty and alcohol, the struggle for education. They have a freshness and authenticity all the more striking for the fact that, although they contain clear messages, they are not overloaded. Naomi's talent for finding a good voice for addressing children did not fail her here.

Naomi's sharp and sympathetic eye for the material details of life informs her children's books as much as those for adults and is an important element in the texture of her writing. Her respect for fundamental creative skills, the making of pots or fishing nets or the beating of metals, gives her an entry into the communities she portrays. From *The Family at Ditlabeng*:

> Mother could make a beautiful, well-curved wall for the inside of a round house out of earth which had been mixed with cow dung into a smooth plaster or she could make this same plaster into the floor of a lapa with a pattern worked onto it. Or she could make other patterns with different colours on the lapa walls. She could make the kind of string kilt that the girls wore at home so that they could save their school or Church

clothes. She could make baskets finely woven to hold grain or meal.[86]

If she could not in fact slip inside an African skin, she could, as a writer, change shape sufficiently to place herself within the lapa walls.

Skara Aphiri, Naomi's companion on at least one hunting trip, commented, 'If she didn't understand, she wanted to.'[87] That wish, that need to understand impelled her writing as well as her involvement in plans and projects. Inevitably there were people whom it alienated. The critical and irritated response from the white, Christian establishment is summed up by a Dr Fuller, who contributed a piece to *Kutlwano* which made a scarcely veiled reference to Naomi:

> Well-meaning persons, including some European agitators who ridiculously try to present themselves as 'more African than the Africans', do disservice ... they romantically plead with Africans to abandon all the moral and social principles they have assimilated in their culture contacts with others.[88]

Naomi of course responded – Dr Fuller had illustrated one of her favourite themes. It was precisely this cultural and religious brainwashing, she argued, the assumption that Africans' 'moral code is inferior to the European one, and that African history is less important than European' which did so much damage.[89]

Yet, though there are times when Naomi's claims to be African seem romantic, she did not forget she was on the outside, and that that position had a particular value. The very title of her book, *Other People's Worlds*, written before her first visit to Botswana, suggests a position on the outside looking in. The worlds she writes of there are not only those she encounters, but her own familiar territory observed by people from beyond its borders.

> Often it is from the critical outsider that we really get a sight of ourselves. And this outsider must be from somewhere beyond the western pattern, and yet not irritatingly certain

that *his* methods are perfect ... We could do with friendly eyes
on us, the warm friendly eyes that can see the awkward joins
and threadbare places in our fabric of society.[90]

Mochudi came to Carradale. Greek Ruele visited to learn about
co-operatives. Francis Phirie came and Naomi took him to tea with
some of the local fishermen and farmers: 'they were charmed with
one another and so admired Francis for being able to whistle a
Highland tune after hearing it once!'[91] Mochudi came to London,
too. Chriselda Molefi, a student in London, visited Dick and Naomi
at Lincoln's Inn. She was suffering from the cold and Dick gave her
a woolly hat.[92] It was important to Naomi to bring these worlds
together but sometimes there is a note of impatience, a suspicion
that she was being taken advantage of, as students came to her door,
in London and Kintyre, expecting help, advice, food.

From 1962, through the seventies and into the eighties, Botswana
was a vivid and commanding strand in her life. It often absorbed
her energies; it fed her writing. Most importantly, in Botswana she
found a clan, a community, and at the least a partly effective
purpose. But Naomi's life had always been multi-stranded, and so
it continued. Africa was an alternative to Scotland, but not a
substitute. 'The loyalty [to Botswana] seemed to parallel rather
than erode my feeling for Scotland,' she wrote.[93] Each affected the
way she looked at the other. There were times when each was used
as a stick with which to beat the other. She was as likely to have
a '100% bloody day' in Mochudi as she was in Carradale.[94] But at
the heart of it all was her own sense of mutuality between Scotland
and Botswana which enabled her to be such a dedicated African.
In an 'Open letter to an African chief', addressed to Linchwe, she
said:

> You know quite well that part of my feeling about our own
> tribe comes from my being partly Highland and knowing in
> myself the warm feeling that we in the Highland area have
> towards our own and our related clans, however much we may
> laugh at it and pretend it is all part of a bad past.[95]

She had willed her way into a Highland identity, through an application of heart and mind. She did the same in Botswana. 'I cling like an old lizard to the rocks of Mochudi,' she wrote in an evocative poem.[96] In conversation in the 1990s, it was to Africa she returned most often.

CHAPTER EIGHT

Something Further

Something further was needed for the sake of making stories.

Early in Orcadia

1

IN 1961, Naomi had reached an age when most men and women are thinking of retiring, or slowing down, if they have not already done so. She was about to embark on another new life. In May of that year, she was interviewed by the *Scottish Daily Express*. 'So this is what it's like to have coffee with a tornado,' was the comment.[1] The following year, the London *Daily Express* featured her in their 'Remarkable mothers' series, in which Naomi said that she thought her children's view of her when young was as 'someone gay, rather pretty, and slightly mad'.[2] But if her energy was not failing her, age was catching up with her in other ways. At the end of that year, her mother died. A few months earlier, Louisa Kathleen Haldane had published her first and only book, *Friends and Kindred*, in which she remembered a world long since gone. It was the world that had produced her daughter, although her daughter is not much mentioned. Her son gets a chapter to himself.

Maya and Cherwell had remained a touchstone of Naomi's life. Her children, especially her sons, had strong bonds with their grandmother. The grandchildren visited when they were small, a new generation being brought up in the context of different assumptions about childcare, and different practical realities, encountering an environment which still had a flavour of Edwardian Oxford. With Maya's death, all that vanished. The contents of the house were disposed of, some of it brought to Carradale. The house itself made way for the building of a new Oxford college. One of Naomi's most powerful ties to England had weakened. (It did not break, however, as Lois settled in Oxford.)

The arrival of part of Cherwell at Carradale House prompted reflections on the resonance of things.[3] There were familiar items transplanted from the world of childhood to the place of the mature adult. The much-loved doll's house arrived, and remains to entertain great-grandchildren but is equally important as a reminder of continuity. A vanished world could not be allowed to mean a vanished past. Yet twenty years earlier, Naomi had recorded in her diary that possessions did not mean a great deal to her. 'I am only attached to such things as typewriter, pen and pencil, which are tools and replacable [sic],' she wrote, but added that 'a clean WC' and 'well fitting shoes' were important for comfort.[4] There were different kinds of attachment to objects. There were those valued because they were needed, and those valued because they were reminders of origins and identity. The latter had always been important to Naomi, whether as emblems of her own life or of the lives she created.

She still spent time in London, she still moved around with apparent restlessness, but Carradale contained most of the things that mattered and was her symbolic home. Mochudi would give her another locus, another home psychologically if not in fact, but there she really did travel light. The only object of hers that remains in Botswana now is the portable typewriter, which sits in the Gaborone office of Charles Bewlay, who came out to teach in Botswana and is now a publishing consultant. Although when in London Naomi entertained Dick's political colleagues, and would make use of his contacts to promote Botswana's needs and interests, Dick's political career did not seem to need her in the way it once had. She no longer participated in active campaigning. They were no longer a political team in the same way as in the early days at King's Norton and Kettering. First Scotland and then Africa shifted Naomi's political centre of gravity.

Labour's victory in 1964 brought a life peerage and a government post for Dick, who was regarded with great respect by many colleagues but was still considered as something of a maverick. Naomi became 'Lady Mitchison', but was dismissive of the honour and rarely used the title. In 1981 she herself received a CBE. She had earlier declined the offer of an OBE and accepted the honour this time because she felt it leant her a little more influence. However, she told no one about it before it was announced.

Dick's 1930s advocacy of aspects of Soviet socialism and his association with the radical Stafford Cripps and Aneurin Bevan had probably held back his political career. His book, *The First Workers' Government* (1934), in which he described a fictional British socialist state, made him suspect. Naomi's activities may have encouraged the suspicion to linger. There were plenty of people in the Labour Party who found her a nuisance. However, she was briefly in favour with the Colonial Office (under a Conservative Government) who encouraged her interest in the young chief designate of the Bakgatla. They soon realized their mistake.[5] The offer to Dick of a peerage was a nudge towards the political sidelines. He was in his seventies, and a cabinet reshuffle of April 1966 brought an end to his political career.

During these years, Dick always spent vacations at Carradale. Christmas was usually celebrated in London, but the family gathered at Carradale for New Year and visited during the summer. In 1982, Naomi recorded that there could be up to a hundred guests at the annual Carradale Hogmannay party.[6] The growing grandchildren got to know their grandparents mainly in the context of Carradale and a house full of cousins, as well, sometimes, as the children and grandchildren of Dick's and Naomi's friends. Their own children were now all married, and had produced substantial families. Yet certain rituals did not change. At meals Dick and Naomi maintained their seats at either end of the long table and exchanged teasing insults. One of Naomi's favourite themes was that she had married far too young, cradle-snatched by Dick.[7]

Some of the youngsters found her an intimidating presence. She was a liable as ever to outbursts of exasperation and disgust. She was not an easy person to approach: they could be overawed by an awareness that she was someone of remarkable assurance and achievement. But when she read or told them stories she was in her element, and some of them, at least, needed no encouragement to listen. For Naomi, the idea of family and kinship was clearly important. She wrote in 1984, 'I think to some extent I am consciously treading the footsteps of my Haldane grandmother who always gathered her family around her.'[8] Carradale became a kind of tribal centre for the Mitchisons, bringing responsibilities which could be trying but also representing connection. There was always work to be done and still today, visitors, whoever they are, may find themselves asked to chop down a tree or do a spot of weeding. The idea of a house as the focal point of extended family life and interests was inherited from Cloan, and Naomi, whether consciously or not, was replicating that inheritance.

In November 1964 came another reminder of mortality, Jack's death from cancer. In 1961, he had left Calcutta to work for the Indian Government's Council of Scientific and Industrial Research, and then was invited by the Orissa State Government to found his own Genetics and Biometry Laboratory at Bhubaneswar. He had little time to see this bear fruit, as the cancer had already been diagnosed and operated on in London. He and Naomi both expressed their anger at the fact that he was led to believe he had longer to live than was in fact the case. Naomi wrote two poems, one probably very soon after his death, the second some time later. Both reflect the importance and the ambivalence of the relationship between brother and sister.

> *The aching head*
> *Hums with the unanswered question,*
> *The thing now for always unsaid.*

What exactly the unanswered question is does not emerge. Naomi seems to be feeling for some definition of her relationship with her brother as well as pondering the nature of death.

> *All joins, all flows,*
> *It is here, the open secret.*
> *Him, but not him: not this: not that. Utterly otherwise.*
> *Who knows?*[9]

The later poem, entitled, like the first, 'J.B.S.H.', was written when Naomi was revisiting India and is more elegiac.

> *The long surf drives in at Puri*
> *Soft in the starlight or moon-edged momently;*
> *The trampled sand smoothes out*
> *And the little crabs run like thistle-down,*
> *Like thistle-down on the fields above Nigg.*
> *I alone swim here,*
> *No more in that cold northern sea,*
> *Soon like you, no more anywhere...*[10]

Swimming in the Bay of Bengal triggers a memory of swimming in the Cromarty Firth half a century earlier, when Jack was a soldier and Naomi soon to become a teenage bride. Through the intervening years, their relationship had been fraught and often fiery. There were rifts and reconciliations, but underlying both was Naomi's feeling that it was impossible to recover their childhood communion. 'Jack is ... always inside a kind of mask,' she had written in 1941. 'I don't feel as if I know him at all.'[11] Although she felt they became closer in later years, there is a persistent sense that he was somewhere beyond the horizon and that she would never catch up. Many versions of Jack appear in her books, and she never ceased to admire him. 'He is really a much bigger person than I am, all round, and I get jealous, as one only can be of one's own family.'[12] The jealousy was part of what bound them.

2

At the same time as Africa provided new territory for writing, Naomi was turning to other sources for her fiction. In 1962, she published her first science fiction novel, *Memoirs of a Space-woman*. This was followed by several short stories and two further novels, *Solution Three* (1975) and *Not By Bread Alone* (1983). The genre was entirely compatible with her fictional preoccupations, allowing her to pursue her interest in quest narratives, as well as enabling her to bring ideas about science, experimentation and ethics into her stories. It also took her into a new territory of human relations. In her historical fiction, she had transplanted human emotions and connections back in time. Now she was placing them in the future, which fascinatingly expanded the possibilities for unusual liaisons.

This at once became apparent in *Memoirs of a Spacewoman*, where the parameters of communication accommodate non-humans and also different aspects of being human. All forms of life are linked, and any division between external and internal becomes blurred. Reproduction is through grafts, and the grafts are both a part of the host and separate. The intensity and sensuality of the relationship between 'mother' and 'child' are among the most memorable aspects of the book.

In each of Naomi's full-length works of science fiction, women feature centrally and in all her shorter science fiction stories they are important. They are scientists, at the frontiers of research. In *Solution Three*, which presents a world where heterosexuality is marginalized (those involved in heterosexual relationships are branded deviants), women are personally and sexually in-dependent of men, and in *Not By Bread Alone* the main female character is a lesbian. In both novels, the emphasis is on men and women working together rather than sleeping together. The result is that women are seen to operate in a world uncluttered by sexual undercurrents, highlighting both their independence and their femininity. Anne, in *Not By Bread Alone*, is a professional scientist who carries on when her male colleague becomes discouraged. She has also the conventional 'soft' feminine qualities of sensitivity, maternalism and a concern for people and their feelings. Naomi portrays lesbian relationships in terms of women who respond to each other's gentlest attributes; there is no place in the picture for a butch masculinity.

These stories are challenging and provocative in a number of ways. It is not future technologies that interest Naomi, although they have a function as part of the future worlds she creates. It is the frontiers of genetics that the stories are founded on. The short story 'Mary and Joe' (1962) introduces some of the ideas that are explored in more detail in the novels. Mary is a geneticist. Her first child, Jaycie, is the product of one of her own experiments, literally fatherless and therefore genetically identical to Mary. Jaycie grows up to become a political leader and agitator. When she is attacked and seriously injured by burns, Mary saves her life, performing a skin graft using her own skin, which can take only because mother and daughter are identical. Jaycie survives to lead a new political movement. Even without the twist on the Christian nativity story, 'Mary and Joe' carries a subversive political charge. Women can reproduce without men; there is no need for the Y chromosome; women are leaders, politically and professionally. The effect of all this on men is suggested at the end of the story. Mary's husband Joe, finding out about their daughter's origins for the first time, looks at her differently. 'Deliberately and with a slow effort he made the hand respond, warmly, gently, normally. For the hand left to itself had wanted to pull away, not to touch her.'[13]

In *Solution Three* and *Not By Bread Alone*, Naomi looks at a future where genetic manipulation has become very sophisticated, which raises new issues of both practical science and ethics. *Solution Three* provides stability, with clones reproducing the species. But what is right for one situation may not be the solution for ever. 'In the days of Her and Him there was a necessary excellence, the sudden emergence of the exact gene combination for that moment in history. But might not a slightly other kind of excellence be needed now?'[14] In other words, scientific experimentation cannot afford to stop, there is no ultimate solution. Similarly, in *Not By*

Bread Alone, the answer to feeding the world seems to have been found through genetic engineering. But it goes wrong, partly because the social consequences of being able to abolish hunger without effort were not considered, partly because the scientific consequences cannot be controlled in the way initially believed. The novel has a vividly contemporary resonance.

Naomi was perfectly aware that in the current of her writing, science fiction was continuity, not change. Her trademark was interpreting a world unfamiliar to her readers, in her science fiction an invented world (which interestingly gets nearer and nearer to a world we recognize) rather than a world distant in place or time, such as Africa or ancient history. In *Solution Three*, she writes, 'The problems facing a world of S.F. are somewhat the same as those of a writer, either of historical fiction, or of stories about people in another culture, with another language.'[15] She is at pains to include the science, to demonstrate how it could happen. Her characters are explorers not of the frontiers of space but of scientific experiment. These books allowed her to give expression to some of her own scientific ideas, but she also learnt a lot from Jack and *Not By Bread Alone* draws on her visits to him in India. The novel is dedicated to her grandson Graeme, and his work and the work of her sons probably also contributed. Lois's descriptions of life in Outer Mongolia, where she worked after Pakistan, were drawn on for *Solution Three*.

It can be argued that in her science fiction, Naomi is more overtly and consistently feminist than she had ever been before, simply through the fact that most of her most interesting and courageous characters are female. The women are not only skilled professionals but have the talent for communion that Naomi so valued. These women are also adventurers, another consistent theme throughout her writing. Communion and community; loyalty both individual and collective; physical, intellectual and technological adventure: these remained her concerns in her final novels, which would again take her back in time.

Coinciding with her venturing into science fiction came a book which can be seen as a kind of sequel to *An Outline for Boys and*

Naomi's science fiction was fairly successful, but she never regained the commanding position she held in the first ten years of her writing career. In the sixties and seventies, she was having to get used to being overlooked by reviewers and to rejection. Her notebooks record lists of publishers who turned her down. It was discouraging, and the pile of unpublished typescripts began to mount. There were also the books she began but never finished, the ideas jotted down in notebooks that were never developed. But the writing continued, and the books came out at the rate of about one a year, slowing down a little in the 1970s. From the 1960s, when she was writing less often for the *New Statesman*, she was writing fairly regularly for both the *Glasgow Herald* and *The Scotsman* and found outlets in other Scottish publications, such as *The Scots Magazine* and *Scottish Field*. Increasingly, her subject matter in Scottish outlets was autobiographical, drawing on memories of her childhood. She was beginning to put together the first volume of her memoirs. She wrote a book, *Hide and Seek*, about her Trotter antecedents where she wove together reminiscence, history and her own thoughts on the nature of inheritance. It was never published.[19] When she came to write the third volume of her memoirs she complained to Lois that it was 'like tripping over tombstones all the time': so many of her friends were dead.[20]

She no longer had a publisher she could count on. The Bodley Head published the first two volumes of her memoirs but rejected the third, which was eventually accepted by Gollancz, who had published her work from time to time over forty years. Several of her children's books were published by Collins. It was not until the late 1970s that her books began to be published in Scotland, first by Canongate (*The Cleansing of the Knife* in 1979) and then by Richard Drew. With both Stephanie Wolff Murray at Canongate and Richard and Lavinia Drew she got on well, and they contributed to a revival of interest in her work. Both published new and old work, though her last two books were published by Balnain Books, based in Nairn. Yet, though Naomi was pleased that her achievement was being recognized in Scotland, the level of return was a reminder that things were not what they used to be. 'I have been offered £100 for a book of short stories,' she wrote to Sandy Grant, 'but am accepting as they have been simply turned down elsewhere. I am madly out of fashion.'[21] This may have been for *Images of Africa*, which Canongate published. For another book, Richard Drew offered an advance of £200. 'I'm at the bottom end now which is annoying but perhaps just.'[22] It was clear that Naomi could not make a living from her writing.

3

Naomi confronted the process of growing old with her usual curiosity. In an article for *Medical World* published in 1961, she reflected on the gains and losses of age. 'One certainly becomes less afraid of death. One feels it would be a nuisance and an interruption, but more and more of one's friends have gone through the experience.'[23] Thirty years later she calmly described an out-of-body experience that came to her when she was very ill with pneumonia. She found it reassuring; it made her realize that death need not be difficult or painful.[24] But age brought losses also. To Bessie Head she had written, probably in the early seventies, 'It is annoying to be too old for a love affair.'[25] She missed 'the curious clarity of perception that used to come with being in love'.[26] She had always felt that love affairs were a creative stimulant. There were health aggravations too. She could not move so easily. Rheumatism which had bothered her for years, was often very painful. In 1981, she had a hip replacement operation in Edinburgh, recuperating with Murdoch and Rowy whose recently-built East Lothian home had no stairs and a garden she could enjoy.

Above all, age brought the loss of people. In the late 1960s, Dick's health began to cause concern after he had a stroke. Towards the end of 1969, he had a second stroke and was in hospital. In January 1970, he had a heart attack, and was taken from Carradale to Westminster Hospital in London by air ambulance. Naomi ensured that Tish Rokeling was able to visit him. Dick's relationship with

Tish had been sustained for thirty years. Although at times Dick showed signs of recovery, he kept relapsing. He died on 14 February. His ashes were scattered in the sea off Carradale, attended by a flotilla of boats. The obituaries paid tribute to his dedication and diligence as an MP. But he was a backroom boy, and in his lifetime received little acknowledgement or reward. Some years later, Naomi wrote in one of her notebooks:

> I would think that Dick, who had in the thirties been involved in the fierce political quarrels of the left, was now a model back bencher, also knew every water main, every post office in his constituency, who always went to endless troubles for his constituents and was also...always ready to help his fellow Labour MPs in their serious difficulties, including the game of turning people's good ideas into a properly drafted Bill or amendment. His heart was in the Commons.[27]

The extraordinary Mitchison partnership was over. But its legacy was everywhere. Without Dick as the fixed centre of her life, a centre that at times she strained against and kicked at, it is hard to imagine how Naomi's excursive existence could have brought the challenges and rewards that it did. His role in her life, like his role in the Commons, was unobtrusive, but it was a necessary presence. Their affection for each other was deep and consistent. There is little doubt that they were each at times wounded by the realities of their principled allegiance to the idea of multiple partners; equally, there is little doubt that an essential loyalty and mutuality survived the damage. In 1960, she had reviewed a book on marriage in terms that revealed no vestige of second thoughts about the path she and Dick had chosen, referring to 'the poor old British professional classes who dowdily stick to the same car, the same fridge and even the same husband or wife for years at a time' and going on to defend polygamy.[28]

The last decade had brought signs of a drift apart. It was not possible for Naomi to knit Mochudi into her marriage in the way that their love affairs had become part of the fabric of their life together. Scotland never meant the same to Dick as it did to Naomi, but Carradale was a place they could share. Mochudi was geographically and emotionally too far away. There were times when, forced to choose between Dick and Africa, she had chosen Africa. She felt the dilemma. She had always wanted to be needed, and this was one of the consequences.

Dick's death brought immediate practical difficulties. Suddenly Naomi became financially vulnerable, as unwise investment had seriously diminished Mitchison funds. The Temple flat was given up, but there was still Carradale House, with its constant maintenance problems, to keep going. (She sold at least one painting, a Lowry, to keep Carradale afloat.) And although Carradale was unquestionably her home, she wanted to retain a foothold in London. This was resolved when she decided to move in to the Arnold-Forsters' Clarendon Road home, but there were inevitable frictions. Naomi wanted to continue her old London life, gathering people around her, inviting them to dinner, perpetuating a lifestyle with herself at the centre of things that was hardly compatible with her daughter's outlook or environment. It became easier when she was able to move into a two-bedroomed flat in the basement. The arrangement continued when Val moved to Blenheim Crescent, where Naomi again occupied the basement.

A pattern evolved of spending winters in London and summers in Carradale, which continued until 1992 when she finally abandoned London. Denny and Ruth were also in London, and Lois was in Oxford. Her marriage to John Godfrey, a protégé of Jack's (who had expressed to Naomi doubts about his suitability) and later a lecturer at the University of Edinburgh, came to a painful end in 1970. Naomi was angry and concerned as she witnessed and tried to mitigate the effects of an acrimonious divorce on her daughter and granddaughters. Lois had published several books, including a novel, *Gillian Lo*, based on her experiences in China where she had spent time as a journalist. But in Oxford she returned to teaching. Denny and Avrion were both pursuing highly successful careers in medical research. Murdoch became professor of natural history at the University of Edinburgh in 1963, where Rowy Mitchison became professor of social history in 1981.

The years did nothing to temper Naomi's experimental curiosity or the need, from time to time, to remind herself that she was a Haldane. In the 1960s, she took part in experiments with mescalin, set up by a doctor in London. In the Temple flat, she took the drug under observation, and herself wrote up the effects. She experienced the first symptoms after three-quarters of an hour – dizziness, nausea, visual distortion. 'I seemed to be falling out of myself.' Everything was intensified, a general hyperaesthesia. 'Anything that touched me, touched me too much.' The after-effects were equally unpleasant, leaving her feeling that she was not the same person as she was before, 'a nasty, lonely feeling'.[29]

Travel had always been part of the spirit of enquiry. It inevitably became more demanding, but it did not diminish in scope. In 1980, Naomi visited the Caribbean, as a guest in Jamaica of Trevor and Barbara Bottomley whom she had known in Botswana. She went ostensibly to ease her rheumatism but it provided material for a children's book, *There and Back*, although it was never published. In February 1987, she was in the Caribbean again, on a cruise, but did not enjoy it. Naomi added another continent to her explorations, going to Australia in 1982 (which provided one of the locations for *Not by Bread Alone*). She liked Australia, visited Cairns, Alice Springs and the north, taking an interest in schools, community, Aboriginal rights. Darwin, she wrote, 'is the only town, in my much-travelled life, where a taxi driver has, in friendliest Australian spirit, taken less than the legal fare.'[30] In 1984, she was lecturing in San Diego, California (she enjoyed American friendliness, as she had fifty years before in the southern states); in 1985, there was a lecture tour in Canada. She was in her eighty-eighth year. Botswana was still very much on the itinerary, although she was no longer going to India.

In Scotland, she was in demand as journalist, author and personality. She was commissioned as a scriptwriter for a BBC series called *Heritage*, which outlined Scottish history and traditions. In September 1974, she was participating in 'Meet the Author' sessions in Edinburgh with Norman MacCaig and Harri

Webb and again with Douglas Reeman and Ted Willis. She enjoyed the second session more than the first, but felt that the men had huge advantages. They led lives protected by 'devoted wives' and were able to write regular hours.[31] On the same day, she went to the James VI exhibition at the Royal Scottish Museum, stopped off at *The Scotsman* offices on North Bridge to see Neil Ascherson – 'nice to talk to journalists again' – and then went on to the Scottish National Portrait Gallery.[32] She showed no signs of flagging, but acknowledged other hints of age – when back in Carradale a few days later she wrote 'My desk is getting terribly cluttered and I find that I am getting increasingly stuck for quite ordinary words, nominal aphasia; they usually come back but what's the good of that?'[33]

The pace scarcely slackened. There was fruit to be picked and rowan and apple jelly to be made. The Coles were visiting. There were planning and paperwork to be done for the house. She had a ride in a helicopter being used for paratroop manoeuvres. Then, on 30 September, she travelled down to London for a Botswana Day party at the Commonwealth Institute. The next day she was at the University of Sussex for the opening of the Mass-Observation Archive.

4

From 1970 Naomi was living life as a single adult woman for the first time. She had been a wife for over fifty years and, however unorthodox the marriage, it had provided stability. As a single woman, her life-style scarcely changed, but the responsibilities stopped with her. There was no Dick to provide advice, to check the accounts, to supply moral and financial support. Carradale House was a concern, and some of the family felt it should be sold, suggesting that Naomi move into the Mains farmhouse next door. Naomi was determined to hang on to it, but it needed constant attention. 'I really get fed up finding funguses growing out of the damp wall above my head – the leaks in the roof seem quite unending,' she wrote to Sandy Grant.[34] There was always some repair required.

The garden was also a major responsibility, but Naomi's attachment to it and all it contained was if anything stronger than to the house. She had nurtured it, planted it, lavished it with attention, and dragooned friends and family into doing the same. She was particularly proud of the dozens of species of rhododendron, with hardly a period of the year when one or other was not in flower. There was usually, but not always, a gardener, but west-coast luxuriance was always threatening to get out of hand. 'I coped with [the garden] alone for a matter of months, aided occasionally by visiting MPs, but it was a wet summer and the weeds were winning the battle,' she wrote in 1960.[35] Naomi underplayed the demands she made on her visitors to contribute hard labour. Without them she could not have coped. Of the first Carradale gardener Naomi was so scared 'that I seldom went into the walled garden during working hours, but made myself a crescent-shaped bed at the far side of the house which nobody else worked on'.[36] But she learned from her gardeners, particularly Percy Edwards who was at Carradale in the 1960s and '70s. He and his wife Emily not only sustained the garden, but also helped to nurse Dick in his last illness and to look after Naomi in the period that followed.

Naomi's interest in plants is reflected in *Not By Bread Alone* and, more incidentally, in much of what she wrote. She played with the idea of starting a nursery business: 'If I were keen to be in a really honest job, unlike writing, which would do no harm to anyone in the community, I would think seriously about seed-growing and nursery-gardening.'[37] But the temptations of a 'really honest job' were not strong enough – and that kind of honest job would have pinned her to Carradale, which was never a serious proposition.

To keep the place going, it was necessary to think of ways the house and the estate could make money. Naomi gave up attempting to run the farm, and let it to a tenant. Some of the property on the estate could be let as holiday homes, and she also decided to use the stretch of land near the shore as a caravan site. This brought some seasonal income, but was dependent on fluctuations in tourism. In 1981, Naomi was concerned that the caravan site was unlikely to make a profit that year.[38] Part of the attraction of Carradale was that, especially since the demise of the Clyde steamers, it was off the usual tourist routes. Carradale became more difficult to get to without a car, and there is still only a one-track road for motor traffic. The village and Carradale House were caught in a quandary that was familiar all over the Scottish Highlands. Although Carradale still maintained a small fishing fleet, tourism was becoming increasingly important to its future. But too many tourists would endanger the qualities that attracted visitors in the first place. It was important for the village to be accessible, but not too much so.

Naomi's difficulties were exacerbated when, in 1969, a fire destroyed the kitchen and some of the outhouses. No one was hurt, but it meant that the kitchen wing of the house had to be rebuilt. The result was a new, larger and much better-equipped kitchen, with basement rooms underneath. Garden produce and fish from Carradale's fishermen went into a new freezer, but shelves were still filled with jam and bottled fruit. Naomi continued to employ local help in the house but the time when domestic help was readily and cheaply available was in the past. For many years, Nettie Mitchell had a key role in maintaining the domestic front, but there was always more to do than pairs of hands to do it. Naomi never overcame her lack of interest in housekeeping and relied heavily on others. Guests were expected to volunteer; some were more adaptable than others to a regime of self-help.

Naomi was single, but not often alone. She expected, and received, support from her children and grandchildren. She had many friends. She rarely sought solitude. Val said that she had never known her mother to go for a walk on her own.[39] She liked to have quantities of people at Carradale and to continue to preside over the long table. She especially encouraged the young to visit. Grandchildren brought their friends, and the grandchildren of Mitchison friends came with their friends. Frances Filson, granddaughter of Tish Rokeling, was a frequent summer visitor, though when she first went to Carradale as a twelve-year-old she found the place overwhelming. When, as an adult, she brought her fiancé Chris Allen, he found it equally difficult to feel comfortable. He remembers sitting with others in the drawing-room one evening, with the rain lashing down outside, when Naomi burst in soaking wet, to announce that the cows had got out and she needed volunteers to help round them up.[40] When Bob Tait and Isobel Murray visited in 1984, they were met by Naomi with a bucket of pigswill in each hand. She asked Bob if he felt like cutting down a few trees before lunch.[41]

Visitors often found the place chaotic, meals uncertain (the sparsity of food is often commented on), unidentified persons of all ages spread over house and garden, but with Naomi incontrovertibly at the centre. In 1955, a profile in *Picture Post* had emphasized the Mitchison hospitality. It catches an impression of Naomi at Carradale as a mercurial presence amidst her assembled company, playing to a diverse audience. It is a picture which many later comments confirm.

> In the often strangely mixed company at Carradale, despite a diffidence, which she shares with her husband, about being the centre of attention, there is always Naomi Mitchison herself, the conscious literary artist, intellectually and emotionally vivid, exciting, unconventional. In her versatility and range of interests, and changing moods, she seems to have something in common with everyone present.[42]

Part of the Carradale experience was often the after-dinner playing of intellectually challenging word games. Not everyone enjoyed them or was good at them; among those who were was the novelist Candia McWilliam. And of course Naomi herself, who liked to win.

At the same time, the formalities were maintained. Naomi, who often during the day would wear odd assemblages of clothes with an accent on comfort rather than elegance, still dressed for dinner in silk and velvet. In 1987, with Naomi's ninetieth birthday approaching, Sue Innes, a journalist, went to Carradale to interview her for *The Scotsman*. She had not been warned about dressing for dinner, and was embarrassed when she discovered that this was expected, as she had nothing suitable to wear. In the event, she converted her daytime attire by donning her silk pyjama top, which seemed to pass muster.[43] In fact, Naomi did not appear to object if others did not participate in this custom; she liked to dress up (but Tabitha Lucas, a granddaughter, remembers that Naomi had a dislike of mirrors) and was not bothered if others did not want to share in the ritual. And the dress enhanced the drama of unpredictability, if there was a sudden need for chasing cattle or if it was felt that a dance or a story was called for.

Naomi no longer had a formal political role in Scotland, but that did not mean that she lost her political voice. One issue which forcibly engaged her attention was that of nuclear weapons, which she energetically opposed. She took a leading role in the early 1960s demonstrations against the American Polaris submarines based in Holy Loch, and later opposed Trident and cruise missiles. The American presence particularly irked her. 'I wish we could get rid of the American army of occupation,' she wrote to Sandy Grant.[44] She visited the women's peace camp at Greenham Common and was a member of Scottish Writers Against the Bomb, which flourished for several years in the mid-1980s.

Nineteen seventy-nine brought a Conservative government under the leadership of Margaret Thatcher, which rapidly began to unpick the fabric of the welfare state which Dick and Naomi and their generation had helped to weave. Naomi was disgusted:

Here everything is being eroded. The public bodies, the Post Office, the Gas Board (both very successful), B.E.A. and so on, all being sold off and I see no reason why we shan't end in hock to some American based international company. The privatization of the N.H.S. goes creeping on and now there is the eroding of the green belts round the cities to please the private builders. People are beginning to wonder what dragon they have unleashed, but it's too late.[45]

She added that the Labour Party was in a mess. The miner's strike of 1984 intensified her concern about the political situation and there seemed to be no effective means of opposition. She had a better chance of influencing politics in Botswana than in Britain. Her belief in a Scottish Assembly remained, but in the 1980s there seemed little prospect of this. The 1987 general election brought no change to the political situation. Naomi voted for Argyll's Liberal candidate as a Labour vote would have been wasted, but she did so reluctantly. That election night she was alone in Carradale House.

In 1981, Mass-Observation, by then existing as an archive located at the University of Sussex, re-started its directives and Naomi began once again to report back. In that year she was concerned about the recession, worrying about university cuts, which affected several members of her family. Money problems nagged. Rates on the caravan site had gone up to £1400 a year and on the river fishing to £450. She did not clear enough on either to pay them. (In 1990 she sold the caravan site.) The recession hit the holiday season that year, and the cottage lets were 'disastrous'.[46] She estimated that at this time she was earning £3000 to £4000 a year from her writing. To maintain the property and the land she needed a great deal more.

It was a difficult year in a number of ways. The arthritis that had been troubling her for a long time intensified, until she finally had a hip replacement operation in October. She was in the Princess Margaret Rose Hospital in Edinburgh for two weeks. Although treatment was on the National Health, she felt she should give a donation to the hospital. On Christmas Day that year, Mark Arnold-Forster died.

Naomi may have felt outside the political arena in Britain, but she had a public presence, in Scotland at least. Four Scottish universities awarded her honorary degrees (the universities of Stirling, Strathclyde and Heriot Watt, and the Open University in Scotland; but none of the older universities). In a notebook dated May 1982 there are some comments under the heading 'Being a woman in Scotland'. 'Definitely inferior ... a great surprise if a woman appears to be really successful.'[47] She was, in some respects, reaping the rewards of success, but in others still felt excluded, as she had so often in the past. Much of the serious business of life was in the hands of men. 'So much happens in Bars ... this is the men's club where they get away from wives'.[48] It had annoyed her when she was a member of the Highland Panel, and still annoyed her.

She visited Edinburgh quite regularly, staying with Murdoch and his family or with her cousin Brodrick Haldane in India Street. She would go for lunch at the Scottish Arts Club in Rutland Square where she could be sure to find people to talk with about art or writing or politics. She felt well and positive about her life. Responding to a Mass-Observation directive of 1984 she rated herself eight out of ten for 'health and well-being' and considered herself to have a high sense of self-esteem.[49] All this time she continued the Alexander technique exercises on which she set great store, although swimming was becoming more difficult.

In 1985 Naomi was invited to lecture at the Royal Museum of Scotland, which she gave without a single note seated in the centre of the platform. She talked about Botswana and totally charmed her audience. Her ninetieth birthday was celebrated both in London and in Edinburgh, where the Scottish Arts Council hosted a party. She was presented with a painting which later went missing, causing great consternation. It turned out that she had left it in the office of her publisher Richard Drew, whom she had gone to see in Glasgow the following day. She was a guest of honour at the opening of the Scottish Poetry Library in Edinburgh in 1984 and again at its fifth birthday celebration in 1989. Students were beginning to write doctoral theses on her. Articles were appearing in Scottish magazines. In October 1984 Isobel Murray and Bob Tait of Aberdeen University recorded a lengthy interview with her for a series of interviews with Scottish writers. She had become a symbol of Scottish women's literary achievement.

5

With her ninetieth birthday approaching Naomi published a new novel, *Early in Orcadia* (1987). The idea had grown from a seed planted on a trip to Orkney when she had been visiting Marjorie Linklater, Eric Linklater's widow. She was going further back in history than she had ever been, to pre-history, where there were no written signposts to guide her. There was no way of knowing the language spoken or the gods believed in, and without language and religion there is a huge gap in understanding of the way people related to each other and the world around them. Yet these are the things that fascinated Naomi and which she made into the substance of her novel. She felt a kinship with the early people of Orcadia – 'Go far enough back and all humankind are cousins'.[50]

With a challenging effort of the imagination she put herself inside the skins of of a neolithic people settling in a land they called 'The Shining', from the way it had shimmered on the horizon from across the sea. She meticulously reconstructs how they might have built a boat capable of crossing the Pentland Firth from Caithness to Orkney, how they might have ferried the animals whose bones archaeologists have found, how they might have learned to weave. She gives them a language, a slightly stilted English, and emotions and fears. Her evocation of an environment and the response to it is commanding. Although inevitably she imposes many of her own views of human relations and how a community is built these do not clash with the context she has created.

Early in Orcadia is in a sense the missing link, that rooted Naomi's story-telling in the origins of humanity. African mythology had enabled her to do something similar, but this novel reveals that it was important for her to complete a connection that was closer to home. There are echoes of many of her favourite themes. A young boy is drowned on the voyage to Orkney: a sacrifice which helps to ensure eventual success. There is a loyal partnership at the core of the novel, but no sexual exclusivity. Family and kinship are the building blocks of the community. Collective effort is essential to survival. These are the tribal values which she saw being eroded in Africa, but which in Orcadia she could make work. But although there are themes which first emerged with her earliest fiction this is a much gentler book than any of the tales of ancient Greece or imperial Rome.

Naomi did not stop with Orkney. A volume of short stories and poems, *A Girl Must Live* (1990), published work that had accumulated over many years, some of it appearing for the first time. They include the realistic and the fantastic, ranging in time and place to give a taste of many of Naomi's main areas of interest. They bring together all sorts and conditions of particularly women, from Laureen of the title story, a pragmatic misfit in contemporary Zambia, to the Scottish female voices and images of the long poem 'The talking oats' which compresses centuries of Highland experience. In 1991 there were two more short historical novels, *The Oath-Takers* set in the turmoil of ninth-century Europe, and *Sea-green Ribbons*, which follows the fortunes of a young girl in Cromwell's England. They are both in a sense quest stories, but the second is the better book. *The Oath-Takers* is fragmented, reflecting perhaps the upheaval of the time but not working successfully as a narrative. *Sea-green Ribbons* began life as a play on the subject of John Lilburne and the Levellers. In the novel the narrative is focused on Sarah, who in Cromwellian London is attracted by the ideas and beliefs of the Levellers. She flees from an abusive husband on her own quest for a just society. Taking her future into her own hands, she learns the hard way about the limitations of a woman's life and the impossibility of a single individual resisting entrenched power. The novel ends on a note of quiet optimism, with Sarah reaching America with her new husband and embarking on a new life.

There is struggle and death in all these novels, but what predominates is the possibility of a better future. Courage, skill and hard work underpin the optimism of both *Early in Orcadia* and *Sea-green Ribbons*. But perhaps what emerges most strongly is the importance of the story-teller's role. 'A writer should be able to wear a hundred masks,' Naomi had written in her unpublished *Hide and Seek*. 'I hope modestly that I can wear at least a dozen and, while

I am wearing each, I shall be able to play the appropriate ritual games.'[51] She saw herself in her nineties, perhaps more clearly than ever, as above all a story-teller with all the sense of ritual and responsibility that that role implies. In both *Early in Orcadia* and *Sea-green Ribbons* she captures the rhythm and cadence of narration that is essential to move a story forward. She was more successful at this when dealing with the past than with the present, as if distance leant her confidence.

In the final story in *A Girl Must Live* rats have inherited the world after the destruction of humanity by 'the Great Darkness'. There are still a few fragments of human history remaining amongst the ruins of the British Museum. Rat historians and story-tellers have chronicled the rise of the 'changed rats' who responded to colour and music, built shelters, developed superior thought processes, and told of how humankind had brought about their own destruction through hatred and rivalry. Surely, the young rats ask, they must have realized the danger of their actions? Yes, is the response: '"if mankind had remained as the most powerful kind of animal, but not killing one another, even progressing, becoming perhaps, as conscious of fine sounds and of the thoughts of others as we rats are, where would we be? If mankind had survived where would the rats be, where our thinking, our consideration for one another, our songs, our beauties? Could there have been room in the world for both?"' And the young rats wonder if the 'almost death of the world' had been necessary for rats to flourish. 'Here were questions which not even the wisest rat amongst all the deeply talented rat historians could answer for certain.'[52]

There are no definite answers. Cycles of destruction and rebuilding can be seen as terrible failures of humanity or as constant renewal. Human nature almost has to believe in the efficacy of sacrifice in order to avoid despair. One interpretation of Naomi's story 'Rat-world' is that humanity, however it happened, has made the ultimate sacrifice for the benefit of a race of superior animals. Another interpretation suggests that humanity, through foolishness, fear and greed, will inevitably destroy itself and all, or almost all, that has been created by human hands, leaving the world to be inherited by animals that humans have invariably feared and hated. Naomi's experience of the twentieth century suggests that both interpretations are equally valid.

In *Early in Orcadia* Hands returns to the mainland to tell the people he left behind that 'the Shining' is land just like theirs, not a mystical 'other place'. Soon they no longer tell tales of 'the Shining'; knowledge has overcome the need to mythologize. But Hands recognizes that myths are essential: 'Something further was needed for the sake of making stories.'[53] From childhood Naomi had gleaned what was needed for making stories, voraciously, sometimes indiscriminately, to feed her endless appetite for story-telling. She was addicted to creating narratives, including many narratives of her own life. As she said more than once in conversation, 'I couldn't do aught else.'[54] She knew there would come a point when she could no longer feed the addiction. 'I think I can still write, but when that goes I had better go too,' she commented in spring 1991. And a little later, writing 'is all I am ... It is my life. I cannot bear to think that my last book is really my life's end.'[55] Her last two books were published in that year.

CHAPTER NINE

Personal and Political

We go with the wave of our time.

You May Well Ask

IN MAY 1970, I was on a flight from Nairobi to London with my two small daughters. There were few people on the plane and we were able to spread out over several seats. It was a night flight, and while I was settling the children to sleep I noticed across the aisle an elderly woman with a battered case, a travelling rug and a typewriter. It suddenly came to me that this was Naomi Mitchison. The next morning I hesitantly accosted her. She smiled, looked slightly embarrassed, but admitted her identity. I told her how I had discovered her novels as a teenager, and how they had brought alive the classical history I was studying at school. I knew little of what she had written since *The Corn King and the Spring Queen*.

I did not meet Naomi again until 1985, when she came to lecture at my place of work, the Royal Museum of Scotland. She talked about how she had met Linchwe and got involved with Mochudi, and I remembered that meeting on the East African Airways flight. She had been on her way back from Botswana. Now her hair was completely white and all the years of the century seemed to be written on her skin. But from time to time her intense blue eyes were lit with mischief and an almost childlike sense of fun. She had, I think, forgotten both meetings when in 1992 I saw her again, to talk about the writing of this book. This is what I wrote at the time:

> I arrive at 11am at the garden flat in Blenheim Crescent, off
> Ladbroke Grove. NM opens the door to me. She greets me with
> warmth, is very friendly, seems pleased to see me. Her clear,
> light blue eyes have a marvellous twinkle. The flat is well lived
> in, a little in need of paint. NM has a large bright
> bed-sitting-kitchen, with an expanse of french window
> opening on to a little patio and garden. There are bowls of
> bulbs on a table on the patio, coming on nicely. There's a desk
> at the window, slightly to one side, papers, a typewriter. It's
> definitely a working room as well as a living room. There are
> books, papers in piles, letters, bills. She has a lot of
> correspondence to deal with and no secretarial help.
>
> A small pine table is laid with two places, but half of it is
> occupied by papers. I am offered coffee, which NM makes in
> a jug. It's very strong. I ask where she would like to sit. She
> decides to sit on the bed, which is piled with cushions on which
> she makes a kind of nest with support for her back. I sit on the
> only armchair. Conversation starts immediately, and
> continues for nearly three hours, almost without pause. It's a
> kind of stream of consciousness, prompted and slightly
> directed by my questions, but I feel these are hardly
> necessary.

On this occasion, Naomi was insistent that the important part of
her life was her books and announced that she was not going to tell
me about her love affairs. She did say that there had been seven.
Later, at Carradale, when I reminded her of this, she looked at me
with that inimitable blue twinkle and said, 'Maybe there were
eight.'[1] I think she was probably at various times and in various
ways in love with six men other than Dick; I don't think she went to
bed with them all. They are all named in this book; there was at least
one other with whom she had a brief sexual encounter. As over the
months I read her books and talked with her, I began to understand
that for Naomi intimacy was enormously important, but that it did

not need to involve sexual congress, just as sex does not necessarily involve intimacy. What was important was choice, and freedom to act on that choice once made. That was where life changed for some women in the 1920s. Naomi, of course, played a part in that change.

In a later, tape-recorded interview, Naomi talked more about relationships. She said:

> For quite a long time, all of us would be, Dick and I would be, very happy just to be with people, in a way very close, but not actually going that far. In a way those were the happiest times. Both of us had these very deeply affectionate feelings about other people and hadn't just stepped over that final —

She broke off and quoted:

> *That's how easily things go wrong,*
> *A sigh to much, a kiss too long.*
> *There follows a mist and blinding rain,*
> *Life is never the same again.*

And added, 'I suppose anybody could have told us, and probably did.'[2]

There is no doubt that in the 1920s, for Naomi and her milieu, sex was political. It was a way of demonstrating freedom, of saying, as Naomi herself put it, 'Here, this is what we're after.'[3] It was feminist; it was socialist, a way of denying the ownership of marriage. It was a way of sharing, of spreading 'kindness', to use Naomi's word. Access to contraception changed the rules of the game, or seemed to. In fact, and in spite of Naomi's confident public statements about 'open marriage', the rules proved undefinable. You cannot legislate for the emotions. It is clear from their letters that their love affairs brought both Naomi and Dick hurt and anxiety as well as comfort and support. It is equally clear that both had a dogged courage in pursuit of what Naomi calls 'right relations'. These relations are not just about individuals, but about families, communities, tribes, nations. In a later interview, Naomi talked about friendship. 'Friendship is life,' she said. 'What are we human beings for except to – I won't say love one another – but at least to like one another?'[4] That seems to me to be as good a description of the purpose of life as any I have come across.

A few months after my first meeting in London, I drove on a beautiful June evening from South Queensferry, near Edinburgh, to Carradale. The countryside was lit from the west by the soft, lambent light you only find in northern summer nights. My route took me up Loch Lomondside to Arrochar, over the Rest and Be Thankful pass to Loch Fyne, and down from Ardrishaig to Tarbert to take the single-track road across to the east side of Kintyre. In the Scottish Highlands, there is no road, highway or single-track, that can mask the delineation of the landscape, the mountains, passes and lochs that dictate the nature of connection between one place and another. I followed the road down the coast, with the silvery mountains of Arran darkening on my left, to Carradale. It was half-past nine when I arrived, bumping along the rutted track to the back door of Carradale House. Naomi had travelled this road hundreds of times.

As I got out of the car, I noticed the scarred and flaking walls of the house. The door opened and I was greeted by Stacey from Australia, part Aborigine, who was staying at the house to help out. Naomi was in the pale blue drawing-room with its lingering smell of wood smoke, dressed for dinner in a Liberty peacock pattern skirt, pink silk shirt and an oriental shawl. She looked marvellous. She took me to her room upstairs. In my notebook I wrote:

> Large desk full of papers, all her books filing a large bookcase, a small bed, clothes draped over chairs. It looks out over the sea. Shortly afterwards she called me back and motioned me to the window. There was an almost full moon, casting a pathway of light across the water.

For me there was a choice of bedrooms, but each was marked by peeling wallpaper and pitted paintwork.

The next morning we began the first of several tape-recorded interviews. At Naomi's suggestion, we sat on cushions on the step of the big doorway that leads out on to the lawn. This is the front door, though it is never used as such. She sat clasping her knees like a teenager. I have seen a photograph of her as a young woman sitting in exactly the same way. On the tape, birdsong and the distant bleat of lambs provides a pleasing accompaniment to her words.

She talked, with a break for lunch which she made herself as Stacey had gone to Campbeltown, until late afternoon. When I suggested we had done enough, she sat herself on one the drawing-room's ample sofas, then suddenly keeled over. For a few moments I was concerned that something had happened to her, then realized that she was simply asleep. She woke half an hour later, rather disorientated, professing not to know where or when she was.

Stacey cooked dinner, and the three of us sat at one end of the huge table to eat. Naomi had, as always, dressed for dinner. I had made a gesture and changed into a skirt. Stacey was in the jeans and sweatshirt she had worn all day. There was a quiet ceremony about the meal which I liked. The table was laid with silver and the candles were lit. Naomi presided almost regally, offering food, pouring wine (though she ate very little herself, and drank almost nothing). We were a tiny island, a rather incongruous trio, in an oceanic dining-room which is well used to accommodating over twenty people. Later that evening Naomi announced that Stacey was a witch. 'There's magic about,' she said.[5]

The following evening, Naomi went upstairs to change and reappeared later on the stair as I was going up. She was wearing a long skirt and a black velvet jacket and looked down at me with one hand on the banisters. In the other she held a large brown envelope, stuffed full. She waved it at me. 'There's a whole love affair here,' she said. I asked her if I could read the letters, and she handed me the packet without a word. If I had had any doubt of her talent for the dramatic gesture, this would have dispelled it. She was superb. I read the letters that night, still reading long after she had retired to bed.

By this time I had become part of the story I was going to tell. The paragraphs I have just written are based on the notes I took at the time. Now I have incorporated them, and myself, into the narrative, just as Naomi's previous biographer, Jill Benton, had done, reflecting her own perspective and her relationship with her theme. The biographer of a living subject cannot avoid stepping on to the stage. In the scene that was played on the stair, I was a character as well as audience.

Each time I visited Carradale, Naomi walked me round the garden, to inspect the peaches and vines in the greenhouses, through the kitchen garden, the half-wild shrubberies, across the lawn, under the trees. On that first visit, we walked down to the shore at her suggestion, and she climbed the stile at the end of the garden, spurning my assistance. The following summer, I arrived at the house to find Naomi rather shaky and walking with a stick. She had had two falls. But in the spring of 1995 she was supervising an enormous bonfire, wielding secateurs with a still powerful hand and flinging branches enthusiastically, almost fiercely, on to the flames. She was an old lady of ninety-seven. The aphasia which had begun to bother her in the seventies was worse. She needed help now to get around, although she hated it. But she was an image of extraordinary strength. That image, in various guises – a competitive tomboy, an impatient young woman, a courageous and curious traveller, an imperious 'Lady' Mitchison – has sat on my shoulder throughout the writing of this book. It is mediated by another, of a kind of aloneness, which comes inevitably with survival beyond colleagues and companions. Angus Calder remembers visiting Carradale and seeing Naomi working by herself in the garden, 'brave and somehow lonely'.[6] Her own sense of existing in a world which had failed to live up to the successive waves of hope and conviction that had driven her increased that isolation.

In April 1992, not long before I made my first visit to Carradale, Naomi had addressed a conference at London's Science Museum which commemorated the centenary of Jack's birth. It was demanding, physically and emotionally, and was followed by her move out of the flat in Blenheim Crescent. Everything was going to Carradale, which would now be her only home. She became ill, so ill that she thought she was dying. But she also acknowledged the experience as a portent: there was not much time left. 'I feel increasingly that time will catch up with me before I have written all I want to write,' she had said in 1988.[7] Now she was trying to tidy things up and sort out papers, and finding it a burdensome task. She was parcelling up papers and sending them to the National Library of Scotland in Edinburgh. I became alarmed when she spoke of throwing things away. She may indeed have destroyed some of the evidence, but equally she may only have been provoking me. I wrote in a letter to Dorothy Sheridan at the Mass-Observation Archive, who had herself worked with Naomi, 'Sometimes I think Naomi is playing games with me, teasing, being mischievous. And age certainly hasn't diminished her sense of theatre.'[8]

Naomi's grandson, Graeme Mitchison, said that she was a woman 'beyond the ordinary', impossible to live up to.[9] I had now come within the magnetic field of her expectations. My interpretation of her life is strongly coloured not only by her own version – few people have provided so extensive a scenario of their own lives, though she warned 'I know that I remember things that didn't happen'[10] – but by a relationship which could never be only professional. When I was in Botswana, word quickly got round that someone had arrived to research a book about Naomi Mitchison. Sandy Grant took me to Mochudi in his pick-up. When he pulled up, a young girl rushed over, shouting, 'Lady Mitchison, Lady Mitchison!' I could smell the beer on her breath, but all the same it was an odd sensation, as if I, to borrow words that Naomi might have used, had adopted the mask of the subject of my book. And in a sense I had, for it was her name that opened doors.

As Sandy helped me track down old Mochudi comrades of Naomi's, we often asked ourselves, what had she really achieved there? We ticked off a list: the library, now a neat, shaded building packed with schoolchildren studying for their exams. The raising of consciousness among women. Had it lasted? Perhaps not, but there was a new women's movement growing now, possibly from seeds planted by Naomi a quarter of a century earlier. The schools and the dozens of youngsters who benefited directly from her help and encouragement. But in fact, to separate what Naomi did in Africa from her achievement elsewhere is misleading. 'Adventure to the adventurous,' was inscribed on the jumble sale jug she treasured. It was the adventuring itself that was at the heart of whatever she achieved, wherever she went.

I stayed in the motel in Mochudi, the only guest apart from a visiting football team on one night. Across a dry, brown, bare space in front of my room there was a dead donkey. I was reading Doris Lessing's book *African Laughter* with the door open. Lizards flickered over the baked earth and goats nibbled at the single straggling tree. Late in the afternoon, a couple of men drove up in a battered pick-up, the universal vehicle in Botswana, and put a torch to the donkey's corpse. When darkness fell, which happened suddenly, it was still a smouldering red heap. Naomi, I thought, would not have watched from a distance. She would have been right there, supervising the flames and noting the precise nature of their effect on the poor dead beast.

She has described herself as a shape-changer, and contends that this is what all writers of fiction have to be. She has indeed played many parts, donned many masks. Others have described how quickly her moods can change. She has never hidden her emotions, has been flamboyant about her likes and dislikes, quick to love and quick to criticize. Beneath all this rapid alteration there has been a deep current of consistency. Her hopes and values as a teenager have remained, informing the whole of her life.

In the context of Africa, she wrote:

> [Africans] understand ... that being one of a tribe is perfectly compatible with being one of a new nation, who understand that tribal society is not something backward and ignorant, but may be the moving force of genuine African progress, as well as being just, fearless and friendly, a focus of human happiness.[11]

Naomi Haldane was a tribal child who was always looking for a tribe of her own. From the gangs of the Dragon School and the

Cherwell chums, through the fellow campaigners and comrades of the 1920s and '30s, to Scotland and then Botswana, Naomi aspired to shape and lead a right-minded community. In 1975, giving the thirty-eighth Haldane Memorial Lecture, she spoke of a teenage fantasy of being one of the Guardians in Plato's republic.[12] She found in traditional tribal Africa a cohesive moral order which in her view was absent in Europe.

> For surely we in Western Europe suffer badly from lack of moral cohesion and ways of strengthening one another? In fact this is why we find the idea of war, with all the getting together which it implies, temptingly acceptable.[13]

It is an experience of Africa at odds with a current picture of much of the continent as beyond redemption, and Botswana is perhaps one of the few African countries which demonstrates the validity of her view. The positive aspects of tribalism could be identified, perhaps because Botswana was independent before the country's valuable mineral resources became known. Although the British had been a colonial presence for decades, it was a part of Africa that escaped the worst of the contests, both African and European, over land and resources.

Naomi's family were part of her community aspiration, and so were her books. In them she explores, examines and experiments over and over again with issues concerning communion and community. Loyalty is at the heart of these. So is love of all kinds, maternal and filial, heterosexual and homosexual, brotherly and sisterly, and infinite combinations and variations of these. Overarching love and loyalty is the idea of comradeship, in adventure and experiment, in war and defeat. Shared goals and shared activity are foundations of much of her life and work. It is reflected in the way she gathered people around her, in the way she celebrated patterns of work in her *New Statesman* articles, for example, where she describes building a hayrick or bringing in the harvest. Or in her support for the brigades in Mochudi, which brought people together to build a dam or repair a road. But she was aware of the dangers of the group. 'Tolerant people do not band themselves together to express their tolerance, but intolerant people have a solidarity which only narrowness of views can give.'[14] Several of her books warn of the terrible destruction that such narrowness can bring.

In one of her last novels, *Early in Orcadia*, Naomi describes the making of clay pots by little Honey and her mother and the other potters. It is a collective activity, dependent for its success on the pooling of experience, passing knowledge on from one generation to the next, and being open not only to learning but to trying out new ideas. At the same time, each pot is the product, the 'child', of an individual. The potters must understand their material and how it behaves when it is fired. They must know what tools to use. They must be able to tell from the feel of the clay whether it is turning out as it should. Naomi is a highly tactile writer. Her focus is on feeling, of the hands as well as of the heart. To write about something, she needed to have felt it herself; and to feel something was to write about it. It is this quality, laced with the imagination, which enables her to translate the felt circumstances into distant times and places, that gives her best writing its characteristic quality.

Naomi's first books were greeted with excitement and praised for their innovative approach to historical material. For a decade or so she was a respected and prominent writer, if never a best-seller. By the Second World War, her reputation was in decline. She was not in tune with the writing favoured by her natural political associates; her patrician background stood in the way of publication in precisely those outlets that she herself approved. Periods of economic depression and unemployment always erect barriers to the achievement of women; the social and economic conditions of the 1930s were against her. When she embarked on another life in Scotland, there was an even rougher road ahead of her. There was a world war, and she was trying to establish herself as a writer in a culture which had with more than average success overlooked the achievement of women. When she turned to Africa, she wrote herself even more firmly into the sidelines as far as

Britain was concerned, although her books for children seemed to maintain more of a presence.

She has written over seventy books, and edited and contributed to many more. She has written hundreds of articles and several short pamphlets. Some of her books are so thoroughly products of their times that they will be read now only for what they can tell us about a period's cast of mind: *The Moral Basis of Politics* and *An Outline for Boys and Girls* for the thirties, *What the Human Race Is Up To* for the early sixties. Some of her novels are interesting efforts, but have deservedly faded: *We Have Been Warned*, *Behold Your King* (1975, about the Crucifixion), *When We Become Men*. But much of her fiction survives impressively: *The Conquered* and most of her 1920s fiction, *The Blood of the Martyrs*, *Travel Light*, *Lobsters on the Agenda*, her three science fiction novels, several of her children's books, many of her short stories all define her as a novelist of unusual skill, intelligence and imagination. Two novels, *The Corn King and the Spring Queen* and *The Bull Calves*, would alone place her in the front rank of twentieth-century writers. As a poet, her output is less distinguished, but she has written some fine poems. Her most ambitious poetry contains her best work, for example 'The cleansing of the knife' and 'The talking oats'. 'The *Alban* goes out; 1939' is a beautifully sustained and resonant work.

Some of Naomi's best writing is contained in newspapers and journals. Her *New Statesman* pieces provide a valuable and immensely readable account of farming in the Scottish Highlands in the 1950s. Scattered through her papers are memorable fragments which seem never to have seen the light of day, and several complete books and plays have not been published. Her memoirs, especially the fist two volumes, *Small Talk* and *All Change Here*, and some of her travel writing are quirky and engaging expeditions into her past and other places. With all this literary activity and the fluctuations of her own success, she has always been keenly interested in the endeavours of other writers, and encouraged and assisted them in many ways.

Much of Naomi's work is now out of print, although this is beginning to change. Isobel Murray, who has taken a lead in re-establishing Naomi Mitchison's reputation, believes that she has been partly the victim of fashion. Bringing her work back into print will make her accessible again and help the process of reassessment.[15] But neither historical fiction nor science fiction has received the attention it deserves from the academic community (with some exceptions of course; there is now a Scott and a Stevenson industry); the odds are still stacked against her.

'Memory can be remarkably inaccurate,' Naomi warns in *You May Well Ask*.[16] In a fragment of typescript, she describes two scenes from her childhood as if they were fiction.

> The girl has only just started her museum. The cousins in New Zealand have sent her the feathers of a bird that can't fly. And she has a lovely string of glass beads from India, but she must be careful of it. The girl likes to be read to, specifically poetry like Tennyson and Browning; she likes the long words in Browning. There are children's books, but most of them are silly except for the Jungle Books, the Wouldbegoods and the Bad Child's Book of Beasts.[17]

> The river is always nice. Father rows, but Boy is almost able. Mother is steering with two ropes ... Sometimes father rows up to the high river, dodging the fallen branches: there are water lilies, white and yellow, and shallows where both the children can paddle across the river, while their father cuts back branches which have grown right across. Then they make a careful fire. The grown-ups have tea and everyone has jam-belows out of the cake shop. If you choose things the day before, a boy will come with it next morning. All shops have boys. Sometimes they get pennies at the houses they go to.[18]

There is an almost filmic quality in these passages, as if we are simultaneously observing through a lens and entering a child's stream of consciousness. Naomi is recreating at the same time as recording, stepping back from the scenes which are related in the third person, but emotionally deep inside them and vividly subjective. 'Boy' is almost able to row, but 'Girl' will learn to row also. It is seniority, not gender, that gives 'Boy' the headstart. Remembering her fantasy of being one of Plato's Guardians, Naomi ruefully notes that she, as a teenager, neglected to take account of the fact that no woman in Plato's Greece could be such a thing, but adds, 'was I in my fantasies ever a female? Probably not.'[19]

Memory generates its own reality; we have to be aware, though, that it may be a reality that no one else recognizes. Naomi makes no secret of the fact that she wrote her life into her fiction, and I have suggested that there are moments when she may have borrowed her actions from her own books. For the story-teller, the boundaries between fact and fiction are nebulous and probably not relevant. In another unpublished work, *Hide and Seek*, she explored her heritage in the context of her Trotter antecedents. No generation can avoid defining itself in terms of the generation that went before; that is part of the human condition. Naomi was very much aware of this, and she was also aware of how this need to define is itself influenced by history.

> History is continuous. It flows through us, sometimes fast, sometimes slow. In a society with little history, in the sense of movements, events, inventions, struggles and newnesses, when movement seems to be slow, the elderly are respected and useful, the keepers of custom; their children want to be like them. This is a conservative society, often a happy one because it is not fragmented, but it is no fun for the innovators, those with new ideas. In a society where historical events crowd in so fast that people cannot keep up with them – which is what most societies are like at present – the old are comparatively useless and only likely to be respected for certain kinds of success, not for qualities of wisdom. Family continuity is no longer sought after. The one thing children don't want is to be like their parents.[20]

Naomi did not want to be like her parents, although she valued her family's origins. She saw herself as an innovator, adventuring beyond accepted social and intellectual frontiers. Yet she valued family continuity, she valued a society founded on custom, she valued ritual, and she, now elderly, felt herself useful and wanted respect. Did she contradict herself? Yes, of course. Consistency, like care, inhibits adventure. She did not like being careful, and equally consistency was not an essential item on her agenda, although I have tried to suggest that the mainsprings of her actions and beliefs have remained remarkably consistent for a woman who has lived through nearly a century of unprecedented change. She relished the idea and the reality of surprising people, confounding their assumptions, and taking risks.

Naomi continued to make efforts to place herself in a continuum of her inheritance and successors. 'Here, now, one is a writer, with some kind of history, some kind of substance of recognition when the name is mentioned,' she reflected in a fragment of typescript which has no date but must be fairly recent. 'So how is one to behave, how is this old writer to meet easily with the people outside her limit of living, including her now white-haired children, grey-haired grandchildren, with their own successes or worries, their own loves and uncertainties?'[21] Where does an old writer and campaigner, an old woman with grandchildren and great grandchildren, fit into a world where she can no longer enact the scenario of her life? The final and most difficult challenge is to write the script for old age.

In an undated letter to Eric Linklater, Naomi talks about security and adventure. 'If one hadn't felt secure one wouldn't have wanted and couldn't have sought adventure.'[22] She had not only the security of class and family, in a country where both still count for a great deal, but also a moral and intellectual security. How else could she have walked into a totally new environment, as she did over and over again, and invented a leading role for herself? She was story-maker as well as story-teller. But there were risks involved, too, in this continual reinvention, and it was risk that both frustrated and enlivened life in her tenth decade. 'I suppose living an ordinary life is risky enough in someone ninety three years old,' she wrote. 'I try not to be looked after and coddled, but cannot avoid it.'[23] She felt she was over-protected and fussed over, and although she appreciated being looked after, she hung onto the idea of taking risks. There was some consolation in the fact that life in one's nineties is *de facto* hazardous.

The poem 'The talking oats' takes us on a half-familiar Mitchison journey, from pre-history to the present day. Whatever the changes and the contradictions, there is continuity, the flow of history, if you find a place where the voices can be heard. One of those places is the Hebrides.

> *Voices in the wind ripple of oats, voices*
> *At the back of the blood, at the back of the brain,*
> *Below the deepest roots of the trees, the blown shouting trees,*
> *Below the oats, below the rocks, below the islands,*
> *Behind the ploughing and sowing, the harvesting and threshing,*
> *At the back of life.*[24]

A picture unfolds of generations of life and work in the Western Isles, coloured by romance but shaped by verisimilitude. Like so many of the worlds she created, which may not be real, it has a rich credibility, composed of people and things, feelings and beliefs. She was an attentive listener to the voices at the back of life.

'We go with the wave of our times,' she said. Most of us do. A few, and Naomi Mitchison was one of them, also make waves.

Notes

Naomi Mitchison herself has been the source of much of the information in this book, through published memoirs and accounts, unpublished diaries, notebooks and letters, and in conversations and recorded interviews. Manuscript material is located in several places. When I began the research there were large quantities of letters, notebooks and typescripts at Carradale House, to which N.M. gave me access. Some items she lent or sent to me. I have credited all of these, as well as the material I saw at Carradale, C.H. for Carradale House. During the five years I have worked on the book N.M. has been sending material to the National Library of Scotland. Some items credited as C.H. are now in their holdings. Material I worked on in the National Library is credited N.L.S. and includes an N.L.S. accession number. In addition, I consulted Mitchison material at the Harry Ransom Humanities Research centre at the University of Texas, Austin (credited H.R.C.), the Wellcome Institute for the History of Medicine and the Mass-Observation Archive at the University of Sussex (M.-O.). Letters with no credited source have been lent to me by their recipients.

As well as five recording sessions with N.M. I have interviewed several members of her family, and a number of friends and associates. I have also had numerous less formal interviews and entirely informal conversations with N.M. herself and many others. I have distinguished between interviews and conversations in the notes below; with the latter, I did not always have a notebook to hand at the time.

Chapter One

1 N.M., quoted in *Small Talk*, in *As It Was*, Glasgow 1988, 41
2 Louisa Kathleen Haldane, *Friends and Kindred*, London 1961, 32
3 N.M., 'Buildings that blend into the landscape', *The Scotsman*, 31 March 1956
4 Ibid.

5 N.M., *Small Talk*, op. cit., 43
6 Ibid., 42
7 Elizabeth Haldane, *From One Century to Another*, London 1937, 111
8 N.M., untitled ts. N.L.S. ACC 10307/3
9 N.M., 'Haldane of Cloan', *Glasgow Herald*, 28 July 1956
10 L.K. Haldane and N.M., 'Dear Andrew', ts, N.L.S., ACC 10852
11 N.M., *Small Talk*, op. cit., 33
12 Ibid., 47
13 N.M., 'Perthshire Sabbath', *Scottish Field*, April 1960, 39
14 Ibid.
15 Ibid.
16 N.M., 'What no lady talked about', *Glasgow Herald*, 20 November 1965
17 N.M., 'Guilt came with the old lace', ibid., 6 November 1965
18 N.M., notebook dated 1981, C.H.
19 N.M., interview with J.C., 13 June 1992
20 L.K. Haldane, op. cit., 179
21 N.M., interview with J.C., 13 June 1992
22 N.M., *Small Talk*, op. cit., 77
23 N.M., 'Hinksey Promising Lad', *Chapman* 50-51, Summer 1987, 8
24 N.M., 'Days of pinafores and sunbonnets', *Glasgow Herald*, 13 November 1965
25 N.M., notebook, C.H.
26 N.M., interview with J.C., 13 June 1992
27 Ibid.
28 L.K. Haldane, op. cit., 211
29 Ibid.
30 Ibid.
31 N.M., interview with J.C., 13 June 1992
32 Ibid.
33 N.M., 'Children's books', *Time and Tide*, 6 December 1929
34 N.M., *Small Talk*, op. cit., 81
35 Ibid., 82
36 Ibid.
37 Her attacker was S. Southwold, author of *The Book of Animal Tales* (1929), who objected to N.M.'s critical review of his book in *Time and Tide*, 6 December 1929. He wrote, 'It is strange how little women understand children and how few can write for them. All children's classics have been, are being, and will be written by men ...' *Time and Tide*, 13 December 1929
38 N.M. to 'Pauline', 28 October [no year], N.L.S., ACC 9634
39 N.M., *All Change Here*, in *As It Was*, 17
40 Ibid.
41 Ibid., 44
42 Ibid.
43 N.M., interview with J.C., 13 June 1992
44 N.M., *All Change Here*, op. cit., 65
45 Ibid., 69
46 Ibid.
47 Ibid.
48 Sybil Bedford, *Aldous Huxley: A Biography*, London 1973, 52
49 N.M., quoted in ibid., 40
50 Ibid.
51 Ibid.
52 N.M., *All Change Here*, op. cit., 89
53 Ibid., 99
54 Gervas Huxley, *Both Hands: An Autobiography*, London 1970, 69

55 Ibid.
56 N.M., *Prisoners of War*, ts, N.L.S., ACC 9151
57 G. Huxley, op. cit., 72
58 N.M., *All Change Here*, op. cit., 94
59 Ibid., 96
60 N.M., interview with J.C., 13 June 1992
61 N.M. *All Change Here*, op. cit., 103
62 N.M., interview with J.C., 13 June 1992
63 N.M., notebook dated 1981, N.L.S., ACC 9119
64 J.B.S. Haldane to N.M., n.d., N.L.S., ACC 10753
65 N.M., *All Change Here*, op. cit., 106
66 J.B.S.H. to N.M., 19 March 1915, N.L.S., ACC 9119
67 N.M., *The Laburnum Branch*, London 1926, 80-1

Chapter Two

 1 N.M., 'War wedding', *Scottish Field*, December 1973
 2 Ibid.
 3 N.M., *All Change Here, As It Was*, 112
 4 Lois Godfrey, interview with J.C., 28 March 1995
 5 N.M., interview with J.C., 13 June 1992
 6 N.M., *All Change Here*, op. cit., 83
 7 Margaret Cole, *The Life of G.D.H. Cole*, London 1971, 83
 8 Quoted in ibid., 84
 9 N.M., *All Change Here*, op. cit., 126
10 N.M. to Elizabeth Haldane, N.L.S., ACC 9186
11 N.M., *All Change Here*, op. cit., 125
12 N.M., 'War wedding', *Scottish Field*, December 1973
13 N.M., *All Change Here*, op. cit., 133
14 N.M., interview with J.C., 13 June 1992
15 J.B.S. Haldane to N.M., 22 January 1916, N.L.S., ACC 10753
16 N.M., interview with J.C., 13 June 1992
17 Ibid.
18 N.M., *All Change Here*, op. cit., 141
19 Ibid., 142
20 N.M., interview with J.C., 13 June 1992
21 Ibid.
22 N.M., *All Change Here*, op. cit., 148
23 N.M., interview with J.C., 13 June 1992
24 Ibid.
25 N.M., *All Change Here*, op. cit., 150
26 N.M., *The Laburnum Branch*, 18
27 N.M., interview with J.C., 13 June 1992
28 N.M., *All Change Here*, op. cit., 153
29 Julian Huxley to N.M., 13 June 1917, N.L.S., ACC 10888
30 N.M., *All Change Here*, op. cit., 153
31 Ibid.
32 Ibid., 154
33 J.B.S. Haldane to N.M., 5 September 1917, N.L.S., ACC 10506
34 N.M., *All Change Here*, op. cit. 154
35 N.M., *The Laburnum Branch*, 81
36 N.M., *All Change Here*, op. cit., 158
37 N.M., 'The Lady in the Big House', BBC Scotland, 13 December 1994

38 N.M., *Comments on birth control, Criterion Miscellany* 12, 1930, 9
39 Ibid., 15–16
40 N.M., *The Laburnum Branch*, 60
41 N.M., interview with J.C., 13 June 1992
42 Ibid.
43 N.M., *The Laburnum Branch*, 57
44 N.M., untitled ts, N.L.S., ACC 10307/3
45 Denis Mitchison, interview with J.C., 21 November 1995; Lois Godfrey,
    interview with J.C., 28 March 1995; Valentine Arnold-Forster,
    interview with J.C., 5 February 1996
46 N.M., interview with J.C., 13 June 1992
47 Ibid.
48 N.M., *When the Bough Breaks*, London 1924, 133–4
49 Ibid.
50 N.M., *You May Well Ask*, London 1979, 27

Chapter Three

1   Margaret Cole, op. cit., 214
2   N.M., interview with Isobel Murray and Bob Tait, 29 October 1984
3   N.M., *You May Well Ask*, London 1979, 70
4   N.M., conversation with J.C., 7 February 1992
5   N.M., *The Conquered*, London 1923, 68–9
6   N.M., *You May Well Ask*, 162
7   N.M., untitled ts, N.L.S., ACC 10307/3
8   N.M., untitled ts, N.L.S., ACC 10888
9   N.M., *You May Well Ask*, 162
10 Raymond Mortimer, 'New novels', *New Statesman and Nation*, 3 May 1923
11 H.C. Harwood, 'New books', *Outlook*, 5 May 1923
12 Richard Haldane to N.M., n.d., N.L.S., ACC 9186
13 E.M. Forster to N.M., December 1923, in *You May Well Ask*, 101
14 Vincent Sheean to N.M., 3 May [no year], H.R.C.
15 Henry Treece, 'My favourite forgotten book', *Tomorrow* X, 11 July
    1951, 61 & 90
16 E.M. Forster to N.M., 1925, in *You May Well Ask*, 103
17 N.M., 'The house on the Mall', ts, dated 1940, C.H.
18 N.M., interview with J.C., 13 June 1992
19 N.M., *You May Well Ask*, 27
20 Ibid.
21 N.M., *The Kingdom of Heaven*, London 1939, 122
22 N.M., *The Blood of the Martyrs*, London, 1939, 41–2
23 Lois Godfrey, interview with J.C., 28 March 1995
24 Val Arnold-Forster, interview with J.C., 5 February 1996
25 Denis Mitchison, interview with J.C., 21 November 1995
26 N.M., *You May Well Ask*, 102
27 Ibid., 113
28 N.M. *Small Talk*, op. cit., 127–8
29 N.M., *You May Well Ask*, 62
30 Ibid., 77
31 N.M., 'Eros or love is god', paper read to the Heretics Society,
    University of Cambridge, November 1925, ts, H.R.C.
32 N.M., 'Some uneasiness', paper read to the English Club, University
    of Oxford, 1930, ts, H.R.C.

33 P.C. Kennedy, 'New novels', *New Statesman and Nation*, 17 December 1925
34 N.M., *You May Well Ask*, 70
35 N.M., *The Laburnum Branch*, 9
36 Denis Mitchison, interview with J.C., 21 November 1995
37 N.M., *Cloud Cuckoo Land*, London 1925
38 N.M., conversation with J.C., 13 June 1992
39 Ibid.
40 Lois Godfrey, interview with J.C., 28 March 1995
41 N.M., *The Listener*, 12 July 1984, quoted in Betty Vernon, *Margaret Cole 1893-1980. A Political Biography*, London 1986, 75
42 Margery Spring Rice to N.M., 29 February 1928, C.H.
43 N.M., *You May Well Ask*, 80
44 N.M., 'Preamble to a contract', ts, N.L.S., ACC 10888
45 N.M. to Mr Bird, n.d., C.H.
46 Margery Spring Rice to N.M., n.d., C.H.
47 Margery Spring Rice to N.M., n.d., C.H.
48 N.M., *The Laburnum Branch*, 80
49 Llewelyn Powys to N.M, 8 February 1927, H.R.C.
50 L. Powys to N.M., n.d. [1927], H.R.C.
51 N.M., *You May Well Ask*, 76
52 Ibid., 52
53 Denis Mitchison, interview with J.C., 21 November 1995
54 N.M., *The Corn King and the Spring Queen*, Edinburgh 1990 [London 1931], 249
55 N.M., 'Back from Achaea', *Time and Tide*, 4 January 1929
56 Ibid.
57 N.M., conversation with J.C., 13 June 1992
58 Theodore Wade Gery to N.M., n.d., C.H.
59 N.M. to Edward Garnett, n.d., H.R.C.
60 N.M. to Dick Mitchison, n.d., C.H.
61 N.M. to Theodore Wade Gery, n.d., C.H.
62 Ibid., 17 February 1931, C.H.
63 N.M., conversation with J.C., 13 June 1992
64 N.M., *Black Sparta*, London 1928, 50
65 L.P. Hartley, *Everyman*, 27 June 1929
66 Review of *Black Sparta Times Literary Supplement*, 14 June 1928
67 J.B.S. Haldane to N.M., 11 September 1928, N.L.S., ACC
68 E.M. Forster to N.M., n.d., in *You May Well Ask*, 104
69 'Shorter notices', *Cape Times*, 30 August 1928
70 N.M., *Black Sparta*, 246
71 Ibid., 306
72 Ibid., 143
73 N.M., *Anna Commena*, London 1928, 20
74 Ibid., 22
75 N.M. to Gabriel Carritt, August 1930

Chapter Four

1 N.M. review of *The Diabolical Principle and the Dithyrambic Spectator* by Wyndham Lewis, *Time and Tide*, 16 May 1931
2 N.M., 'The book and the revolution', *Time and Tide*, 17 January 1930
3 Ibid.

4 N.M., *You May Well Ask*, 34
5 N.M., *Comments on Birth Control, Criterion Miscellany* 12. 1930, 5
6 Ibid.
7 Ibid., 15–16
8 Ibid., 21
9 Ibid., 25
10 'Critic's commentary', *Time and Tide*, 7 June 1930
11 Stella Browne, review of *Comments on Birth Control, The New Generation*, June 1930
12 N.M., *Comments on Birth Control*, 8
13 N.M., *The Corn King and the Spring Queen*, London 1931, 212
14 Ibid., 213
15 Ibid., 214
16 W.W. Hadley, review of *The Corn King…, Sunday Times*, 30 May 1931
17 Review of *The Corn King…, Birmingham Post*, 26 May 1931
18 Winifred Holtby, 'A new subject for fiction', *News Chronicle*, 4 June 1931
19 Neil Ascherson, *Black Sea*, London 1996, 211
20 Stella Browne, review of *The Corn King…, New Generation*, July 1931
21 Interview, *The Star*, 9 December 1929
22 Interview, *Yorkshire Observer*, December 1931
23 'She makes the past live', *Daily Herald*, 27 March 1931
24 'Women to the fore', *Weekly Scotswoman*, 30 January 1932
25 Margaret Cole, *The Life of G.D.H. Cole*, London 1971, 145
26 N.M., *You May Well Ask*, 183
27 N.M., 'Remembering 1926', *The Delicate Fire*, London 1933, 355–60
28 Eric Hobsbawm, *The Age of Extremes*, London 1995 [1994], 102
29 Dick Mitchison to N.M., 9 December 1930, C.H.
30 M. Cole, *Growing Up into Revolution*, London 1949, 140
31 Ibid.
32 Betty Vernon, *Margaret Cole*, London 1986, 68
33 M. Cole, op. cit., 142
34 Ibid.
35 Dick Mitchison to N.M., n.d. [from South Africa]
36 Dick Mitchison to N.M., n.d.
37 M. Cole, *The Life of G.D.H. Cole*, 145
38 N.M., *An Outline for Boys and Girls and their Parents*, London 1932, 4
39 N.M., 'Two prophets', *Time and Tide*, 26 July 1930
40 N.M., untitled ts, N.L.S., ACC 9152
41 N.M., *Lancashire Daily Post*, 19 June 1931
42 N.M. to Stella Benson, quoted in *You May Well Ask*, 137
43 Lewis Gielgud to N.M., n.d., H.R.C.
44 L. Gielgud to N.M., 10 November 1931, H.R.C.
45 N.M., ts, C.H.
46 N.M., ts, C.H.
47 Gabriel Carritt, interview with J.C., 19 March 1994
48 John Pilley to N.M., 23 July 1932, C.H.
49 Ibid.
50 M. Cole to N.M., 2 July 1932, C.H.
51 M. Cole, *Growing Up into Revolution*, 143
52 N.M., Russian diary, ts, 12, C.H.
53 J. Pilley to N.M., 11 July ?1932, C.H.
54 N.M., *You May Well Ask*, 192
55 N.M., Russian diary, ts, 8, C.H.
56 Ibid., 65
57 Ibid.

58 Ibid., 75
59 Ibid., 118
60 Ibid., 94
61 Ibid., 209
62 Ibid., 211
63 Ibid., 175
64 Ibid.
65 Ibid., 245
66 Ibid., 246
67 Ibid., 249-50
68 Aldous Huxley to N.M., quoted in Sybill Bedford, *Aldous Huxley: A Biography*, London 1973, 263
69 N.M., Russian diary, ts, 251
70 Ibid., 253
71 N.M. to J. Pilley, July 1932, C.H.
72 N.M. to J. Pilley, July 1932, C.H.
73 N.M., 'Midsummer eve 1933', *Chapman* 50-51, Summer 1987, 8
74 N.M., 'Since there's no help', *The Delicate Fire*, 301
75 N.M., 'Archaeology and the intellectual worker', in *Twelve Studies in Soviet Russia*, ed. M. Cole, London 1933, 257
76 Ibid., 257-8
77 N.M., *The Delicate Fire*, 230
78 N.M. to Edward Garnett, 8 September ?1932, H.R.C.
79 N.M., 'Two men at the salmon nets', *The Delicate Fire*, 63
80 N.M., *The Moral Basis of Politics*, xiii
81 N.M., *We Have Been Warned*, London 1935, 380
82 Ibid., 304
83 Ibid., 490
84 Ibid., 259
85 Ibid., 260
86 N.M. to E. Garnett, in *You May Well Ask*, 173
87 N.M. to E. Garnett, ibid., 174
88 Victor Gollancz to N.M., ibid., 177
89 N.M. to Constable, ibid., 178
90 N.M. to J.C., n.d. [1993]
91 N.M. to E. Garnett, 8 September ?1932, H.R.C.
92 N.M., Housing Diary, ts, N.L.S., ACC 10879
93 Ibid.
94 N.M., untitled ts, N.L.S., ACC 10879
95 N.M., *You May Well Ask*, 196
96 N.M. to E. Garnett, 8 September ?1932, H.R.C.
97 N.M. to J. Pilley, n.d. ?1933, C.H.
98 N.M., *Naomi Mitchison's Vienna Diary*, London 1934, 9
99 Ibid., 10-11
100 Ibid., 15-16
101 Ibid., 32
102 Ibid.
103 Ibid., 218
104 N.M. to Kgosi Linchwe, 5 July 1965, C.H.
105 Julius Deutsch to N.M., 17 June 1934, H.R.C.
106 Dick Mitchison to N.M., 24 February 1935, C.H.
107 N.M. to J. Pilley, n.d., C.H.
108 N.M., *You May Well Ask*, 205
109 Harry Pollitt to N.M., 27 January 1936, H.R.C.
110 N.M., *You May Well Ask*, 206
111 N.M., election address, 1935, C.H.

112 Lois Godfrey, interview with J.C., 28 March 1995
113 Murdoch Mitchison, interview with J.C., 12 July 1996
114 N.M., 'Why do the boys run after me?', ts, H.R.C.
115 N.M., 'The Rock', *Manchester Guardian*, 13 May 1954
116 N.M., *The Home and a Changing Civilization*, London 1934, 37
117 Ibid., 41
118 N.M., 'The Snowmaiden', in *The Fourth Pig*, London 1936, 79
119 N.M., *You May Well Ask*, 148
120 Ibid., 149
121 N.M. to V. Gollancz, 31 August 1932
122 N.M., *The Moral Basis of Politics*, 33
123 Zita Baker to N.M., 16 November 1933, C.H.
124 N.M. to Dick Mitchison, 21 February 1935, C.H.
125 Ibid.
126 Ibid.
127 Ibid.
128 N.M. to Dick Mitchison, 22 March 1935, C.H.
129 George Orwell to N.M., 17 June 1938, H.R.C.
130 N.M., 'The glen path', ts, C.H.
131 N.M., *You May Well Ask*, 212
132 L.K. Haldane, op. cit.
133 Elizabeth Longford, *The Pebbled Shore*, London 1986, 78
134 Ibid., 131
135 Olaf Stapledon to N.M., n.d., in *You May Well Ask*, 140–141

Chapter Five

1 N.M., *The Moral Basis of Politics*, London 1938, 35
2 Ibid., 351
3 Francis Burdett, 'Caught in a distorted world', *Catholic Herald*, 24 November 1939
4 Frank Swinnerton, 'From ancient to modern', *Observer*, 22 October 1939
5 Harold Brighouse, 'From Nero to Hitler', *Manchester Guardian*, 10 October 1939
6 Review, *Christian World*, 16 November 1939
7 John Mair, 'New novels', *New Statesman and Nation*, 7 October 1939
8 N.M. to John Lehmann, n.d., H.R.C.
9 John Lehmann, comment added to letter from N.M., n.d., H.R.C.
10 Neil Gunn to N.M., 3 June 1941, N.L.S. ACC 10201
11 C.E.M. Joad, 'Complaint against lady novelists', *New Statesman and Nation*, 19 August 1939
12 Ibid., 26 August 1939
13 World War II diary, ts, 83, C.H.
14 G.D.H. Cole, 'A place called Carradale', *New Statesman and Nation*, 19 August 1939
15 Ibid.
16 N.M., *You May Well Ask*, 221
17 Ellen Wilkinson to N.M., n.d., H.R.C.
18 'Clemency Ealasaid', *The Bull Calves*, London 1947, 9
19 Ibid.
20 Ibid., 10
21 Ibid.
22 A copy of the typescript is with the Mass-Observation Archive at the

University of Sussex. Another was loaned to me by N.M. I have quoted from the latter. Part of the diary was published as *Among You Taking Notes. The Wartime Diary of Naomi Mitchison 1939-45*, edited by Dorothy Sheridan, 1989. Where I quote from the published version I have acknowledged it accordingly.

23 N.M., *Among You Taking Notes*, ed. Dorothy Sheridan, London 1989, 35
24 N.M., interview with J.C., 13 June 1992
25 N.M. to Aldous Huxley, n.d., N.L.S. ACC 10140
26 N.M., interview with J.C., 13 June 1992
27 N.M., *Among You Taking Notes*, 42
28 N.M., WWII diary, ts, 32
29 Ibid., 23
30 Ibid., 62
31 N.M., letter to *Glasgow Herald*, 21 October 1939
32 N.M., *The Cleansing of the Knife*, Edinburgh 1978, 17
33 N.M. to Tom Harrisson, 6 October 1942, M.O.
34 N.M., *Among You Taking Notes*, 58
35 N.M., *The Cleansing of the Knife*, 26
36 N.M., *Among You Taking Notes*, 56-7
37 N.M., *The Cleansing of the Knife*, 5
38 Ibid., 6
39 Ibid., 9
40 N.M., WWII diary, ts, 145
41 N.M., *Among You Taking Notes*, 65
42 N.M., WWII diary, ts, 146
43 Ibid., 153
44 Ibid., 167
45 Ibid., 174
46 Ibid., 83
47 Ibid., 219
48 N.M., ms notebook, C.H.
49 Margaret Cole, *Growing Up into Revolution*, London 1949, 142
50 Ibid.
51 N.M., *Among You Taking Notes*, 85
52 N.M., WWII diary, ts, 239
53 Ibid., 242-3
54 Ibid., 248
55 Ibid., 438
56 Ibid., 493
57 Louise Annand, interview with J.C., 27 July 1993
58 N.M., WWII diary, ts, 691
59 N.M., conversation with J.C., 19 July 1993
60 N.M., WWII diary, ts, 534
61 Ibid., 328
62 Ibid., 326
63 N.M., *Among You Taking Notes*, 103
64 Ibid., 104
65 N.M., *The Cleansing of the Knife*, 47
66 N.M., *Among You Taking Notes*, 106
67 N.M., WWII diary, ts, 344
68 N.M., *The Cleansing of the Knife*, 47
69 N.M., WWII diary, ts, 357
70 Ibid., 1270
71 Ibid., 355
72 Ibid., 532
73 Ibid., 1124

74 Lois Godfrey, interview with J.C., 28 March 1995
75 N.M., WWII diary, ts, 661
76 Ibid.
77 Ibid., 888
78 N.M., *The Bull Calves*, 92
79 Louise Annand, conversation with J.C., 27 July 1993
80 N.M., WWII diary, ts, 721
81 Ibid., 744
82 Ibid., 930
83 Untitled ts, C.H.
84 N.M., WWII diary, ts, 538
85 N.M., *Among You Taking Notes*, 133
86 Ibid.
87 N.M., 'Jim McKinven: March 1941, *Chapman* 50-51, July 1987, 41
88 Ibid., 42
89 N.M., *Among You Taking Notes*, 117
90 N.M., WWII diary, ts, 1071
91 Ibid.
92 N.M., WWII diary, ts, 1043
93 Ibid., 897
94 Ibid., 1044
95 Ibid., 1298
96 Ibid., 1084
97 Ibid., 1088
98 Ibid., 1477
99 Ibid., 1261
100 Ibid., 473
101 Ibid., 827
102 Ibid., 954
103 N.M., interview with J.C., 14 June, 1992
104 N.M., *Among You Taking Notes*, 301
105 Lois Godfrey, comment on draft to J.C., 29 August 1996
106 N.M., *Among You Taking Notes*, 323
107 Louise Annand, interview with J.C., 27 July 1993
108 N.M., WWII diary, ts 1594

Chapter Six

1   N.M., *Saltire Self-Portraits 2*, Edinburgh 1986, 5
2   N.M. to Tom Harrisson, 9 October 1944, M.O.
3   N.M., *Saltire Self-Portraits 2*, 6
4   N.M., 'MP's wife', ts, C.H.
5   Ibid.
6   Ibid.
7   Ibid.
8   Ibid.
9   'The house on the Mall', ts, C.H.
10 N.M., 'MP's wife'
11 Louise Annand, interview with J.C., 27 July 1993
12 N.M. to Compton Mackenzie, 194[?]
13 N.M., *Saltire Self-Portraits 2*, 8
14 Ibid.
15 N.M., 'Argyll County Council', ts, C.H.

16 N.M. to Bettie Baxter, n.d., probably 1950s, M.O.
17 N.M. to Tom Harrisson, 18 May 1950, M.O.
18 N.M., 'Argyll County Council', ts, C.H.
19 N.M., Highland Panel', ts, C.H.
20 N.M., *Saltire Self-Portraits 2*, 10
21 N.M., letter to *New Statesman and Nation*, 23 December 1944
22 Minutes, Highland Panel, 23 December 1958, C.H.
23 N.M., memo to Highland Panel, 23 March 1960, C.H.
24 John Gibson, interview with J.C., 23 April 1994
25 N.M., comments on the *West Highland Survey*, C.H.
26 Ibid.
27 N.M., memo to the Highland Panel, November 1951, C.H.
28 J.A. Ford, conversation with J.C., 18 June 1994
29 N.M., *Lobsters on the Agenda*, London 1952, 44
30 Ibid., 167
31 Ibid., 175
32 Ibid., 178
33 Ibid., 130
34 John Gibson, interview with J.C., 23 April 1994
35 N.M. to Bettie Baxter, 1 January 1949, M.O.
36 N.M., 'Lean harvest,' *New Statesman and Nation*, 26 March 1955
37 N.M., interview with J.C., 16 July 1992
38 N.M., 'Lean harvest,' *New Statesman and Nation*, 26 March 1955
39 Minutes, Highland Panel, 22 December 1955, C.H.
40 N.M., interview with J.C., 16 July 1992
41 N.M. to Bettie Baxter, n.d., probably 1957, M.O.
42 N.M., WWII diary, ts, 964
43 N.M. and Denis Mackintosh, *Spindrift*, London 1951, 19
44 Copies of both typescripts are in the National Library of Scotland.
45 N.M., *Other People's Worlds*, London 1958, 1
46 N.M., 'Writers in the USSR', *New Statesman and Nation*, 6 September 1952
47 N.M., 'Year of the good hay', ibid., 30 July 1955
48 N.M., 'Thoughts on growing grass', ibid., 11 June 1955
49 N.M., 'Summer work', ibid., 29 June 1957
50 N.M., 'Big mill', ibid., 26 November 1955
51 N.M., 'Think of a number', ibid., 11 February 1956
52 Ibid.
53 N.M. to Bettie Baxter, n.d., ?1956, M.O.
54 N.M. to Bettie Baxter, 25 December 1954, M.O.
55 Lois Godfrey, conversation with J.C., 19 July 1993
56 Review of *The Big House*, *Times Literary Supplement*, 17 November 1950
57 Naomi Lewis, 'Under the mountain', *New Statesman and Nation*, 2 December 1950
58 *Scotland's Magazine*, December 1950
59 N.M., *The Rib of the Green Umbrella*, London 1960, 124
60 N.M., 'Writer and the child', *New Statesman and Nation*, 12 February 1955
61 Elizabeth Longford, foreword, *Travel Light*, London 1984, vii–xi
62 N.M., *The Swan's Road*, London 1954, 14
63 N.M., *Travel Light*, London 1984 [1953], 56
64 N.M., *Mucking Around*, London 1981, 13
65 Ibid., 15
66 Ibid., 16
67 N.M., 'Cold War', ts, N.L.S., ACC 10888

68 N.M. to Robert Graves, n.d., N.L.S., ACC 9198
69 N.M., 'Cold War', ts, N.L.S., ACC 10888
70 Ibid.
71 Ibid.
72 Ibid.
73 N.M., *Mucking Around,* 85
74 N.M., notes on India, N.L.S., ACC 10810
75 N.M., notes on women in Bangladesh, N.L.S., ACC 10810
76 Review of *Judy and Lakshmi, Hindu,* Madras, 9 August 1959

Chapter Seven

1   N.M., *Mucking Around,* London 1981, 34
2   Ibid., 115
3   Ibid., 117
4   N.M., 'Split mind of Ghana', *New Statesman and Nation,* 23 March
    1957
5   N.M., *Other People's Worlds,* 1
6   N.M., interview with J.C., 14 June 1992
7   Ibid.
8   Kgosi Linchwe, interview with J.C., 31 October 1994
9   Ibid.
10 N.M., interview with J.C., 14 June 1992
11 N.M., *Ketse and the Chief,* London 1963, 15
12 N.M., 'Installation of an African chief', *The Scotsman,* 14 April 1963
13 Ibid.
14 N.M., *Other People's Worlds,* 15
15 Ibid., 155–6
16 N.M. to Eric Linklater, 23 May, N.L.S., ACC 10282
17 David Maine to N.M., 22 July 1964, C.H.
18 Norman Molomo, interview with J.C., 28 October 1994
19 N.M., ms diary, ?1966, N.L.S., ACC 10888
20 N.M., 'Children's plight in a parched land', *The Scotsman,* 30 October
    1965
21 N.M. to Dick Mitchison, 2 February 1965, C.H.
22 Ibid.
23 Patrick von Rensburg, interview with J.C., 28 October 1994
24 N.M. to Bessie Head, n.d. N.L.S., ACC 10888
25 N.M. to Lois Godfrey, 5 November 197[?]
26 N.M., 'Naomi Mitchison finds herself asking questions', *Kutlwano* VI,
    October 1967, 28
27 Kathy Linchwe, interview with J.C., 4 November 1994
28 Ibid.
29 Ibid.
30 Ibid.
31 Greek Ruele to N.M., 1 July 1968, N.L.S. 10888
32 N.M., 'Borejane dam', *Manchester Guardian,* 19 July 1965
33 Fiona Moffat, interview with J.C., 27 October 1994
34 N.M., ms diary, ?1966, N.L.S., ACC 10888
35 N.M., 'Botswana contradictions', *African Affairs* 77, 307, April 1978,
    233
36 N.M., *Return to the Fairy Hill,* London 1966, 69
37 N.M. to Linchwe, 22 September 1967, C.H.

38 N.M. to Bettie Baxter, 29 May 1963, M.O.
39 N.M. to Linchwe, December ?1962 or 63, C.H.
40 N.M. to Linchwe, n.d. C.H.
41 Linchwe to N.M., 8 November, C.H.
42 N.M., ms diary, 1964, N.L.S., ACC 10807
43 N.M., ms diary, n.d., C.H.
44 Ibid.
45 N.M., ms diary, N.L.S., ACC 10888
46 Linchwe to N.M., January 1965, C.H.
47 N.M., ms diary, C.H. This diary is not dated, but the comment probably reflects the community centre after Sandy Grant had ceased to be involved.
48 Ibid.
49 N.M., *Return to the Fairy Hill*, 142
50 N.M. to Bettie Baxter, 28-[?]-69, M.O.
51 N.M., ms diary, n.d., N.L.S., ACC 10888
52 Kenneth Koma to N.M., 6 July 1966, C.H.
53 Amos Pilane to N.M., 23 August 1973, C.H.
54 Sandy Grant and Struan Robertson, a photographer based in Johannesburg who photographed the Independence Day celebrations, both made this analogy in conversations with J.C.
55 N.M., *African Heroes*, 7
56 N.M. to Linchwe, 22 September 1967, C.H.
57 Didon Faber, conversation with J.C., 3 November 1994
58 Kathy Linchwe, interview with J.C., 4 November 1994
59 Sandy Grant, *The Guardian Independence Supplement* (Botswana), 24 September 1993
60 Brian Egner to J.C., 25 October 1994
61 Ibid.
62 Fiona Moffat, interview with J.C., 27 October 1994
63 Linchwe, interview with J.C., 31 October 1994
64 N.M., ms diary, dated 1979, N.L.S., ACC 10888
65 N.M. to Professor Proctor, 27 August 1968, N.L.S., ACC 10325
66 N.M., 'Import-Expert', *African Affairs* 74, 294, January 1975, 61
67 N.M., 'One party rule', *The Roundtable* 289, 1984, 38
68 Ibid.
69 N.M. to Linchwe, 22 July ?1970, C.H.
70 N.M. to Linchwe, 8 August ?1970
71 N.M., *African Heroes*, 189
72 Ibid., 8
73 Ibid., 7
74 Ibid.
75 N.M. to Henry Treece, January 1964, H.R.C.
76 N.M. to Henry Treece, n.d., H.R.C.
77 Linchwe, interview with J.C., 31 October 1994
78 N.M., *When We Become Men*, 220
79 John Fuller, 'Around Sharpeville', *New Statesman and Nation*, 8 January 1965
80 N.M. to Linchwe, n.d., C.H.
81 N.M., *Return to the Fairy Hill*, 76
82 Ibid., 83
83 Ibid., 190
84 N.M., *The Family at Ditlabeng*, London 1969, 71
85 N.M., *Ketse and the Chief*, 31
86 N.M., *The Family at Ditlabeng*, 71
87 Skara Aphiri, conversation with J.C., 26 October 1994

88 Dr Charles Fuller, letter, *Kutlwano* VI, 9, September 1967, 2
89 N.M., letter, *Kutlwano* VI, 12, December 1967, 7
90 N.M., *Other People's Worlds*, 118
91 N.M. to Sandy Grant, 8 July 1984
92 Chriselda Molefi, conversation with J.C., 26 October 1994
93 N.M., *Saltire Self-Portraits 2*, 32
94 N.M., ms diary, dated 1965, N.L.S., ACC 10779
95 N.M., 'Open letter to an African chief', *Journal of Modern African Studies 2*, 1, 1964
96 N.M., untitled poem in a letter to Professor Proctor, 15 January 1969, N.L.S., ACC 10325

Chapter Eight

1   William Grant, 'So this is what it is like to have coffee with a tornado'. *Scottish Daily Express*, 2 May 1961
2   'Remarkable mothers', *Daily Express*, 3 April 1962
3   N.M., notebook, C.H.
4   N.M., W II diary, ts, 217, C.H.
5   Murdoch Mitchison, conversation with J.C., 12 July 1996
6   N.M., response to Mass-Observation directive, winter 1982, M.O.
7   Graeme Mitchison, interview with J.C., March 1996
8   N.M., response to Mass-Observation directive, winter 1984, M.O.
9   N.M., 'J.B.S.H.', *Chapman* 50–51, Summer 1987, 44
10 Ibid.
11 N.M., WW II diary, ts, 509
12 Ibid., 234
13 N.M., 'Mary and Joe', *Nova One*, London 1970, 178
14 N.M., *Solution Three*, London 1975, 122–3
15 Ibid., 5
16 N.M., *What the Human Race Is Up To*, London. 1962, 6
17 Ibid.
18 J.B.S. Haldane in ibid., 400
19 The typescript of *Hide and Seek* is in the National Library of Scotland, ACC 9914.
20 N.M. to Lois Godfrey, n.d.
21 N.M. to Sandy Grant, 20 September ?1981
22 N.M. to Lois Godfrey, n.d.
23 N.M., 'Ageing from inside', *Medical World*, March 1961, 259
24 N.M., conversation with J.C., 12 June 1992
25 N.M. to Bessie Head, n.d., probably 1970s, N.L.S., ACC 10888
26 N.M., 'Ageing from inside', op. cit., 260
27 N.M., notebook, dated July 1983 – February 1984, N.L.S., ACC 10461
28 N.M., 'Choosing partners', *New Statesman and Nation*, 27 August 1960
29 N.M., 'Yet I shall be tempest tost', ts, N.L.S., ACC 104/61
30 N.M., notebook, N.L.S., ACC 10888
31 N.M., diary, C.H.
32 Ibid.
33 Ibid.
34 N.M. to Sandy Grant, 9 October 1978
35 N.M., 'Winds and seedlings', *New Statesman and Nation*, 9 April 1960
36 Ibid.
37 Ibid.
38 N.M., response to Mass-Observation directive, autumn 1981, M.O.
39 Val Arnold-Forster, interview with J.C., 5 February 1996
40 Chris Allen, conversation with J.C., 20 June 1996

41 Isobel Murray, interview with J.C., 24 May 1996
42 Malcolm K. Macmillan, 'Naomi, friend of the Gaels', *Picture Post*, 8 October 1955
43 Sue Innes, conversation with J.C., 7 May 1996
44 N.M. to Sandy Grant, 23 May ?1981
45 N.M. to Sandy Grant, 28 April ?1979
46 N.M., response to Mass-Observation directive, autumn 1981, M.O.
47 N.M., notebook dated May 1982, N.L.S., ACC 9119
48 Ibid.
49 N.M., response to Mass-Observation directive, spring 1984, M.O.
50 N.M., introduction, *Early in Orcadia*, Glasgow 1987, 6
51 N.M., *Hide and Seek*, ts, N.L.S., ACC 9914
52 N.M., 'Rat-world', *A Girl Must Live*, Glasgow 1990, 253
53 N.M., *Early in Orcadia*, 73
54 N.M., conversation with J.C., June 1992
55 N.M., response to Mass-Observation directive, spring 1991, M.O.

Chapter Nine

1 N.M., conversation with J.C., 7 July 1992
2 N.M., conversation with J.C., 13 June 1992
3 N.M., interview with J.C., 7 February 1992
4 N.M., interview with J.C., 14 June 1992
5 N.M., conversation with J.C., 13 June 1992
6 Angus Calder, conversation with J.C., 17 August 1996
7 N.M., response to Mass-Observation directive, summer 1988, M.O.
8 J.C. to Dorothy Sheridan, 12 September 1993
9 Graeme Mitchison, interview with J.C., 29 March 1996
10 N.M., interview with J.C., 13 June 1992
11 N.M., untitled ts, N.L.S., ACC 10879
12 N.M., 38th Haldane Memorial Lecture, ts, C.H.
13 N.M., 'The future of Christian missions in Africa', *The Listener*, 18 July 1963
14 N.M., untitled ts, N.L.S., ACC 9914
15 Isobel Murray, interview with J.C., 24 May 1996
16 N.M., *You May Well Ask*, 14
17 N.M., ts, N.L.S., ACC 10888
18 Ibid.
19 N.M., untitled ts, C.H.
20 N.M., *Hide and Seek*, ts, N.L.S., ACC 9914
21 N.M., untitled ts, C.H.
22 N.M. to Eric Linklater, *A Girl Must Live*, 137, N.L.S., ACC 10282
23 N.M., 'The Talking Oats'

Bibliography

The work of Naomi Mitchison which has been published in book or pamphlet form, listed chronologically according to first publication in the UK.

The Conquered, Jonathan Cape, London, 1923

When the Bough Breaks, and other stories, Jonathan Cape, London, 1924

Cloud Cuckoo Land, Jonathan Cape, London, 1925

The Laburnum Branch: Poems, Jonathan Cape, London, 1926

Anna Commena, Representative Women series, Gerald Howe, London, 1928

Black Sparta: Greek Stories, Jonathan Cape, London, 1928

Nix-Nought-Nothing: Four Plays for Children, Jonathan Cape, London, 1928

Barbarian Stories, Jonathan Cape, London, 1929

The Hostages, and other stories for boys and girls, Jonathan Cape, London 1930

Comments on Birth control, Criterion Miscellany No 12, Faber and Faber, London, 1930

Boys and Girls and Gods, World of Youth series, Watts & Co, London 1931

Kate Crackernuts: a Fairy Play for Children, Aldan Press, Oxford, 1931

The Corn King and the Spring Queen, Jonathan Cape, London, 1931

The Price of Freedom (play), with Lewis Gielgud, Jonathan Cape, London, 1931

The Powers of Light, Pharos, London, 1932

An Outline for Boys and Girls and their Parents, ed., Gollancz, London, 1932

The Delicate Fire: Short Stories and Poems, Jonathan Cape, London, 1933

'Archaelogy and the intellectual worker', in *Twelve Studies in Soviet Russia*, ed. Margaret Cole, New Fabian Research Bureau, London, 1933

'Anger against books', in *Contemporary Essays*, ed. Sylvia Norman, no publisher, 1933

Naomi Mitchison's Vienna Diary, Gollancz, London, 1934

The Home and a Changing Civilisation, Twentieth Century Library, The Bodley Head, London, 1934

We Have Been Warned, Constable, London, 1935

Beyond This Limit, Jonathan Cape, London, 1935

The Fourth Pig, Constable, London, 1936

An End and a Beginning (play), Constable, London, 1937

Socrates, World Makers and World Shakers, with Richard Crossman, The Hogarth Press, 1937

The Moral Basis of Politics, Constable, London, 1938

'The *Alban* goes out: 1939' (poem), Raven Press, Harrow, 1939

As it Was in the Beginning, (play), with Lewis Gielgud, Jonathan Cape, London, 1939

The Blood of the Martyrs, Constable, London, 1939

The Kingdom of Heaven, Heinemann, London 1939

Historical Plays for Schools, 2nd series, Constable, 1939

Re-educating Scotland, ed., Scottish Convention, [Glasgow], 1944

Nix-Nought-Nothing and Elfin Hill: Two Plays for Children, Jonathan Cape, London, 1948

Men and Herring: a Documentary, with Denis Macintosh, Serif Books, Edinburgh, 1949

The Big House, Faber and Faber, London, 1950

Spindrift (play), with Denis Macintosh, Samuel French, London, 1951

Lobsters on the Agenda, Victor Gollancz, London, 1952

Travel Light, Faber and Faber, London, 1952

Graeme and the Dragon, Faber and Faber, London, 1954

The Swan's Road, Naldett Press, London, 1954

Highlands and Islands, Unity Publishing, Glasgow, 1954

To the Chapel Perilous, Allen and Unwin, London, 1955

Little Boxes, Faber and Faber, London, 1956

Behold Your King, Frederick Muller, 1957

Five Men and a Swan, Allen and Unwin, London, 1957

The Far Harbour, Collins, 1957

Other People's Worlds, Secker and Warburg, 1958

A Fishing Village on the Clyde, with George Paterson, People of Britain, Oxford University Press, Oxford, 1960

Judy and Lakshmi, Collins, London, 1959

The Rib of the Green Umbrella, Collins, London, 1960

The Young Alexander the Great, Max Parrish, London, 1960

Karensgaard: The Story of a Danish Farm, Collins, London, 1961

Presenting Other People's Children, Hamlyn, London, 1961

Memoirs of a Spacewoman, Victor Gollancz, London, 1962

The Young Alfred the Great, Max Parrish, London, 1962

What the Human Race is Up To, ed., Victor Gollancz, London, 1962

The Fairy Who Couldn't Tell a Lie, Collins, London, 1963

Alexander the Great, Longman, London, 1964

A Mochudi Family, no publisher, Wellington, 1965

Ketse and the Chief, Nelson, London, 1965

When We Become Men, Collins, London, 1965

Return to Fairy Hill, Heinemann, London, 1966

The Big Surprise, Kaye & Ward, London, 1967

African Heroes, The Bodley Head, London, 1968

Don't Look Back, Kaye and Ward, London, 1969

The Family at Ditlabeng, Collins, London, 1969

The Africans, Blond, London, 1970

'Mithras My Saviour', in *The Penguin Book of Short Stories*, ed J.F. Hendry, Penguin, 1970

Cleopatra's People, Heinemann, London, 1972

The Danish Teapot, Kaye and Ward, London, 1973

A Life for Africa: Bram Fischer, Merlin Press, London, 1973

'My brother Jack', in *J.B.S. Haldane Reader of Popular Scientific Essays,* Mockna, USSR, 1973

Small Talk: Memoirs of an Edwardian Childhood, The Bodley Head, London, 1973

Solution Three, Dobson, London, 1973

Sunrise Tomorrow: a Story of Botswana, Collins, London, 1973

'What do you think yourself?', in *Scottish Short Stories,* Oxford University Press, Oxford, 1973

Oil for the Highlands?, Fabian Society, London, 1974

All Change Here: Girlhood and Marriage, The Bodley Head, London, 1975

'The Hill Modipe', in *Scottish Short Stories,* Oxford University Press, Oxford, 1975

'Mary and Joe', in *Nova One,* ed. Harry Harrison, Robert Hale, London, 1975, USA, 1970

'Miss Omega Raven', in *Nova Two,* ed. Harry Harrison, Robert Hale, London, 1975, USA, 1971

'The Factory', in *Nova Three,* ed. Harry Harrison, Robert Hale, London, 1975, USA, 1972

'Out of the waters', *Nova Four,* ed. Harry Harrison, Robert Hale, London, 1976

'The red fellows', in *Scottish Short Stories,* Oxford University Press, Oxford, 1975

Snake, Collins, London, 1978

'Call me', in *Scottish Short Stories,* Oxford University Press, Oxford, 1976

'The little sister', in *Pulenyani's Secret,* ed. Mary Kobel, Oxford University Press, Oxford, 1976

Sittlichkeit, Haldane Memorial Lecture, Birkbeck College, London, 1977

The Cleansing of the Knife and Other Poems, Canongate, Edinburgh, 1978

'The sea horse', in *Modern Scottish Short Stories,* eds. Fred Urquhart and Giles Gordon, Hamish Hamilton, 1978

The Two Magicians, with G.R. Mitchison, Dobson, London, 1978

You May Well Ask: a Memoir 1920-1940, Victor Gollancz, London, 1979

The Vegetable War, Hamish Hamilton, London, 1980

Images of Africa, Canongate, Edinburgh, 1980

Mucking Around: Five Continents Over Fifty Years, Victor Gollancz, London, 1981

Margaret Cole 1883-1980, Fabian Society, London, 1982

What Do You think Yourself?, Paul Harris, Edinburgh, 1982

Not by Bread Alone, M. Boyars, London, 1983

Among You Taking Notes: Wartime Diary 1939-45, ed. Dorothy Sheridan, Victor Gollancz, London, 1985

Beyond this Limit: Selected Shorter Fiction, ed. Isobel Murray, Scottish Academic Press, Edinburgh, 1986

Saltire Self-Portraits 2, Saltire Society, Edinburgh, 1986

Early in Orcadia, Richard Drew, Glasgow, 1987

A Girl Must Live: Stories and Poems, Richard Drew, Glasgow, 1990

The Oath-Takers, Balnain Books, Nairn, 1991

Sea-green Ribbons, Balnain Books, Nairn, 1991

Naomi Mitchison's journalism is extensive. At different times she wrote regularly for *Time and Tide* and the *New Statesman and Nation*, less often for several newspapers, including the *Manchester Guardian, The Observer, The Scotsman* and the *Glasgow Herald*. She contributed poems, stories and articles to a huge range of journals and magazines, particularly in the UK and Africa.

There is little critical work on Naomi Mitchison. It includes:

Benton, Jill *Naomi Mitchison, A Biography*, Pandora Press, London, 1990

Calder, Jenni 'Men, women and comrades', in *Gendering the Nation: Studies in Modern Scottish Literature*, ed. Christopher Whyte, Edinburgh University Press, Edinburgh, 1995

Calder, Jenni 'More than merely ourselves: Naomi Mitchison', in *A History of Scottish Women's Writing*, ed. Douglas Gifford and Dorothy Macmillan Porter, Edinburgh University Press, Edinburgh, 1997

D'Arcy, Julian *Scottish Skalds and Sagamen*, includes a chapter on

'Naomi Mitchison', Edinburgh University Press, Edinburgh, 1996

Dickson, Beth 'From person to global: the fiction of Naomi Mitchison', *Chapman* 50–51, vol 10, 1 & 2, Summer 1987

Hendry, Joy 'Twentieth-century women's writing: the nest of singing birds', in *The History of Scottish Literature* vol 4, ed. Cairns Craig, Aberdeen University Press, Aberdeen, 1987. Includes comment on N.M.

Murray, Isobel 'Novelists of the Renaissance', in *The History of Scottish Literature* vol 4, ed. Cairns Craig, Aberdeen University Press, Aberdeen, 1987. Includes N.M., with Eric Linklater and Lewis Grassic Gibbon.

Murray, Isobel 'Human relations: an outline of some major themes in Naomi Mitchison's adult fiction', *Studies in Scottish Fiction: Twentieth Century*, Scottish Literary Studies 10, ed. Joachim Schwend and Horst Drescher, Frankfurt am Main, 1990

Smith, Alison 'The woman from the big house: the autobiographical writings of Naomi Mitchison', *Chapman* 50–51, vol 10, 1 & 2, Summer 1987

Index